NICOLA STURGEON

Nicola Sturgeon

Ian Mitchell

Volume 1: the Years of Ascent (1970-2007)

Volume 2: the Years of Decision (2007-2014) *(forthcoming)*

Volume 3: the Years of Power (2014-2022) *(forthcoming)*

By the same author:

The Cost of a Reputation (1998)

Isles of the West (1999, 2005)

Isles of the North (2005)

The Justice Factory (2020)

Russia and the Rule of Law (forthcoming)

Nicola Sturgeon

a citizen's biography

of a driven woman in a drifting parliament

Volume 1: the Years of Ascent

Ian Mitchell

Burnside Studios
Burnside Street
Campbeltown
Scotland

To register interest in volume 2 (or to comment or contribute), please mail:

sturgeonbook@gmail.com

Table of Contents

Author's note   1

Dramatis Personæ   7

Another day at the office…   15

1. The Early Years   17
2. Into Parliament   29
3. Talking the Talk   62
4. The Second Parliament   74
5. The Talking Shop   100
6. Holyrood   136
7. Deputy Leader   177
8. The Wind Shifts   219
9. Victory!   241

Appendix: Popular *versus* Parliamentary Sovereignty   277
Source note   309
Acknowledgements   315
Sustainability Statement, by Hamish Gobson   317
Index – consolidated in volume 3

To

the memory of J.S.B.P.

"…while the Germans had their pincers at Minsk,

the Russians had their mincers at Pinsk…."

R.I.P.

Author's Note

This is a "citizen's biography". It is neither a journalistic portrait nor an academic assessment. It is not even a political biography in the fullest sense of the word, because I have concentrated on Nicola Sturgeon's *parliamentary* contribution to Scottish politics. My main source is the *Official Report* of the proceedings in the Holyrood chamber since that is where the democratic heart of devolved Scotland ought to beat. Sturgeon has been a Member of the Scottish Parliament (MSP) from the first day of its existence, so her story is also in part its story.

If I have an overarching theme, it is the rule of law. I have lived for many years outside Scotland, including when young in *apartheid* South Africa and more recently in Vladimir Putin's Russia. Both offered valuable lessons about the necessity of government by consent if society is to minimize institutional violence. My forthcoming book, *Russia and the Rule of Law* will explain how the English-speaking world and the Russian-speaking one evolved from a common root into two societies which are now indirectly at war with each other due to the Russian belief in the utility of violence as both a diplomatic and a social management tool. Apartheid South Africa had a similar outlook, as did much of medieval Scotland. At that time, Highland/Gaelic society was evolving into a system of government very different from Lowland/British society, where the rule of law, rather than the supremacy of the sword, began to emerge as a novel civic ideal.

The essence of the rule of law is *reciprocity* between those who make the rules within any given society and those who have to obey them. This is what democracy is designed to achieve and what Vladimir Putin's "power vertical" is determined to crush. But Scotland has its own tradition of authoritarianism, as anyone who has lived for any length of time in the shadow of Empire, among the Scots abroad, will know. At home, even the history of the church has illustrated this, especially in the period after the General Assembly became a more accurate reflection of national opinion than the parliament. Examples are the killing of Covenanters in the seventeenth century; the attempt to impose religious uniformity after the Union of 1707; and the sustained campaign on the part of the Kirk after 1922 to send economic migrants from Catholic Ireland back to the newly formed Free State whose poverty and narrow horizons they wanted to avoid. Despite all that, there were other sorts of Scot, from Adam Smith and David Hume onwards who had a strong belief in the importance of personal freedom, intellectual diversity and equality between citizens. This is expressed in the popular saying that "we're a' Jock Tamson's bairns".

The novelty of Scotland's situation today is that we have a semi-autonomous, semi-democratic parliament which some people, including many MSPs, think is not working as it should. Nationalists say it is unsatisfactory because it lacks full sovereign powers; devolutionists allege that it has failed in its main task of holding the government to account on behalf of the citizens. Other controversies surround the relationship of the bureaucracy to devolved democracy, the developing habit of government secrecy, the attempt to police private opinion, and the increasingly tenuous relationship between voters and those they elect to represent them in parliament.

Those are not the only difficulties, but floating high above any specific issue is the unarguable fact that, democratically speaking, any problems with the Scottish "constitution" are ultimately *British* problems. It was the Westminster government which created the Scottish parliament, and it is *Westminster's* responsibility to make sure devolution works for *all* Britons, in *all* parts of the United Kingdom, including Scotland. Reciprocity denied in the Hebrides is reciprocity denied by London just as much as it is by Edinburgh.

As Secretary of State for Scotland in 1997, Donald Dewar was the principal architect of the Holyrood parliament as an institution. He made the rules. He was responsible for devising the unusual electoral system, and he made some critical choices, like how the debating chamber was laid out. Early on, he made this important claim: "The Scottish parliament will be marked by a new kind of politics." In this, he was reflecting the aims of the Consultative Steering Group which recommended the procedural approach for the new institution. It had said, "The establishment of the Scottish parliament offers the opportunity to put in place a new sort of democracy in Scotland." In the same vein, and more recently, Nicola Sturgeon, the most influential figure to date in Dewar's parliament, said when announcing her electoral pact with the Green Party in mid-2021, "This is a new way of doing politics."

What form is all this political novelty actually taking? Or are we simply seeing old-fashioned power politics in a new disguise? Many people voted for the establishment of the parliament in 1997 thinking, as I did, that it would be an opportunity to dispense with irrelevant and/or inappropriate controls over life in Scotland, some of which had been drafted at late-night sittings in Westminster without much thought for their application north of the border. Many people expected more sensible legislation to result from a new parliament in Edinburgh. The hope in 1997 was that it would disavow the authoritarian tradition I have mentioned while retaining the practicality and relevance that was customary in the phrasing of Scots law. I thought, naively as it turned out, that devolution would make life in Scotland *freer*. I ignored the old truism that the more bodies you have making rules, the more rules will be made. Like nature, power abhors a vacuum.

The most noticeable feature of modern Scottish politics has been its focus on nationalism, or independence. Nationalism is an attempt to give geographical definition to perceived ethnic, cultural, linguistic and other differences. However, throughout history, survival has depended to a significant extent on the opposite, namely size, alliances and co-operation with others who have comparable political principles. In Europe, such relationships have been governed since the Reformation by some approximation to the developing idea of international law.

I have written two books about law—*The Cost of a Reputation* and *The Justice Factory*—and two which are about sailing among the Scottish and Norwegian islands: *Isles of the West* and *Isles of the North*. The latter pair explore the dangers of powerful bureaucracies, including charities, which throw their self-righteous weight about in small communities like islands, undermining social cohesion and individual liberty. In retrospect,

I see these, too, as threats to the rule of law since ultimately state violence is implicit in the aggressive remodelling of society by government, especially when claims to "moral virtue" are used to justify limitations on traditional freedom.

You do not have to live long on the west coast to appreciate that Edinburgh is, for political purposes, almost as remote as London. Based, as I have long been, in seaward Argyll I meet many people who have intelligent and informed views on the topics raised in this book. I have not quoted such people individually, partly because so many are reluctant to draw attention to themselves by speaking "on the record".

Instead, I have put their comments into the mouth of Hamish Gobson, a composite character who lives on Great Todday—strictly, Todaidh Mór—the island made famous by Compton Mackenzie in his popular farces, of which the best known is *Whisky Galore*. This is a technique which I adopted, for different reasons, in *The Justice Factory* when interviewing Court of Session judges.[1] They talked to me only on condition that they could not be identified individually since there are conventions of judicial conduct which they did not wish to abuse. The College of Justice in Edinburgh is a small society, as is the world of the Hebrides, however geographically dispersed the latter may be. Both deserve the respect of discretion in return for their candour.

Hamish Gobson is not part of the Hebridean world as Compton Mackenzie would have known it. He lives by the shore and studies seaweed, crabs and life on the intertidal frontier. But he makes his living online at *Todday Today*, a website compiled on Great Todday from which I quote occasionally below. If Gobson has an overarching theme, it is that in a consumer world most politicians—but not *all*—cling to their personal self-interest as tenaciously as seaweed to a rock. Politics comes second for all but the most dangerous. We should be extremely suspicious of anyone who seeks power over his or her fellow citizens in peacetime.

Sometimes at dusk in calm weather when "the dimness comes on the kyles", as Sorley Maclean put it in the English text of "Hallaig", you can almost see the dark mass of Great Todday rising out of the western sea.

---

[1] *The Justice Factory: Can the Rule of Law Survive in 21st Century Scotland?* Ian Mitchell (2020)

Likewise, when the great and the good of Holyrood swoop down by helicopter for another selfie-opportunity among their local political partisans and the broken-down ferries, you could be forgiven for thinking, as Maclean also put it, that "the dead have been seen alive". It is to assert a general right to reciprocity with the helicopter heroes that Hamish Gobson publishes his comments on this gentry. "They read the polls," he says, "while I read the runes, which tend to be more reliable on a 'whole earth' basis."

My own position is simpler. I voted for the Scottish National Party for thirty years before leaving for Russia in 2006. My reasons were the same as for supporting the proposed Scottish parliament in 1997. I thought Scotland would be a freer society if ruled *domestically* by Scots. Coming home after twelve years in Moscow, I began to notice ominous parallels between nationalism there and nationalism here. Personal freedom has been the main casualty in both cases, and centralised authoritarianism the main cause of that. I discussed the background to this at some length in *The Justice Factory*, Part II, so will restrict myself here to observing that it is not enough in either country to have a "benevolent Tsar"; we need an *institutional framework* in which honest opinion can be channelled fearlessly upwards to people who are listening to more serious feedback than the opinion polls. Without that, reciprocity between the rulers and the ruled is a practical impossibility. In a parliamentary democracy, the foundation of the institutional framework should, of course, be the parliament. That is why I decided to write this book with two subjects—the chamber and its champion, if you like.

I want to stress that this is a *parliamentary* biography. I have no interest in Ms Sturgeon personally. I have never met her, and so far as I know, we have no friends in common—certainly no family. We come from completely different social, cultural, political, educational and professional backgrounds. She has often said she thinks private life should be separated from public life. I agree entirely. The reader hoping for domestic scandal below will be disappointed. My aim is to discover her *political personality*, as revealed by her performance in parliament.

This has nothing to do with prosaic issues like *policy*. Party policies evolve from day to day, and change as circumstances do or as opportunities present themselves. The essence of an individual in a position of long-term power from the citizen's point of view is not their policies at any given moment, but their public *character*. That is what I want to elucidate in Sturgeon's case. I assume her speeches in parliament are at least "politically" sincere because if what she says in the chamber does not represent her real thoughts on national issues, then we really are in a Putin-style world of mirrors and sleight of truncheon. Accordingly, it is Nicola Sturgeon's words, as printed in the Scottish parliament's *Official Report* and duly contextualised, which form the basis of this story.

Readers will come to their own conclusions about Ms Sturgeon. Whatever their view, I trust most will think it worthwhile to have tried to exercise the freedom that all Scots still have, but which Russians no longer have, to examine the words and public attitudes of those who run their country, and to write about them from their own point of view as *citizens*. To me, that means to write fairly, of course, but always in your *own personal style and from your own individual perspective*. I hope others will take up the idea of citizens' biographies, either for their intrinsic interest or because they feel that historical memory is being distorted by those with an axe to grind.

Today, it is only free citizens who can look at some of the important but controversial issues we face without prior intellectual restraint or institutional self-censorship. You don't have to be qualified to write books, just as you don't have to be qualified to be a politician. Each trade can look the other in the eye. Neither is academically respectable. Therefore, let each text, including this one, stand on its own merits rather than on those of its untenured and unelected author. In a free Scotland, we can all be Jock Tamson's biographers.

Campbeltown
Kintyre
Autumn 2022

Dramatis Personæ
(MSPs mentioned below, 1999-2007, with principle ministerial positions)

Brian **Adam** (SNP) born Morayshire 1948; biochemistry Aberdeen University; biochemist; North-east Scotland "list" 1999-2003, Aberdeen North constituency 2003-2007. Died 2013

Bill **Aitken** (Conservative) born Glasgow 1948; Glasgow Caledonian University; financial services, local councillor, District Court Judge, Deputy Lord Lieutenant of the City of Glasgow; Glasgow "list" 1999-2007

Wendy **Alexander** (Labour) born Glasgow, 1963; history University of Glasgow; management consultant; special advisor to Donald Dewar; Paisley North constituency 1999-2007; variously Minister for Communities, Enterprise, Lifelong Learning and Transport 1999-2002

Jackie **Baillie** (Labour) born Hong Kong 1964; University of Strathclyde; community economic development manager; Dumbarton constituency 1999-2007; Minister for Social Justice 2000-1

Shiona **Baird** (Green) born Hereford 1946; University of Edinburgh; farmer; North-east Scotland "list" 2003-7. Party leader 2004-7

Richard **Baker** (Labour) born Edinburgh 1974; University of Aberdeen, President of National Union of Students in Scotland; charity officer; North-east Scotland "list" 2003-7

Chris **Ballance** (Green) born Worcester, 1952; bookshop owner, playwright; South of Scotland "list" 2003-2007

Mark **Ballard** (Green) born Leeds 1971; economic and social history University of Edinburgh; editor *Reforesting Scotland;* Lothians "list" 2003-2007; elected Rector of Edinburgh University 2006, ahead of Magnus Linklater, journalist, and Boris Johnson, politician

Scott **Barrie** (Labour) born St Andrews 1962; University of Edinburgh; social worker; Dunfermline West constituency 1999 - 2007

Sarah **Boyack** (Labour) born Glasgow 1961; modern history and politics

university of Glasgow; town planner and environmentalist; constituency
Edinburgh Central constituency 1999-2007; Minister for Transport and
Planning 1999-2001

Rhona **Brankin** (Labour) born Glasgow 1950; University of Aberdeen; special
needs teacher, Midlothian constituency 1999-2007; Deputy Minister for
Culture and Sport 1999–2000; Deputy Minister for Environment and Rural Development 2000–2001; Deputy Minister for Health and Community
Care 2004-5; Minister Environment and Rural Development 2005-7; Minister for Communities 2007

Robert **Brown** (Liberal) born Newcastle-on-Tyne 1947; law University of Aberdeen; solicitor, Glasgow City Councillor; Glasgow "list" 1999-2007

Bill **Butler** (Labour) born Glasgow 1956; University of Stirling; teacher; Glasgow Anniesland constituency 1999-2007, following death of Donald
Dewar.

Rosemary **Byrne** (Scottish Socialist) born Irvine 1948; teacher, trade union activist; South of Scotland "list" 2003-2007

Dennis **Canavan** (Independent) born Cowdenbeath 1942; University of Edinburgh; maths teacher; Falkirk West constituency 1999-2007 (MP Falkirk
West (Labour) 1974-2000)

Malcolm **Chisholm** (Labour) born 1949; University of Edinburgh; teacher;
Edinburgh North and Leith constituency 1999-2007; Minister for Health
and Community Care 2001-4, Minister for Communities 2004-6. Resigned
in protest at Trident replacement plans (MP for Edinburgh North and
Leith 1992-2001)

Cathy **Craigie** (Labour) born Stirling 1954; local councillor; Cumbernauld and
Kilsyth constituency 1999-2007

Bruce **Crawford** (SNP) born Perth 1955; human resource manager Scottish
Office, local councillor; Mid-Scotland and Fife "list" 1999-2007

Roseanna **Cunningham** (SNP) born Glasgow 1951; law Universities of Western Australia, Stirling, Aberdeen; solicitor, advocate; Perthshire South and
Kinross-shire constituency 1999-2007 (MP Perth and Kinross 1995-7)

Frances **Curran** (Scottish Socialists) born Glasgow 1961; lecturer; West of
Scotland "list" 2003-7; ex-Militant Tendency; organiser of protest against
G8 meeting at Gleneagles 2005

Margaret **Curran** (Labour) born Glasgow 1958; economic history University
of Glasgow; community worker; Glasgow Baillieston constituency 1999-

2007; Minister for Communities 2002-4, Minister for Parliamentary Business 2004-7

Donald **Dewar** (Labour) born Glasgow 1937; law University of Glasgow; solicitor, politician, talk show host; Glasgow Anniesland constituency 1999-2000 (MP Aberdeen South 1966-70, Glasgow Garscadden then Anniesland 1978-2000). First Minister 1999-2000. Died 2000

Lord James **Douglas Hamilton** KC (Conservative) born Dungavel House 1942; law Universities of Oxford and Edinburgh; Lothian "list" 1999-2007 (MP Edinburgh West 1974-99) From 1997, Baron Selkirk of Douglas

Helen **Eadie** (Labour) born Stenhousemuir 1947; local councillor; Dunfermline East then Cowdenbeath constituencies 1999-2007. Died 2013

Dorothy-Grace **Elder** (SNP/Independent) born 1942; journalist; Glasgow "list" 1999-2003 (1999-2002 SNP; 2002-3 Independent)

Fergus **Ewing** (SNP) born 1957; law Glasgow University; solicitor; Inverness East, Nairn and Lochaber constituency 1999-2007. Son of Winnie Ewing

Winnie **Ewing** (SNP) born Glasgow 1929; law Glasgow University; solicitor; Highlands and Islands "list" 1999-2003 (MP Hamilton 1967-70, Moray and Nairn 1974-9; MEP Highlands and Island 1979-99) Mother of Fergus Ewing, "Mother of the House" 1999

Patricia **Ferguson** (Labour) born Glasgow 1958; public administration Glasgow College of Technology; health services administrator, trade unionist; Glasgow Maryhill constituency 1999-2007; Deputy Presiding Officer 1999-2001. Married to Bill Butler

Alex **Fergusson** (Conservative) born Wigtownshire 1949; Scottish Agricultural College; farmer; South of Scotland "list" 1999-2003, Galloway and Upper Nithsdale constituency 2003-7. Knighted in 2016. Died 2018

Brian **Fitzpatrick** (Labour) born 1961; law Glasgow University; solicitor, advocate; Strathkelvin and Bearsden constituency 2001-3

Colin **Fox** (Scottish Socialists) born Motherwell 1959; mathematics Strathclyde University; accountant, political activist (Militant Tendency); Lothians "list" 2003-2007

Murdo **Fraser** (Conservative) born Inverness 1965; law University of Aberdeen; solicitor; Mid-Scotland and Fife "list" 2001-2007

Phil **Gallie** (Conservative) born Portsmouth 1939; electricity station manager, local councillor; South of Scotland "list" 1999-2007 (MP for Ayr 1992-7) Died 2011

Rob **Gibson** (SNP) born Glasgow 1945; University of Dundee; teacher, local councillor; Highlands and Islands "list" 2003-7

Karen **Gillon** (Labour) born Edinburgh 1967; University of Birmingham; community education; Clydesdale constituency 1999-2007

Annabel **Goldie** (Conservative) born Glasgow 1950; law University of Strathclyde; solicitor; West of Scotland "list" 1999-2007. Now Baroness Goldie, Minister of State for Defence

Donald **Gorrie** (Liberal) born India 1933; Classical Mods and History, University of Oxford; teacher, local government councillor; Central Scotland "list" 1999-2007 (MP Edinburgh West 1997-2001) Died 2012

Christine **Grahame** (SNP) born Staffordshire 1944; arts, law University of Edinburgh; teacher, solicitor; South of Scotland "list" 1999-2007

Iain **Grey** (Labour) born Edinburgh 1957; physics University of Edinburgh; teacher, charity fund-raiser; Edinburgh Pentlands constituency 1999-2003. Minister for Social Justice 2000-1; Minister for Enterprise, Transport and Lifelong Learning 2002-3

Robin **Harper** (Green) born Thurso 1940; University of Aberdeen; teacher; Lothians "list" 1999-2007

Patrick **Harvie** (Green) born Vale of Leven 1973; Manchester Metropolitan University; youth worker, civil servant; Glasgow "list" 2003-7

John **Home Robertson** (Labour) born Edinburgh 1948; West of Scotland Agricultural College; local councillor, politician; East Lothian constituency 1999-2007 (MP East Lothian 1978-2001)

Gordon **Jackson** KC (Labour) born 1948; law University of St Andrews; advocate; Glasgow Govan constituency 1999-2007

Cathy **Jamieson** (Labour) born Kilmarnock 1956; fine art, Glasgow School of Art; art therapy, social work; Carrick, Cumnock and Doon Valley constituency 1999-2007. Minister for Education and Young People 2001-3; Minister for justice 2003-7

Alex **Johnstone** (Conservative) born Stonehaven 1961; farmer; North-East Scotland "list" 1999-2007. Died 2016

Andy **Kerr** (Labour) born East Kilbride 1962; social science Glasgow Caledonian University; local councillor, consultant; East Kilbride constituency 1999-2007. Minister for Finance and Public Services 2001-4; Minister for Health and Community Care 2004-7

Richard **Lochhead** (SNP) born Paisley 1969; politics University of Stirling; environmental development officer; North-East Scotland "list" 1999-2006, Moray constituency 2006-7

George **Lyon** (Liberal) born Rothesay 1956; farmer, President of National Farmers Union Scotland; Argyll & Bute constituency 1999-2007

Kenny **MacAskill** (SNP) born Edinburgh 1958; law University of Edinburgh; solicitor; Lothians "list" 1999-2007

Jack **McConnell** (Labour) born Irvine 1960; University of Stirling; teacher, political activist; Motherwell and Wishaw constituency 1999-2007; Minister for Finance 1999-2000, Minister for Education, Europe and External Affairs 2000-1, First Minister 2001-7. Now Baron McConnell of Glenscorrodale

Margo **MacDonald** (SNP, Independent) born Hamilton 1943; Dunfermline College of Physical Education; teacher, politician; Lothians "list" 1999-2007(1999-2003 SNP; 2003-7 Independent) (MP Glasgow Govan 1973-4; Deputy Leader SNP 1974-9) Died in 2014

Jamie **McGrigor** (Conservative) born London 1949; French, University of Neuchâtel; financier, farmer; Highlands and Islands "list" 1999-2007. Now Sir James McGrigor, Bt.

Ken **Macintosh** (Labour) born Inverness 1962; history University of Edinburgh; television journalist; Eastwood constituency 1999-2007

Angus **MacKay** (Labour) born Edinburgh 1964; politics University of Edinburgh; chaity officer, political advisor, local councillor; Edinburgh South constituency 1999-2003; Minister for Finance 2000-1

Henry **McLeish** (Labour) born Fife 1958; town planning Heriot-Watt University; footballer, town planner; Central Fife constituency 1999-2003; Minister for Enterprise and Lifelong Learning 1999-2000, First Minister 2000-1 (MP Central Fife 1987-2001; Minister of State at the Scottish Office 1997-1999)

David **McLetchie** (Conservative) born Edinburgh 1952; law University of Edinburgh; solicitor; Lothians "list" 1999-2003, Edinburgh Pentland constituency 2003-7; Leader Conservatives 1999-2005. Died 2013

Michael **McMahon** (Labour) born Motherwell 1961; welder, trade union activist; Hamilton North and Bellshill constituency 1999-2007

Maureen **Macmillan** (Labour) born Oban 1943; English literature Edinburgh University; teacher; Highlands and Islands "list" 1999-2007

Michael **Matheson** (SNP) born Glasgow 1970; occupational therapy Queen Margaret University; occupational therapist; Central Scotland "list" 1999-2007

Brian **Monteith** (Conservative) born Edinburgh 1958; Heriot-Watt University; political researcher, public relations; Mid-Scotland and Fife constituency 1999-2007

Mary **Mulligan** (Labour) born Liverpool 1960; shop worker, local councillor; Linlithgow constituency 1999-2007

Alex **Neil** (SNP) born Irvine 1951; economics University of Dundee; Labour Party activist, SNP activist; Central Scotland (list) 1999-2007

Irene **Oldfather** (Labour) born Glasgow 1954; politics University of Strathclyde; lecturer, researcher; Cunninghame South 1999-2007

Norah **Radcliffe** (Liberal) born Aberdeen 1946; University of Aberdeen; Gordon constituency 1999-2007

Keith **Raffan** (Liberal) born Aberdeen 1949; University of Cambridge; politician, broadcaster; Mid-Scotland and Fife "list" 1999-2005 (MP (Conservative) Delyn 1983-92)

George **Reid** (SNP) born Clackmannanshire 1939; history University of St Andrews; TV producer, politician; Mid-Scotland and Fife "list" 1999-2003, Ochil constituency 2003-7; Presiding Officer 2003-7 (MP Clackmannan and Eastern Stirlingshire 1974-9) Knighted 2012

Shona **Robison** (SNP) born Yorkshire 1966; social sciences University of Glasgow; social worker; North-East Scotland "list" 1999-2003 Dundee East constituency 2003-2007

Euan **Robson** (Liberal) born 1954; public relations, local councillor; Roxburgh and Berwickshire constituency 1999-2007

Mike **Rumbles** (Liberal) born Tyneside 1956; education Sunderland Polytechnic; Royal Army Education Corps; West Aberdeenshire and Kincardine constituency 1999-2007

Mark **Ruskell** (Green) born Edinburgh 1972; environmental science University of Stirling; Mid-Scotland and Fife "list" 2003-7

Michael **Russell** (SNP) born Bromley 1953; theology, history University of Edinburgh; media producer, author; South of Scotland "list" 1999-2003

Alex **Salmond** (SNP) born Linlithgow 1954; economics and history University of St Andrews; economist, politician; Banff and Buchan constituency

1999-2002; Leader SNP 1990-2000, 2004-7 (MP Banff and Buchan 1987-2007)

Tavish **Scott** (Liberal) born Inverness 1966; business studies Napier College; political support worker, farmer, local councillor; Shetland constituency 1999-2007; Minister for Transport and Telecommunications 2005-7

Tommy **Sheridan** (Scottish Socialists) born Glasgow 1966; economics University of Stirling; political activist and campaigner; Glasgow "list" 199-2007, Scottish Socialists 1999-2006; Solidarity 2007

Richard **Simpson** (Labour) born Edinburgh 1942; medicine University of Edinburgh; doctor; Ochil constituency 1999-2003, Mid-Scotland and Fife "list" 2003-7

Elaine **Smith** (Labour) born Coatbridge 1963; economics and politics Glasgow College; teacher; Coatbridge and Chryston constituency 1999-2007

Margaret **Smith** (Liberal) born Edinburgh 1961; Edinburgh West constituency 1999-2007

Sir David **Steel** (Liberal) born Kirkcaldy 1938; law University of Edinburgh; politician; Lothians "list" 1999-2003; Presiding Officer 1999-2003 (MP Roxburgh, Selkirk, and Peebles 1965-1983, Tweeddale, Ettrick, and Lauderdale 1983-1997) Created Lord Steele of Aikwood in 1997

Nicol **Stephen** (Liberal) born Aberdeen 1960; law University of Aberdeen; solicitor, financier, local councillor; Aberdeen South constituency 1999-2007; Minister for Transport 2003-5, Minister for Enterprise and Lifelong Learning 2005-7; Leader of Liberals 2005-7 (MP Kincardine and Deeside 1991-2)

Stewart **Stevenson** (SNP) born Edinburgh 1945; University of Aberdeen; software engineer; Banff and Buchan constituency 2001-7. Claims to have been the most prolific speaker in the parliament, having made 284 speeches in his first six years

Jamie **Stone** (Liberal) born Edinburgh 1954; history University of St Andrews; local councillor; Caithness, Sutherland and Easter Ross constituency 1999-2007

Nicola **Sturgeon** (SNP) born Ayr 1970; law University of Glasgow; solicitor; Glasgow "list" 1999-2007

John **Swinney** (SNP) born Edinburgh 1964; politics University of Edinburgh; management consultant; North Tayside constituency 1999-2007; leader SNP 2000-4

Jean **Turner** (Independent) born Glasgow 1939; medicine University of Aberdeen; doctor; Strathkelvin and Bearsden 2003-7

Kay **Ullrich** (SNP) born Prestwick 1943; social work Queen's College, Glasgow; social worker; West of Scotland "list" 1999-2003. Died 2021

Ben **Wallace** (Conservative) born Farnborough 1970; Sandhurst; Army officer; North-East Scotland "list" 1999-2003. Now Secretary of State for Defence

Jim **Wallace** KC (Liberal) born Annan 1954; economics and law University of Cambridge; advocate; Orkney constituency 1999-2007; Leader Liberals 1992-2005; Deputy First Minister 1999-2005 (MP Orkney and Shetland 1983-2001) Now Lord Wallace of Tankerness

Mike **Watson** (Labour/Independent) born Cambuslang 1949; economics Heriot-Watt University; trade unionist; Glasgow Cathcart constituency 1999-2005; Minister of Tourism, Culture and Sport 2001-3 (MP Glasgow Central 1989-1997) Created Lord Watson of Invergowrie 1997

Maureen **Watt** (SNP) born Aberdeenshire 1951; politics University of Strathclyde; teacher, personnel manager, local councillor; North-East Scotland "list" 2006-7

Sandra **White** (SNP) born Glasgow 1951; local councillor; Glasgow "list" 1999-2007

Another day at the office...

Shona Robison (North-East Scotland) (SNP): For the record, the Health and Community Care Committee took evidence on 8 May and 15 May. Both Nicola Sturgeon and I were present for all the oral evidence during those meetings. Perhaps the convener of the Health and Community Care Committee would like to take the opportunity to withdraw her remarks.

Mrs Margaret Smith (Edinburgh West) (LD): I will not withdraw the remark, because I know for a fact that Nicola Sturgeon was not in her seat on that occasion.

Nicola Sturgeon: I was at the toilet.

Mrs Smith: I remember thinking at the time that she had been away long enough to send a press release. That is what I thought that she was doing—

   [*Interruption.*]

The Deputy Presiding Officer: Order.

Shona Robison: Perhaps Margaret Smith should check the *Official Report* before making such comments in the chamber. I have the *Official Report* here and it says that Nicola Sturgeon and I were present for all that evidence.

Mrs Smith: On a point of order. As far as I am aware, the minutes of any meeting simply say that someone was present at a meeting. I did not say that Nicola Sturgeon was not present at the meeting. I said that Nicola Sturgeon was not there to hear all the evidence that was given. That is not the same thing.

Nicola Sturgeon: What about you?

Mrs Smith: I was there actually, apart from going to the toilet once. I did not say—

   [*Interruption.*]

The Deputy Presiding Officer: Order. I do not regard that as a point of order.[2]

---

[2] *Official Report*, 20 June 2002, col. 10003

Chapter 1

The Early Years

Nicola Ferguson Sturgeon was born on Sunday 19 July 1970. She spent the first year of her life in Prestwick, a town on the south-west coast of mainland Scotland better known for the visit that Elvis Presley paid there while on army service in 1960. After his aircraft landed, the King of Rock 'n' Roll famously asked, "Where am I?"

Part of Sturgeon's mother's family came from Leeds, but otherwise her background is Scottish. Her father was an electrician, and in 1971 he moved, with his wife and child, into a council house in Dreghorn, another unremarkable small town, near Prestwick, on the Kilmarnock road outside Irvine. Dreghorn's most famous son was John Boyd Dunlop, who was born there in 1840. He is widely credited with having invented the pneumatic tyre which, as Hamish Gobson points out, enables us all to drive about on pressurised, and therefore hot, air.

More seriously, Gobson shares the old Hebrideans belief that birth is important, both socially and chronologically. Anyone born on 19 July in the Gregorian calendar is a Cancer, the symbol of which is a crab. Sturgeon shares a birthday with two figures Gobson considers symbolically relevant to the story below. The first is Vladimir Mayakovsky, the Cossack-Ukrainian "Futurist" poet who, in 1930, fell into despair due to the centralising ("top down") nature of Stalin's single-man government. Vengeful philistine functionaries were put in charge of fields like "art production". Constant, ill-informed snooping by politically correct bureaucrats stifled creativity. Mayakovsky tried to resist by doing what little he could to preserve the freedom and diversity of Russian cultural life. But Stalin was implacable. "Finally," Gobson writes, "in the name of art,

Mayakovsky went the extra mile and shot himself."

A more modern Cancerian in whose life Gobson sees another illuminating analogy is that of Harold Egbert Camping, the celebrated
American evangelist and radio star who predicted that the world would
end on 21 May 2011. That was just days after the election in which Sturgeon's Scottish National Party (SNP) achieved the first overall majority
for any party in the Scottish parliament. Some thought that in itself was
a sign that the world was coming to an end. But when nothing had happened, either in Edinburgh or "the wider universe", by midnight on 21st,
Pacific Daylight Time, Holyrood was able to convene on 25th and ap-
point a new First Minister and his Deputy, Nicola Sturgeon. Camping
was compelled to revise his forecast. He rescheduled "UniBang2" for 21
October. When the result then was equally disappointing, the unhappy
Camping resigned his church positions, abjured further prophesy and
said to his bewildered followers, "We humbly acknowledge we were
wrong."

Beyond their powerful claws, crabs are well-armoured, having a
tough outer shell which encourages introversion and individual self-suf-
ficiency. One of the Crab's "perceptible characteristics is being inward-
looking." Psychologically, Cancerians are said to be "capricious and dramatic", with a need "to feel love, if only from the general public." Above
all else, they hate "mockery and not being taken seriously". Crabs, as a
species, are not known for their sense of humour, which might be why,
Gobson suggests, Sturgeon acquired the nickname "Nippie".

Recent support for Gobson's view has come from Mandy Rhodes,
the editor of *Holyrood*, the magazine which covers Scottish politics and
personalities. She knows Sturgeon better than most and, soon after she
became First Minister, Rhodes wrote of her:

> [Sturgeon] is an incredibly private person doing a very public job and has
> become adept at giving the impression of being just like you and me, elevat-
> ing 'being normal' to an art form… Paradoxically, *she is more at ease*, it seems,
> *with strangers*, where she is not having to give of herself, than she is with
> closer acquaintances, where more personal investment might be required."[3]

---

[3] *Scottish National Party Leaders,* eds. James Mitchell & Gerry Hassan (2016), p. 356

(emphasis added)

Sturgeon herself admitted as much in an interview with Alastair Campbell in 2015. "I am quite a shy person," she said. "In my younger days that manifested itself as [being] cold and overly reserved."[4]

Crabs are famous for the tenacity of their grip, and determination is Sturgeon's most noticeable political characteristic, after her emotional reticence. She has always had a single, over-riding professional aim in life: to destroy the United Kingdom as political entity. The scale of her ambition was always colossal, but that is not uncommon among politicians with few close acquaintances or intellectual interests outside politics. What is unusual is that Sturgeon has the will to match the ambition.

One other general observation is worth making at the outset. Mandy Rhodes also wrote about Sturgeon's position in the nexus of class affiliation and national identity which is so important to nationalist activists in Scotland today:

> Sturgeon stands out from other professional politicians, not only because she is a woman, but because she appears authentically Scots; *state-educated, working-class, left-leaning,* and *believably human.*[5] (emphasis added)

To be "authentically Scots", it would seem, you have to be born into the right class. That is an accident of birth and therefore an attribute rather than an attainment. Reliance on inheritance is the opposite of meritocratic. Rhodes's observation is acute as it is the common boast of politicians who grew up thinking themselves "working class" that those who did not have that privilege cannot speak for the "real" (i.e. "authentic") Scotland. Jimmie Reid, the moving spirit of the Upper Clyde Shipbuilders work-in, put this point clearly in a speech to shipyard workers when Sturgeon was just a year old:

> Today Scotland speaks. Not the Scotland of the lairds and the lackeys. They've never represented Scotland. *Here in this meeting today is the real Scotland.* The Scotland of the working people. No title, no rank, no Establishment honour can compare with the privilege of belonging to the Scottish working

---

[4] *GQ Magazine*, 13 March 2017, interview from November 2015

[5] *Ibid.,* p. 364

class.[6] (emphasis added)

Since Sturgeon has, throughout her political life, tried to ridicule and dismiss what she sees as the Tory "establishment", a further comment from Jimmy Reid is relevant to the issue of defensive self-assertion:

> In the last analysis, workers can only depend on themselves, on their fellow workers, on the unity of their class. There are those in society who try to diminish our self-confidence as workers. They *try to inculcate in ourselves a self-belittlement of our own ability and our own intelligence*, to try and inculcate into us almost from childhood that we're here to be ruled, and somebody else is here to rule us.[7] (emphasis added)

The problem with inverse elitism is what happens when you "move up a class"? Today, Sturgeon lives in Charlotte Square in Edinburgh's New Town, dresses in expensive designer clothing, employs servants, moves about in chauffeur-driven cars and buys large houses. Is she still "authentic"? Does she still represent what Jimmy Reid called "the real Scotland"? Or is she now part of a socio-economic group which has "never represented Scotland"? A century ago, upwardly mobile "Scots on the make" changed their accent when they moved to the New Town, or to London. Today they change cars, clothes and the size of their houses. Is there any important difference between classical snobbery and the modern variety? Or are both equally "inauthentic"? Does it matter?

No, says Hamish Gobson, who regards "authenticity" as "but the guinea's stamp". A crab's a crab for a' that, he maintains. As he knows from life by the Todday shore, these animals multiply with astonishing speed. They lay eggs by the thousand and spawn numberless, almost identical young. The mother makes no personal investment in her offspring. Perhaps that is why Sturgeon has so often been criticised by "inauthentic" Scots for having followers who reproduce her opinions in a way which suggests that they do not think for themselves individually, and behave more like an army of crabs.

That is where the analogy breaks down. Sturgeon is not responsible

---

[6] Reid can be seen saying the words on the YouTube film "upper clyde shipbuilders 1", 1971.

[7] *Ibid.,* "The Sounds of the Clyde", 1971, at 9 minutes

for the conformist attitudes of her human followers. Moreover, she has told us *herself* that she has a personal investment in every young Scot. Though childless herself, she has said that, as First Minister, she is the "first mother" of Scotland. Talking to social activists at a Global Care Family Gathering at her old school in 2018, Sturgeon illustrated Rhodes's point by describing herself as "the chief corporate parent in Scotland. Chief Mammy, as I prefer to describe it!"[8]

***

The future Chief Mammy went to school locally, at Greenwood Academy in Dreghorn, a new institution, established in 1972 with the motto "Aye to learn". That was the year in which, on St Andrew's Day, Compton MacKenzie died in Edinburgh. He had been the first prominent English incomer to take up the Scottish nationalist cause. He was voted Rector of Glasgow University in 1931 by students who were experiencing the early stirrings of Scottish nationalism. Soon afterwards, he helped establish the SNP. Mackenzie had first come to Scotland after he bought the Shiant Isles (in the north Minch) in the 1920s, before moving to the isle of Barra in 1930. He is buried there in a small Catholic cemetery overlooking the Big Beach, or Traigh Mhor, where the flights from Glasgow now land. The true story on which he based *Whisky Galore* concerns the stranding, in winter 1941 off Eriskay near Barra, of a ship with quarter of a million bottles of over-proof whisky in the holds. Curiously, the name of the real ship was the SS *Politician*.

Early in life, Sturgeon gave signs of both introversion and humourlessness. She would retreat under the dining room table to read when parties were in progress, sometimes her own. She recalls wanting to become an author "like Enid Blyton". Despite this, young Nicola had something in common with Britain's second female Prime Minister, Theresa May, who was once asked in an interview what was the "naughtiest" thing she had ever done. She said that, as a child, she "ran through fields of wheat".[9] Sturgeon's equivalent involved her younger sister,

---

[8] She was speaking at Greenwood Academy, Dreghorn, on 27 October 2018.

[9] *Telegraph*, 5 June 2017

Gillian, who now advertises herself as a Tarot reader. Gillian had a Barbie-type doll with plastic hair, and her older sister took a bladed weapon and cut off a lock. This is a widely reported story which Sturgeon now denies. But, rather than laughing it off as childish trivia, she took the matter seriously when asked about it.

"I deny the allegations levelled at me by my sister," she said. "I'm sure I didn't cut the hair off her Barbie doll. But if I did – and it's an if – then there would have been some provocation involved, I'm sure of it."[10]

As a teenager, Sturgeon read Nigel Tranter, the historical novelist and dreamy nationalist who, when he was not writing Westerns, published tales of Jacobite heroism and romance. She idolised Cilla Black, the Liverpudlian singer. "She still holds a special place in my affections," Sturgeon told Alastair Campbell. "One of my earliest memories was a tantrum at Littlewoods in Ayr. I was about four and I wanted a Cilla Black album and my parents said no, and my grandad came along and bought it for me."[11] Despite romantic Cilla, as a teenager Sturgeon had a poster of Jim Sillars, the rugged hero of the gritty Left in "authentic" Scotland, on her bedroom wall. In between times, she liked to go ice-dancing in nearby Ayr to Duran Duran, a band of "new romantics" from West Bromwich in the Black Country.[12]

***

Sturgeon was first introduced to politics by an older woman, Kay Ullrich, a social worker who lived close by. Ullrich felt strongly that nuclear submarines should not be stationed on the Clyde. She had already stood for parliament as a Nationalist in order to try to get them moved. Before the 1987 general election Sturgeon offered to help Ullrich with her campaign, despite the fact that she was still at school. The motivation Sturgeon has cited many times since for taking so intense an interest in

---

[10] BBC News 14 November 2014

[11] *GQ Magazine, op. cit.*

[12] For a fuller account of Sturgeon's pre-political, and private, life as well as the media's interaction with her, see *Nicola Sturgeon: a political life*, David Torrance (2016).

politics so early in life was "hatred of Margaret Thatcher".[13] That, she says, was "the motivation for my entire political career." Ironically, it was England's "Iron Lady" who gave life to the political personality of Scotland's "Iron Woman".

Sturgeon has never forgiven Thatcher, even though she fell from power while Sturgeon was still at university, and died in 2013, before she became leader of the SNP. Despite the fact that it was Mrs Thatcher's housing policy which allowed her family to buy their council house in Dreghorn, Sturgeon's negative attitude to the Tory leader has been uncompromising. Thatcher stood for the United Kingdom, and Sturgeon stands for its destruction. Where sovereignty is concerned, politics is a zero-sum game.

Though Thatcher was still riding high when Sturgeon got involved in Ullrich's campaign in 1987, support for the SNP was rising, albeit very slowly. The Party's share of the national vote in the general election that year rose from 1.1% (in 1983) to 1.3%. In Scotland, the SNP attracted 12.2% of the popular vote. This was less than half the Conservative figure north of the Border and only a quarter of the Labour one. Unionist parties attracted over 85% of the vote. The uncomfortable truth for nationalists was that most Scots did not hate Mrs Thatcher as much as they did. Separatist activism was *not* a safe career choice in those days. But that did not discourage Sturgeon.

"I hated the fact that [Thatcher] was able to do what she was doing yet nobody I knew in my entire life had voted for her," Sturgeon said much later.[14] Here again, the singleness of purpose is evident, even during a period when she experimented with cannabis. ("It made me sick; I really didn't like it," she told one journalist.)[15] Though she says she did not know any Tories, Dreghorn was in the constituency of Cunninghame South, and before 1987 both Cunninghame North and neighbouring Ayr were held by Tories. There must have been plenty of them about. Indeed in her own constituency 6,095 people voted Tory, beating

---

[13] *Scottish National Party Leaders, op. cit.,* p. 358

[14] *Sturgeon,* Torrance, *op. cit.,* p. 26

[15] *Ibid.,* p. 27

Ullrich, who received only 4,115 votes for the SNP.[16] Can it really be true that Sturgeon never in her "entire life" met any such people? Or was this a case of retrospective memory management?

The SNP won three seats in 1987, which was up from two in 1983 but still an indifferent performance. However, that did not deter Sturgeon. In any case, there were straws in the wind. The election saw the first retreat by Thatcher's Tories, who lost 21 seats overall, half of them in Scotland where they were reduced from having 21 MPs in 1983 to just 10. This was also the election in which Alex Salmond, then a slim, smooth-talking but huffy banker, was first elected to parliament. It was during the election campaign that Sturgeon's future husband, Peter Murrell, started to work for Salmond, the man who was to become Sturgeon's political mentor. Politically, Scotland was, and is, a small country.

According to a later BBC profile, Sturgeon really joined the SNP in a fit of pique at being assumed to be a potential Labour supporter.

> Ms Sturgeon's English teacher was a Labour councillor and assumed his pupil would also join the party, because of her interest in politics and antipathy for the Tory government.
>
> When he handed her a membership form, she said it was the catalyst for joining the Nationalists.
>
> "I thought: 'Stuff you, I'm going to join the SNP'," she said in an interview.[17]

In other accounts, Sturgeon has given credit to Nelson Mandela. Three weeks before starting at university, on 18 July 1988, she went to her first political rally, which was to mark Mandela's 70th birthday.

> "To me," she recalled in 1999, "he was just the personification of everything I thought was ideal in politics."
>
> [She claimed] in one interview that events in South Africa "made [her] a Nationalist."[18]

It is a measure of her *political* self-confidence that Sturgeon has never felt it necessary to explain how she could support a man who had once

---

[16] The Labour candidate, David Lambie, received 22,700 votes.

[17] BBC News, 5 September 2012

[18] *Sturgeon,* Torrance, *op. cit.,* p. 30

been a terrorist. Mandela had been a co-founder of Umkhonto we Sizwe (Spear of the Nation) which was the military wing of the African National Congress (ANC). It committed acts of sabotage throughout the 1960s in protest against the National Party and its policy of separatism. It would be interesting to know how that clash of nationalisms—National Congress *versus* National Party—made Sturgeon a nationalist.

She has also said that she used Mandela to put her "nationalism in an international context". For all Mandela's immense and justified distinction as a pioneer of non-racial South Africa in later years, it is hard to know how Sturgeon could have formed any view more profound than that of a fan in 1988. She had never visited Africa, and at the time she went to the rally, Mandela was still in Pollsmoore prison with his positive achievements yet to come. Might this have been another example of retrospective memory management?

***

Around the time of the Mandela rally, Sturgeon graduated from Greenwood Academy. Two months later she enrolled at Glasgow University. Her life-long fixity of purpose did not let her take a "gap year" as students often do if they want to broaden their horizons. Many go out to Africa, for example, to help deprived communities through teaching, building schools or working in hospitals. Sturgeon's internationalism did not yet extend to international travel.

At university, the same fixity of purpose took her straight into the Young Scottish Nationalists. She was soon in the thick of student politics, though she made little impact. But she never gave up. For example, in the 1990/91 General Poll for the Student Representative Council she came last. But she persisted and, later that year, she managed to get herself elected to committees on sexual harassment and "women's issues". It was a start.

Rather in the way that Glasgow University a generation earlier brought together so many of the important faces in the Labour Party— Donald Dewar, Derry Irvine, John Smith, etc.—it provided Sturgeon with many of her future friends in nationalist politics, like Angela Constance, Alasdair Allan, Shona Robison and Stewart Hosie. SNP activists would rest from their labours by going "doon the watter" to Dunoon for tea and a scone. There, Sturgeon met and discussed issues such as how to avoid paying the poll tax with future luminaries of the SNP like Fiona Hyslop, who grew up in England, Roseanna Cunningham, the semi-Australian republican, and Angus Robertson, who was born in England but whose mother was German. Perhaps vicarious travel also helped put Sturgeon's "nationalism in an international context".

The portrait painted by journalists of the future First Minister in those days is not flattering. She was considered by many to be "po-faced", "humourless" and a bit of a Plain Jane. Despite being called "Nippie", or even "the Nippie sweetie", Iain Macwhirter, the *Herald* political commentator, described her as "slightly mannish".[19] Some say less kindly that had earned her another nickname at University: Seaweed—allegedly because "not even the tide would take her out."

Politics was a more reliable world. The Young Scottish Nationalists supplied many of her friends and future followers. Apart from the names just mentioned, they included a future leader of the Party, John Swinney, and others, like Derek Mackay and Humza Yousaf, who will appear later in this story. Meanwhile, Sturgeon put all her energy into the "Youth for Salmond" campaign, wearing pro-Salmond T-shirts and other forms of political marketing paraphernalia, while trying to keep abreast of her studies.

***

In July 1992 Sturgeon graduated in Public International Law. The subject was central to her interest in independence. But not everyone was impressed with her performance as a student. Professor Alastair Bonnington of the Glasgow University Law Faculty has commented:

> I taught Nicola Sturgeon when she was in law classes at Glasgow University. I seem to have failed to instil in her the most basic rules of how the institutions of government work in the free world. We tried to teach that a one-party government which tramples on the independence of the other arms of the state, and indeed the independence of its own members, is the very

---

[19] *Sturgeon,* Torrance, *op. cit.,* p. 56

antithesis of true democracy. How sad that we failed.[20]

The reason for Sturgeon's deficient understanding might have had something to do with the fact that she was not primarily interested in law. As she told Scottish Television soon after graduation, "I spent more time involved in politics than I did studying law."

Whatever her private enthusiasms, Sturgeon now had to establish a career. She took a diploma in legal practice at the University the following year, then served a legal apprenticeship with the prominent firm of McClure Naismith. It had once been known as a pillar of the Protestant Ascendency in the west of Scotland, having started as a debt recovery operation in 1826. That was a time when Catholics were still barred from the legal profession (and much else besides). It is a credit to Sturgeon's political flexibility that she was prepared to go to work for an organisation which carried with it the legacy of sectarian division. However, for reasons never stated, McClure Naismith decided that after Sturgeon completed her two-year apprenticeship they would not employ her on a full salary. "There was no question of Nicola staying on," one of the partners has been quoted as saying. "I don't think she was surprised by that decision."

Sturgeon next went to work for a small, new law firm in Stirling called Bell & Craig. Gordon Craig was a dedicated SNP member, but it is not known if he hired Sturgeon as a gesture of kindness to a fellow nationalist "in distress". This cannot be ruled out as the firm mainly did conveyancing work which, though profitable, is rarely exciting and certainly does not call for a background in public international law. The closest the firm came to any geographical initiative was to open a branch office in Falkirk.

Sturgeon has been reticent to the point of secrecy about what she did at Bell & Craig, though the Law Society has provided some information due to a complaint made about her work by one of her clients. The allegation was that Sturgeon had done nothing effective to help a battered wife who was being pursued by her violent husband and that it was only after she left the firm that the victim was able to make the application

---

[20] *Scotsman*, 21 July 2016

for legal aid which she wanted. Whatever the truth, in the end Bell & Craig waived the outstanding fee for the battered wife and let the caged politician go. Sturgeon is unconcerned but uncandid, saying only: "I've got nothing that I want to confess."[21]

After Bell & Craig, she moved back to Glasgow and joined the Drumchapel Law Centre. Once again, this was not the sort of establishment where there was much call for expertise in public international law. But she earned a reputation for effectively focussed advocacy in the sort of unglamorous cases where law and life clash unpityingly, and it is only the lawyers who emerge unimpoverished. As the Law Centre was a not-for-profit organisation, and therefore did not pay well, it cannot have been the money which took her to Drumchapel. Most probably politics was the driver. At any rate, it was in Glasgow that she hoped to find a stepping stone to parliament or, failing that, a council.

Sturgeon did not stay in Drumchapel long. She decided to stand in the first Scottish parliamentary election, to be held in May 1999. She had her sights on a constituency called Govan, named after a decaying suburb of inner-city Glasgow where the nationalist protest vote could be expected to be strong. The last remaining shipyard on the upper Clyde was located there, but its future was uncertain. Her long apprenticeship among the SNP activists had paid off and she was adopted as the official candidate.

As the legal book closed, so the political one opened wide.

---

[21] *Daily Express*, 5 April 2021

Chapter 2

Into Parliament

Sturgeon's assault on elected office in May 1999 was not her first. In fact there had been five previous ones. Her maiden campaign was for the Irvine North ward on the Cunninghame District Council in 1992, which she fought while still at university. She lost to Labour by a substantial margin, as she did in the UK general election in the same year, when she stood for Glasgow Shettleston. She received slightly less than a third of the votes of the winning Labour candidate. Undaunted by another defeat, she stood for Baillieston/Mount Vernon in the 1994 Strathclyde Regional Council election. She came second, getting less than half the vote of the successful Labour candidate. More disappointment was to follow. She stood for Bridgeton in the Glasgow City Council elections the following year and was beaten comprehensively, attracting just 16% of the vote compared with the winning Labour candidate's 84%.

In 1997 Sturgeon stood again for the House of Commons in the election which saw New Labour returned to office with Tony Blair as Prime Minister. Her target constituency was now Govan which, though it had been Labour for most of the time since 1918, had been won for the SNP in spectacular circumstances *twice*. In 1973 the vocal and colourful Margo MacDonald took it away from Labour for a few months and in 1988, Sturgeon's teenage political heartthrob, Jim Sillars (by then Margo MacDonald's husband), won the seat and represented Govan for four years. Perhaps the journeyman solicitor thought she could emulate such protean feats?

In the event, she lost by 3,000 votes to a popular Muslim, Mahommad Sarwar, whose son is now leader of the Labour faction in the

Holyrood parliament. Sarwar turned out to be a successful MP, being re-elected twice and serving eventually for thirteen years. After leaving the House of Commons, he was elected to the Pakistani Senate and served two terms as Governor of the Punjab, retiring only in 2022. Though that was in the future, Sturgeon illustrated her early command of the essential political skill of character assault combined with self-promotion when she said of Sarwar: "He wants Govan because he wants to be Britain's first Muslim MP. I want Govan because I want to do whatever I can to help the people of Govan."[22]

Defeat made no impression on Sturgeon's characteristic determination to "help the people". She entered the lists for Govan again in the first Scottish parliament election, in May 1999. Once again, she was beaten into second place by the Labour candidate who, on this occasion, was Gordon Jackson QC, the advocate who went on to defend Sturgeon's mentor, Alex Salmond, in the "sexual harassment" case in 2020 (as will be discussed in volume 3). Third in that election was the Conservative candidate, Tasmina Ahmed-Sheikh, who subsequently changed party and became Salmond's assistant on his Russian television show. Many of the characters in the Holyrood drama were already on stage.

Overall, the SNP did not do badly in this election, getting about a quarter of the vote and securing seven democratically elected seats, as against the Conservatives' nil. True, the Liberal Democrats won 12 democratic seats while the Labour Party won 53. The computer-generated allocations in the bureaucratically-allocated "list" seats changed the balance significantly. (The difference between democratic and bureaucratic seats in the Scottish parliament will be explained below.) Labour won 790,000 "list" votes for which it was awarded 3 additional seats. The SNP won 639,000 "list" votes, for which it was awarded a further 28 seats. The Tories received 319,000 "list" votes and were awarded an additional 18 seats. In round terms, Labour needed 263,000 votes per "list" seat; the SNP 23,000 and the Tories 18,000. The consequences of this computer-based gerrymandering have been felt in all Scottish elections to this day. It renders local opinion meaningless as what you win on the democratic swings you lose on the bureaucratic roundabout. Only the

---

[22] *Sturgeon,* Torrance, *op. cit.* p. 62

broad national swing is intelligible. Elections ostensibly intended to select local representatives move one step closer to being crude national
plebiscites. Constituency responsibility, and hence personal contact between MSPs and voters is compromised. Politics moves one step away
from the people; reciprocity is threatened; centralisation encouraged;
parliament devalued.

Surprisingly in the context of Sturgeon's commitment to promoting
women in politics, the SNP was far behind Labour in terms of gender
balance. Labour won 56 seats, of which 23 were men and 23 women.
The SNP had 20 men and 15 women; the Conservatives 15 men and 3
women; and the touchy-feely Liberal Democrats 15 men and only 2
women. (Henceforth, I will refer to them simply as "Liberals" for con-
venience.) The proportion of women among MSPs was to sink from
43% in 1999 to 26% in 2007. By then, the SNP's percentage had been
overtaken even by the Conservatives.[23]

The gender imbalance in the SNP was of long standing, and was a
harbinger of things to come. Some said it was not the SNP's fault. Kay
Ullrich was one of the female minority in the first parliament. She
blamed Britain for Scottish chauvinism. "As long as Westminster retains
power over the relevant legislation, Scottish ministers' ability to make
the [Scottish] Executive's equality strategy effective will be very limited."[24]

Sturgeon's second place in Govan had been won by hard work. She
canvassed so relentlessly that she occasionally suffered from "brain
fade". A conspicuous example was a press conference in mid-April. With
the election just three weeks away, she made the point that she wanted
"foreign" languages taught in primary schools, but froze when asked
which ones. Michael Russell, the conspicuously cultured chief executive
of the party, came to her rescue with a few suggestions. In her defence,
it must be emphasised that Sturgeon had led a sheltered life and not
travelled much. She had studied French at the Greenwood Academy, but

---

[23] See *The Modern SNP: from protest to power*, ed. Gerry Hassan (2009), p. 44

[24] *Official Report*, 8 November 2000, col. 1456. For quotations below for which the
source is clearly the *Official Report*, only the date and column reference will be
given.

never claimed to be able to speak it well. Her "internationalism" had not extended to learning other people's languages.

If there was one criticism which did stick to her, it was of her image as a Cancer, that is to say a crab which hides beneath its hard shell, in its own crevasse in the rock, and is not comfortable moving too far beyond the sheltering screen of floating seaweed. She did not naturally have the expansive, open-jacketed self-confidence that Salmond, for example, did. She seemed to take little interest in anything outside politics, including ordinary social life. Journalists noticed how far she was prepared to go in sublimating her natural self in order to project her political self. Even something as uncool as make-up seemed legitimate in a higher cause. Three days before the ballot, one reported with glee: "Nicola Sturgeon has been spotted wearing lippie."[25]

***

Sturgeon's second place in Govan did not mean she failed to get into parliament. Rejected democratically, she was able to get in on the bureaucratic roundabout. This distinction needs to be explained as the composition and behaviour of the Scottish parliament from then till now can hardly be understood otherwise.

The ruling elite in the British Labour Party, having won the 1997 Westminster general election by a massive margin, and the referendum on the establishment of a Scottish parliament by an even wider one, wanted to devise a constitution for that parliament which would allow Labour to continue its historic domination of democratic politics in Scotland, but without making that dominance offensively obvious.[26]

One hope for the new parliament was, as George (now Lord) Robertson famously put it, that it would "kill nationalism stone dead." In the 1997 election, Labour had received 46% of the votes in Scotland and

[25] *Sunday Herald,* 2 May 1999

[26] Between the Great Reform Act in 1832 (before which elections were held on the grossly undemocratic franchise of the pre-1707 Scottish parliament) and the arrival of full democracy, soon after the First World War, the Liberals were electorally dominant in Scotland. Between then and the early 1960s there were ebbs and flows. For the remainder of the twentieth century it was Labour that was "the Scottish party".

78% of the Scottish seats, while the SNP had received 22% of the votes and 8% of the seats. (The Tories got 18% of the votes and won no seats at all.) If a small, single-chamber half-parliament were to work, a system had to be devised that would sacrifice pure democracy to Scottish reality, and cloak "tribal" uniformity in fake variety. Hence the willingness to replace some of the elected seats by appointed ones. By this means, losing parties could be allocated seats they could not win in straight contests in actual constituencies.

The freedom to distort national voting patterns was not the only reason for departing from the Westminster system. Donald Dewar was been Secretary of State for Scotland from 1997, and therefore responsible for devising the new political architecture. The result was the Scotland Act (1998) which introduced what I will refer to below as "the Dewar Constitution".

Dewar's hope was that the new parliament would abandon adversarial politics and operate by "consensus". He explained his thinking in 1997:

> The House of Commons chamber at Westminster, with government and opposition at two sword-lengths apart, is without doubt the most atmospheric debating chamber in the world. But its shape reflects the first past the post voting system. The Scottish parliament will, of course, be elected on a proportional system, and that will change how we do things, perhaps more than people realise… The Scottish parliament will be marked by *a new kind of politics*.[27] (emphasis added)

Consensus, of course, has it place, but that is generally when there are no difficult decisions to be made about important issues. When there are, consensus can be the enemy of democracy as it is either natural, in which case it would have been arrived at anyway, whatever the structure of the parliament, or it is artificial, in which case it is to an extent authoritarian, and always centralising. Even when it works, it focusses artificially on the uncontroversial centre of public discourse and marginalises broad swathes of opinion, especially innovative opinion on either side. It encourages the conventional and discourages creativity.

---

[27] Speech to the 1997 conference of the Centre for Research into Elections and Social Trends, 21 November 1997, quoted on gov.scot archive website for that date.

One of the best-known examples of forced consensus was the McCarthy-ite anti-Communist drive in the United States in the early 1950s. It created a widespread fear of being found to be outside the mainstream. If elected representatives in any democracy act in unreasoning conformity with others, they betray their responsibility to those who have voted for them. The same happens with strict whipping in parliaments—a point that was to become a major problem in the Scottish parliament later.

Either way, the effect of artificially promoted consensus is to create a centrist bloc which is likely to become a permanent regime, with all the evils associated with politicians who get too comfortable with their hands on the levers of power. Everyone knew that the Labour Party in post-war Glasgow was the local "establishment". Pork barrel politics dominated, rather as they did in post-independence Ireland and still do in the European Union. Dewar, who grew up in Glasgow, wanted to avoid replicating that type of government in the new national parliament. He could see the dangers of a tribalized legislature and wanted to remove them, even though it was his own tribe which was dominant.

Dewar's motives were pure but his methods disastrous. Initially, he pressed for full proportional representation, but that was diluted to having 56 seats allocated by proportional representation, and the other 73 on the traditional British "individual constituency" basis. Scotland's main constitutional authority has explained the reason for the hybrid electoral system:

> Electoral reform [i.e. proportional representation] was the price of Liberal Democrat participation in the Scottish Constitutional Convention. For Labour, which had most to lose from the introduction of any form of proportional representation, it seemed to offer a guarantee against a possibility that the SNP might win an outright majority, and in so doing re-open the devolution "settlement".[28]

Under the Dewar Constitution, the 73 "democratic" seats followed, with few changes, the 72 then existing constituencies for the

---

[28] *Constitutional Law of Scotland*, Alan Page (2015), p. 49, para. 4-05

Westminster parliament.[29] The 56 "proportional representation" seats were, and still are, allocated to eight multi-member "hyper-constituencies" similar to those once used for elections to European parliament. There are about half a million electors in each, which makes any personal link between voters and representatives impossible. As Hamish Gobson puts it: "Not even Liberace had that many friends."

Worse still, the candidates are chosen by central party managers, not by local constituency associations, which is why I have called them "bureaucratic" seats, unlike the ordinary ones, which I have called "democratic". Officially, the former are referred to as "list" seats, since candidates have to be on a registered party list in order to be allowed to stand. This is reminiscent of the question put to individual travellers in the Soviet Union by Intourist receptionists: "Good morning, sir. Are you a group?" Similarly, the Scottish parliament classifies any *individual* standing in such seats as a "party of one". Margo MacDonald became one of the best known of these after she was ejected from the SNP (see below). At this writing, there is not a single independent in the parliament.

Unlike many systems of proportional representation, in Scotland we have what is called a "closed list" system, which means that voters do not even have the chance to express an opinion on which candidate on their preferred party's list they vote for. As you may vote for a *party* only, it is the *party managers* who decide which of their "list" candidates will have the chance of becoming an MSPs, not the electorate.

Tipping the balance further against the voters and in favour of the political managers at central headquarters is the fact that candidates do not even have to choose between democracy and bureaucracy. They may stand for both types of seat. You may offer yourself for a democratic one then, if you lose, be elected for a super-constituency on the "list". Personal risk for politicians is minimised in this way. Sturgeon's own career illustrates this. She stood for Govan in 1999 and failed, yet she was elected in the same poll for the super-constituency called "Glasgow", which included Govan. Same in 2003. But in 2007 she was elected for Govan itself (most of it by then called Glasgow Central), and so

---

[29] This has since been reduced to 59 MPs in order to redress the representational imbalance with England created by the Scottish parliament.

abandoned the seat she had held for eight years, allowing the party bureaucrats to bump everyone else on the "list" ladder one place up. She
seems to have abandoned "Glasgow" without regret, which says something about the lack of a strong link between voter and MSP in these
huge "list" seats. They represent human interaction in name only, not
substance. Even Liberace gave a farewell concert.

Dewar believed that "consensus" could be achieved only by giving
seats to failed candidates in this way.[30] The result is that elections are
only indirectly decided by the electorate. The electoral system is a ma-
nipulable hybrid of public voting and behind-the-scenes bureaucratic
control. That was not the original idea by any means. All the bodies involved in structuring the new parliament agreed with the principle that
"political power should be shared rather than concentrated in the hands
of the government."[31]

The most dramatic example of the problems that can arise from devaluing the democratic vote will be described at the end of this volume
as it occurred in the general election of 2007. That was when the SNP
came to power for the first time, but it did so *solely due to the computer
allocation of "list" seats.*

I say "computer" allocation because "list" seat the results are calculated electronically using something called the "d'Hondt formula". That
refers to a mathematical equation devised by a Belgian lawyer called Victor d'Hondt (1841-1901). The d'Hondt formula allocates seats by giving
each party a quotient for additional (i.e. "list") seats after the democratic,
or constituency, results have been decided. It has to be done in that order
as the "list" could not otherwise be used to distort the democratic result.
The quotient per party is equal to the total number of "list" votes for
that party divided by the number of seats already allocated to it by the
electors at the democratic stage—starting at 0—plus one. Few understand how this works in practice.[32]

---

[30] Prof. Page puts it like this: "The allocation of regional [i.e. "list"] seats tends to com-
pensate parties who did less well in winning constituencies [i.e. "democratic" seats]."
Ibid., p. 48, para. 4-04

[31] *Ibid.,* p. 47, para. 4-02

[32] The d'Hondt system is also called "the greatest divisors" method. It is one of the least
proportional of the various methods of deciding proportional representation. It is

Due to complexity and public ignorance, Scottish elections offer endless opportunities for gaming the system, as will be seen below. It may be a "new kind of politics", but it is an odd kind of democracy which favours party managers over the voters. Two things can be said with certainty. First, the vast majority of Scots have no idea how their "list" vote is used to arrive at parliamentary seat numbers, which is the key to all elections. Secondly, there can hardly be a more naked form of electoral abuse than a system which is understood only by the party insiders who run it. The result has been the evolution of the sort of corrupting elitism which Dewar wanted to avoid.[33]

There is more to the Dewar Constitution than this—for example, the unicameral parliament in which the debating chamber is laid out as a "flat crescent", and which looks more like a lecture hall than a debating chamber. That and other related problems will be discussed in context below. The main point here is that a body structured to achieve consensus has brought about the opposite, namely the polarisation of Scottish politics. Dewar's attempt to "improve" Scotland by "de-tribalising" it has failed in its own terms.

Hamish Gobson argues that Scotland will always be a country which is happy with its traditional divisions of clan, class, confession and, more recently, constitutional view. The English, he says, like sporting contests with rules and a referee, while Scots still prefer clan warfare which has no rules or umpires. The first is reflected in the etiquette and rituals at Westminster, which Dewar wanted to improve upon, and the second in Holyrood, where the "improvement" has resulted in an apparently permanent majority for his party's bitterest enemies, the SNP.

Well-informed commentators saw this coming, even in 1999. The veteran Glasgow journalist, Murray Ritchie, immediately understood that you cannot have sporting etiquette when voters prefer clan warfare: "Most of us came to the view long ago that the Scottish general election

---

used in bodies like the European Parliament, where a simple democratic vote is not possible due to the lack of an EU-wide "*demos*", or single electorate.

[33] In a posthumous tribute to Dewar in a collection of essays about him, the SNP constitutional "guru", Professor Sir Neil MacCormick (see below), appeared to be sceptical of the wisdom of this arrangement: "The mixed system of constituency and list members is not ideal and *may in due course be superseded*." (emphasis added) (*Donald Dewar: Scotland's first First Minister*, ed. Wendy Alexander (2005), p. 144)

is in fact an independence referendum." He detected a longer-term danger in this:

> This election is becoming a referendum on independence, exactly what Labour did not want, far less envisage. What is more, *it appears likely to be the pattern of every Scottish general election until the SNP wins one.*[34] (emphasis added)

***

The new parliament first convened in the Church of Scotland building on the Mound in Edinburgh, above Waverley station, as construction of a purpose-built palace of democracy had not yet started. The first meeting had an element of ceremonial about it. Due to her seniority, and her experience in the European and Westminster parliaments, Winnie Ewing was informally considered the "Mother of the House" and therefore the correct person to preside over the opening formalities. But she was an SNP stalwart and not above putting a deceptive spin on the background to the great event.

Ewing announced that the Scottish parliament was hereby "reconvened", after having been "adjourned" in 1707. In fact, it was not adjourned then; it was *abolished* on its own motion, just as the English parliament was.[35] The new Edinburgh parliament had nothing in common with its predecessor beyond the name. For a start, Dewar's brainchild was at least partly democratic, which the old Scottish parliament never was. It was a feudal parliament, with seats allocated on property-based criteria. This history is described in more detail in the Appendix below.[36]

---

[34] *Scotland Reclaimed: the Inside Story of Scotland's First Democratic Parliamentary Election* (2000), p. 51. Weeks into the new parliament, Ritchie was writing: "In [many] areas our MSPs are showing a willingness to debate matters which are reserved to Westminster, a sign that many Members are already impatient with the restrictions on their legislative powers." (p. 218) Of that, much more below.

[35] Strictly speaking, the parliament was adjourned on 25 March, and *dissolved* on 28 April, 1707. The new state of Great Britain came into existence on 1 May 1707. The first meeting of the parliament of Great Britain took place on 23 October 1707.

[36] Readers who wish to study the old parliament should consult, first, *The Parliaments of Scotland*, Robert Rait (1924) and, for a deeper view of the crucial 1603-1707 period, *Thoughts on the Union between England and Scotland* by A.V. Dicey and Robert Rait (1920). "The Records of the Parliaments of Scotland", an internet site compiled by the

The whole of official Scotland continues to use the words "reconvened" and "adjourned" as if they represent historical truth. Two decades later, Sturgeon herself was still repeating them:

> I was there in the chamber, and it was an incredibly emotional moment ... to see the woman who had served in the House of Commons as champion of a Scottish Parliament, served in the European Parliament, to come to a third parliament and declare it *reconvened* in the way she did.[37] (emphasis added)

The doyen of Scottish legal historians, Professor David Walker, wrote shortly after the opening:

> The Scottish Parliament created was *not* a revival or recreation of the parliament dissolved in 1707, which was differently constituted... It is a subordinate body to which certain powers have been devolved.[38] (emphasis added

The parliament's first duty was to elect someone to moderate its debates. But even that was controversial. Dennis Canavan, the veteran Labour politician and independence campaigner, objected to there being a *secret* ballot for the position of Presiding Officer (the equivalent of Speaker). His exchange with the Mother of the House is revealing:

> **Dennis Canavan:** On a point of order, Dr Ewing. Will you give us guidance on whether we can have an open, recorded vote rather than a secret ballot? We have waited for our first Scottish Parliament for nearly 300 years—indeed, this is our first ever democratically elected Scottish Parliament—and the Parliament was supposed to herald a new era of open democracy, but our first vote is to be a secret one. That seems rather strange. Surely we

Scottish Parliament Project based at the University of St Andrews, contains a short summary, clearly explained. Reference is made to many other more detailed studies. Here the main point to stress is that the old Scottish parliament was not even intended to be democratic. It represented key stakeholders only and its purpose was to translate the king's will into law. It retained to the end a basically medieval (i.e. feudal) franchise, unlike its English equivalent, which slowly moved beyond feudalism to (some) recognition of individual representation. Winnie Ewing's history was fake. It was also elitist. Perhaps because she was a Nationalist, she seemed less concerned by the fact that the old parliament was undemocratic than that it was *Scottish*.

[37] BBC "Political Heroes", 12 March 2018

[38] *Scottish Legal System,* David Walker (2001), p. 192. Prof. Walker also commented on the d'Hondt formula saying it is a "complicated system" which "stresses party affiliation of candidates and plays down voters' personal regard for candidates." (p. 192).

should behave like an open democracy, rather than a secret society… Even in the House of Commons [Canavan had been an MP for 26 years] there is an open, recorded vote on every occasion, including the election of the Speaker. Would you be prepared to accept, from me, a motion that we have an open recorded vote rather than a secret ballot on this important, historic, first vote of our first ever democratically elected Scottish Parliament?

Winnie Ewing: My heart is with you, but the standing orders are against you. At the moment, I will obey the standing orders. If there is any other person who wants to say that we should not obey the standing orders, perhaps they should enter the discussion now. There is no one else so, Dennis, while my heart is with you, the standing orders have to settle the matter for now. Perhaps in future we can reform ourselves.[39]

A week later, Sturgeon spoke in a debate on the appointment of junior ministers in terms which also invoked fundamental principles:

We, as members of the first Scottish Parliament, must be guided by the principles that guided the consultative steering group. That group envisaged an *open, accessible Parliament* in which power would be shared between the Parliament, the Executive and the Scottish people, with *an Executive that would be accountable to the Parliament and a Parliament that would be accountable to the Scottish people.*[40] (emphasis added)

***

The formal opening of the parliament took place six weeks later, on 1 July. Though the Prime Minister had more important things to do that day, the Queen was happy to preside. She brought a festive atmosphere to the ceremony, helped by the numerous civic dignitaries in attendance and many displays of national symbolism.

Dewar made the keynote speech. He talked in sentimental clichés about welders in the Clyde shipyards, the eighteenth century "Enlightenment" and "the distant cries of the battles of Bruce and Wallace". He also invoked Robert Burns, the "national Bard" whose political reputation is tainted for some by his willingness to get involved with slavery

---

[39] 12 May 1999, col. 7
[40] 19 May 1999, col. 113

when he was broke. Dewar ignored that and concentrated on the Bard after he made money, when the world's first claret egalitarian wrote, "A man's a man for a' that."[41]

Burns's poem was sung and Dewar commented: "At the heart of that song is a very Scottish conviction: that honesty and simple dignity are priceless virtues, not imparted by rank or birth or privilege but part of the soul." Either Dewar's words were a statement of the obvious—that "the rank is but the guinea's stamp" as Burns put it in his poem—or they carried the snide implication that the English, Welsh, Irish and other peoples are not so generously endowed with "honesty and simple dignity", since those are "very *Scottish* convictions".

The Queen, by contrast, was more tactful, despite the guinea's stamp which hung about her like a rope of pearls. Dressed in a "thistle-coloured frock coat and matching dress", she graciously ignored Tony Blair's "too busy to attend" snub and, with Prince Philip, did her best to bring the proceedings to life. She talked of the same Scottish qualities as Dewar had but did not attempt to derive a message of moral superiority from them. Instead she said that "the grit, determination, humour and forthrightness" exhibited by so many Scots are "qualities which contribute so much to the life of the United Kingdom."[42]

The only parliamentarian who avoided anodyne clichés that day was Tommy Sheridan, leader of the Scottish Socialists. He accused the Queen of being "unelected" and spoke of "the privileged inheritors of stolen fortunes" who were officiating that day amid "a whole parade of wigs, robes and funny trousers." He referred to them as

> feudal relics [who] show off their fineries a stone's throw from the fabulous wealth salted away in the vaults of modern financial capitalism up the Royal Mile – £150 billion of it to be specific. In the same country where the Royal

---

[41] Burns bought his ticket to Jamaica, intending to become an apprentice slave-master, in 1786 and wrote the poem Dewar referred to in 1795. It is relevant that the case which established that slavery was unlawful in Scotland, *Knight v Wedderburn*, came to the Court of Session nine years *before* Burns decided to go slaving abroad. In 1777, Joseph Knight, a slave, was successfully defended by, amongst others, Henry Dundas, whose statue now stands in St Andrew Square in Edinburgh, but who is reviled by people who blame him for favouring slave traders when in government during the Napoleonic wars.

[42] BBC, 4 July 1999

Bank of Scotland and the Bank of Scotland each declared £1,000 million profits last month, one in three children and one in four families are officially classified poor.[43]

Clearly, there was work to be done.

***

The first words which Sturgeon spoke in any parliamentary debate were: "I would like to make a point not of substance but of form."[44]

It was a typically careful start. Apart from being called "Tommy Sheridan in drag" and saying "there was no room for complacency" on drugs policy, Sturgeon did not feature much in the first few months of the parliament's existence. When she did speak, she tended to be cautious, sometimes to the point of pessimism. Notably, she contributed to a debate on the Scottish economy in a way which was a portent of woes to come. Presciently considering future troubles, she was worried about the imminent closure of the Kvaerner shipyard in Govan, her hoped-for constituency. She wanted the British government to come to the rescue with an order for £250 million's worth of roll-on, roll-off ferries as a way of making the yard seem more viable, and therefore attractive to potential buyers. Otherwise it might shut.

She had a wide range of bodies she said were responsible for the imminent destruction of Scottish shipbuilding. Previously it had been only the British government. Now she added the Korean one and the International Monetary Fund.

> What can the Executive do to protect the Scottish economy and its industries from the inappropriate economic policies pursued by Westminster.... The Minister will be aware that the global competition faced by our shipbuilding industry is unfair... *South Korea is illegally subsidising its shipbuilding industry using International Monetary Fund loans to run its shipyards at a loss.*[45] (emphasis added)

---

[43] BBC, 1 July 1999. Curiously, the (American) band commissioned to celebrate the day with a concert in Princes Street Gardens was called Garbage.

[44] 2 June 1999, col. 165

[45] 18 November 1999, col. 722

"The Executive", it should be explained, was the term then in use to denote what is today called the Scottish Government, though it was officially distinct from "the Scottish Ministers", which was really the Scottish Cabinet. Confusingly, the civil service was also called the "Scottish Executive". The term Executive will recur below until 2007, when the terminology was changed unilaterally by the new SNP government, though this was retrospectively legalised in 2012 by a new Scotland Act.

The outstanding feature of Sturgeon's long political career manifested itself early, namely her "grit and determination" (to use the Queen's words). One wonders what took this serious-minded, shy, bookish, quick-witted but socially unconfident woman into a nastily competitive world where she would have to start meeting Tories? She could have continued in quiet but "authentic" obscurity at the Drumchapel Law Centre, doing good and being paid badly for it. Instead she chose to put herself in the public spotlight, and sacrifice her life and privacy in the thieves' kitchen of politics. As things stood in 1999, she had no realistic hope of getting into government so conviction must have trumped career in her mind.

An early incident would have opened her eyes to the authoritarian centralism which disfigured nationalist politics even then. Ian Blackford, now an SNP MP, was treasurer of the Party and custodian of its enormous overdraft. Being a businessman, Blackford reckoned he could recognise a deficit when he saw one, so he began calling for economies. This of course affected the leadership. Alex Salmond was forced to admit that he had claimed for taxis to the tune of nearly £18,000 over the last two years (perhaps double that in today's money, say around £300 a week) and £6,159 for two years' worth of airfares for his wife when they went on trips abroad. But the SNP has long had a clan-style "no criticism" rule about its leaders. Suddenly, the national treasurer who had raised the point was an enemy of the current leader. Salmond said, "I do not regard Mr Blackford as important."[46] As a result, Blackford was humiliated in the re-election for treasurer. Arms must have been twisted because he was voted out of his job by 632 votes to 142.

The "no criticism" policy is worth noting as it was to become much

---

[46] *Salmond*, Torrance, *op. cit.*, p. 207; wife's travel expenses, p. 251

more pronounced in future years, especially after Sturgeon became leader. (A formal policy of forced consensus was introduced in 2015, as will be described in volume 3.) This was popular in the Party early on. Few even wanted reciprocity. The senior *Times* journalist, Kenny Farquharson, noted right at the start: "Most SNP members are stubbornly loyal to the leadership, regardless of whether the incumbent is to their personal taste. When it comes to a crunch vote, *their instincts are usually to back the boss.*"[47] (emphasis added)

While others made a noise in the chamber and thumped their chests outside it competing for status, Sturgeon's "eyes-down" persistence reminded Hamish Gobson of T.S. Eliot's "ragged claws" in the way she "scuttled across the floors of silent seas", ingesting paperwork, digesting arguments and producing debating points with a neatness and precision few others could match. She had another important skill, too. Though she took a while before venturing into major debates, she was quick with the one-liners right from the start.

> **Nicola Sturgeon (Glasgow) (SNP):** Will Mary Mulligan answer the question that Des McNulty refused to answer when it was posed by John Swinney—whether more students or fewer students will pay the new deferred tuition fee than paid the old up-front tuition fee? It is a simple question that requires a simple answer.
>
> **Mrs Mulligan (Linlithgow) (Lab):** I have never known Nicola Sturgeon to ask a simple question.
>
> **Nicola Sturgeon:** I have never known Mary Mulligan to give a simple answer.
>
> **Mrs Mulligan:** As the minister said, under the new scheme, no student will be worse off.
>
> **Nicola Sturgeon:** That was not the question.
>
> **Mrs Mulligan:** Last November, I was honoured to be asked by West Lothian College…[48]

She was equally nippy with a Liberal, Robert Brown, who tried to intervene when Sturgeon herself was talking. Unlike Mulligan, she did not allow the interjection, saying instead: "If I were Mr Brown, I would

---

[47] *Sunday Times*, 18 June 2000

[48] 27 January 2000, col. 580

be trying to keep a low profile," and then resuming her speech.[49]

If Donald Dewar had hoped the Scottish parliament might become better than the Westminster one because it operated by "consensus" rather than by debate about the choice between alternatives, early signs like these were not encouraging. Sadly, Dewar did not live long enough to be able to stamp his vision of mature but non-competitive debate on the institution. On 11 October 2000, the tribune of Scottish parliamentarianism died of a brain haemorrhage.

Dewar was seen as a pivotal figure and widely mourned. Gobson wrote in *Todday Today* about the irony of scattering his ashes at the small town of Lochgilphead in mid-Argyll where he had family roots (his middle name was Campbell). The town, Gobson said, is "a nest of public sector nationalists due to the Argyll & Bute Council there." Subsequently a statue was erected outside Buchanan Galleries, a shopping arcade in the centre of Glasgow. Buried among nationalists, Dewar was memorialised among consumerists, though he had never been in sympathy with either group. But his successor as leader of the Labour Party, Henry McLeish, caught the mood of apotheosis in the political world: "Donald was our nation's trustee and did not fail his native land."[50]

Gobson, however, was sceptical. "Dewar," he wrote, "was a good man who fell amongst socialists. He now stands in bronze on a high plinth, looking down through unglazed spectacles on competitive materialists as they shop till they drop in an American-style mall in the centre of a city whose fortune was substantially derived from slaving. *Sic transit gloria tribuni…*"

***

Even while she was still finding her feet in parliament, Sturgeon was not a cross-party consensus builder. She reserved her most abusive and cutting comments, not for the administration, but for other parts of the Opposition, especially the Tories. Curiously, she treated the administration with respect, and even on occasion with open admiration. Power

---

[49] *Ibid.,* col. 598

[50] *Dewar*, Alexander, *op. cit.,* p. 174

talks louder than principle, it seems, but not so loud as prejudice. She conveyed the impression of loathing Tories *on principle*. Instead of disagreeing with them, which is the function of politicians from differing parties, she seemed to *detest* them in the same embittered, personal way she hated Margaret Thatcher. This was closer to class war than to modern, individualist politics. It was based on the "authenticity" principle, with its hereditary privileges of social acceptability. It was blind to the variety of human life, and its constant evolution without rules. It was fundamentally hostile to both meritocracy and equal justice for all.

To take a representative example from the first year of the new parliament: the SNP resisted a proposal to create a children's commissioner for Scotland who would "ensure that children's views are positively promoted." This was the first of many initiatives the future "Chief Mammy" undertook in relation to children *en masse* when she was, successively, SNP shadow minister for Children and Education, and for Health and Community Care. But her positive feelings about young people were not always so strong as her negative ones about Tories, as was seen when she went into battle with Brian Monteith, the Conservative spokesman for Education, Culture, the Arts and Sports:

> **Mr Brian Monteith (Mid Scotland and Fife) (Con):** I welcome Nicola Sturgeon's comments about consulting children. Unlike Jim Wallace, I see no difficulty in supporting her amendment. Were we in government, we would accept it.
>
> **Nicola Sturgeon:** I am glad that the Tories have learned from their mistakes and are now in favour of consulting people; that is not something that they were good at when they were in office.[51]

Later in the debate, Monteith summed up for the Tories, beginning with another unequivocal statement of support for Sturgeon's party:

> **Mr Brian Monteith:** I reiterate the Conservatives' agreement not just with the motion but with the SNP's amendment.[52]

Monteith clearly wanted to agree with Sturgeon, but she was having none of it. She rejected Tory support with ill-concealed contempt:

---

[51] 24 February 2000, col. 115

[52] *Ibid.,* col. 131

Nicola Sturgeon: In spite of the efforts of Tory members, we have had a constructive debate. It is cheering that all members—excluding the Tories—believe that the law should be changed.[53]

A minute later there was this exchange:

Nicola Sturgeon: Cathy Jamieson [Labour] said it all—let us have a reasonable, calm and rational debate and let us allow members to express their views. I regret that, on today's evidence, the Tories—Lyndsay McIntosh and Brian Monteith—have failed to engage in this complex debate. There are no easy answers, but instead of trying to offer something constructive to the debate, the Tories have done what the Tories often do—fallen back on easy answers and glib arguments. They have fallen back on the answers that they think will attract popular support.

Mr Monteith: It is just common sense.

Nicola Sturgeon: Common sense means constructive engagement in debate. Mr Monteith would do well to reflect on that.[54]

Leaving aside the patronising last sentence, Sturgeon's point both then and later was the clannish one that Tories have to be opposed at all times, *even when they agree with you.*

Not everyone in the SNP was so negative. A completely different attitude to children was taken by another SNP MSP, Dorothy-Grace Elder:

All members will agree that this Parliament should not turn into some sort of Mary Poppins for adults, acting as a national nanny to parents by wagging its finger at them and telling them how to bring up their children. As a parent, I am not qualified to do that just because I have a wee plastic badge that says that I am an MSP. *I used to be a marvellous parent, but that was before I had children.* I knew it all in those salad days; before having three children, I would never have dreamed of using any form of physical chastisement on a child and was a tut-tutter if I saw it in public. Then I had my own children, woke up and smelt the coffee.[55] (emphasis added)

---

[53] *Ibid.,* col. 133

[54] *Ibid.,*

[55] *Ibid.,* col. 126. Elder subsequently lent credence to Rhodes's point about Sturgeon's inability to deal with individuals rather than categories of people. She said Sturgeon "had never been a team player… She *didn't speak to me in the three years* I was in the SNP

***

Two months later, Sturgeon was involved in a debate about school boards, in which she said a measure that was damaging when introduced under the Tories was beneficial when the Labour Party were in government:

> **Mr Brian Monteith (Mid Scotland and Fife) (Con):** Did not the SNP oppose school boards when the Conservative Government introduced them? If so, why has the SNP changed its position on that?
>
> **Nicola Sturgeon:** From somebody who voted no and advocated a no vote in the referendum but who now sits in the Scottish Parliament, that is rich. Thankfully, life has moved on since the dark days of the Tory Administration. School boards were the creation of a malevolent Tory Government, but in many areas of Scotland they have risen above that to contribute greatly to the life of Scottish education.[56]

Since she and Monteith were in broad agreement on the matter before the chamber, Sturgeon had to express the inherited superiority of the "authentic" Scot against an "inauthentic" Tory in off-topic rhetoric:

> Does Mr Monteith never get embarrassed when he stands in the parliament talking about support for teachers, given that he backed a government which, for 18 long years almost victimised Scottish teachers, underfunded Scottish education and created many of the problems in our education system?[57]

This sort of slashing political sectarianism was popular with the SNP rank and file, and Sturgeon's stock in the Party began to rise. Though it was only Tories she attacked consistently in this way to begin with, she soon began to take pot-shots at other targets.

In April she contributed to the debate on an SNP motion about

---

group and *shared the same office.*" (*Daily Record*, 21 March 2021, emphasis added) Elder resigned from the SNP, alleging that her warnings about male bullying within the party were being ignored. She became an Independent member in 2002. She did not stand for election in 2003.

[56] 22 March 2000, col. 816

[57] *Ibid.*, col. 819

"public services". Alex Neil, a defector from the Labour Party who harboured secret thoughts which were later to earn him the nickname "the silent Brexiteer", had restated the Nationalists' creed in these words:

> We are in an ironic position. We are one of the wealthiest nations in Europe—and not only in terms of oil, although Scotland is western Europe's biggest producer of oil. We produce 30 per cent of Europe's natural gas. Scotland is one of the best food producers in Europe and one of the greatest centres of the electronics industry. Our universities are among the best in the world. By any measure, Scotland is potentially a very wealthy nation. Why is one of the potentially wealthiest nations in Europe one of the poorest nations in Europe?

Neil went on in words which were to presage the SNP's arguments at the time of the 2014 referendum on independence, in particular that Scotland's wealth should not be shared with anyone else, and certainly not "the British":

> The official UK forecast for oil revenues over the next five years is £20 billion; I am prepared to accept Gordon Brown's assumptions. If we had 85 per cent of that—as we would be entitled to—we could start to raise the levels of investment in education, housing and health in Scotland to European levels. This is a constitutional issue, because until we change the constitutional relationship between Scotland and England—and between Scotland and Europe—Scotland, which is *potentially the wealthiest nation in Europe*, will continue to be one of the poorest nations in Europe thanks to mismanagement by the three right-wing British unionist parties, which have been so miserable in their contributions to this debate.[58] (emphasis added)

George Lyon, a Liberal, responded to SNP claims about how much oil money it would be able to spend by saying the "technique used in SNP speeches is that on no account should a sense of fiscal responsibility be allowed to get in the way of economic policy."[59]

Janis Hughes, a Labour member, saw a different danger in the Nationalists' approach:

> The [SNP] motion is unhelpful in its intentions, inaccurate in its assertions

---

[58] 6 April 2000, cols. 1389, 1391

[59] *Ibid.*, col. 1387

and designed simply to create further divisions between this Parliament and Westminster. I am sorry to say that despite all the hopes of new politics emerging in the Scottish Parliament, the SNP continues to act in a divisive and troublemaking way.[60]

Sturgeon responded with ostentatious contempt:

There have been times this morning when I have felt that I was at school. We have had school-marm Janis Hughes telling us to stop making trouble, and I am convinced that one of these days George Lyon will skip his speech altogether and run straight down to the front of the chamber with an apple for the minister. His contribution was truly nauseating.[61]

Dewar-style consensus depends on courtesy in debate, but that is undermined when some in the room talk so aggressively about others present. Many commentators started describing Sturgeon as a "formidable debater"—some still do. But abuse is not debate, and a posture of in-yer-face loathing does not make a person "formidable", merely unpleasant. Sturgeon went so far in this debate as to belittle ministers, saying they were "mere puppets" without individual initiative:

The motion that we are debating today is about ambition. It is about lifting our sights and being confident about what we could achieve if we had the powers and freedoms that other Parliaments all over the world enjoy and take for granted—the power and freedom to make this Parliament, the Government and the Minister for Finance genuinely accountable to the people of Scotland, instead of mere puppets at the whim of the Westminster Government.

The Finance Minister, Jack McConnell, intervened to ask Sturgeon where money could be found to cover the £4 billion fiscal deficit that Scotland could run due to Westminster subsidies. She "lifted her sights" and answered confidently:

There is no £4 billion deficit, as Jack McConnell knows only too well. Oil prices have doubled since he published that devastating critique.[62]

---

[60] *Ibid.*, col. 1391

[61] *Ibid.*, col. 1393

[62] *Ibid.*, col. 1394

McConnell tried to intervene in her speech again, but Sturgeon would not let him.

Right from the start, shipbuilding has been one of Sturgeon's consistent themes. Today, all Scots are conscious of the SNP's controversial approach to the construction of roll-on roll-off ferries to serve the Scottish islands. In 2000, the focus of attention was still on Kvearer's Govan shipyard, formerly Fairfields. Since then, it has changed hands again and now thrives as part of BAE Systems, the largest armaments conglomerate in Europe. However, then its future was in doubt. But Sturgeon's language in debate was provocative. Referring to the then Minister for Enterprise and Lifelong Learning, Henry McLeish, she said:

> He will be aware of speculation that Govan might build only one of the roll-on-roll-off ferries required by the MOD [Ministry of Defence]. Is he aware that that would not in itself be enough to keep the yard open for the two years until it is due to start work, with Scotstoun, on the type 45 prototype [a naval destroyer]? Is he further aware that what Govan needs to fill that gap is work equivalent to 28,000 tonnes of steel—that is equivalent to four roll-on-roll-off ferries? … Will he confirm that is what he will press the UK Government to deliver and that anything less would be a betrayal of the workforce at Govan?[63]

McLeish replied despairingly, saying, "It is a pity that such questions are laced with words such as betrayal."

Within a week of the ferry debate, Sturgeon was on the attack again. In the course of a session devoted to "Discipline in Schools", she accused Brian Monteith of "focussing on only the high-profile cases" and indulging in "10 minutes of scaremongering". He had not in fact drawn attention to any particularly "scary" cases, high-profile or otherwise, but concentrated on general judgements and statistics. However, he had spoken first, so when Sturgeon stood up, she was free to misrepresent his argument.

The main statistic Monteith produced concerned the number of incidents of either physical violence or verbal abuse which teachers and school staff had been subjected to by pupils. "There were 1,388 recorded incidents against teachers and 517 against ancillary workers", he said,

---

[63] 27 April 2000, col. 141

referring to the figures for 1998-1999, which were the most recent available.[64]

Sturgeon started her response by saying,

> The Tory motion is another example of the way in which the Tories are, only now, addressing an issue that they failed to do anything at all about during 18 long years in government...
>
> The results of a survey that was published earlier this year revealed that, in 1998-99, nearly 2,000 violent attacks on teachers and school staff took place. That survey should not be ignored by any member of this Parliament.[65]

So Monteith's "scaremongering" consisted of saying 1,905 incidents of violence and abuse had taken place when the actual total was "nearly 2,000". Gobson wondered if Sturgeon had actually been listening to Monteith, or was just reading from a prepared script.

It was left to Jamie Stone, for the Liberals, to give the only specific example of "scaremongering", if by that is meant quoting an individual case of terrifying hooliganism:

> When I was a pupil at Tain Royal Academy, we had a bad boy who not only filled a fire extinguisher with weedkiller and sugar in an attempt to blow up the school—that was his ultimate act—but I remember that he put sugar in the rector's petrol tank. That lad was expelled.[66]

Gobson wrote in *Todday Today* that he was proud to hear of a Scottish schoolboy chemist with the imagination to leverage ordinary weedkiller in this way. Wha's like us?

***

The designers of the Scottish parliament had decided right at the start that it would help make it more Jock Tamsonish if it sat from time to time in other cities in Scotland. So it was that in May 2000, the whole circus betook itself to the former Strathclyde Regional Council debating

[64] 4 May 2000, col. 282
[65] *Ibid.*, col. 289
[66] *Ibid.*

chamber in Glasgow to discuss "Glasgow Regeneration". There was no mechanism for *listening* to Glasgow while there. This was an exercise in attention-seeking rather than reciprocity.

The proceedings opened at 10 a.m. with the non-denominational Time for Reflection which starts every parliamentary week. The reflector on this occasion was S.L. Garjee, president of the Hindu Mandir in Glasgow. He talked about the Upanishads, saying that it was "ignorance [which] makes us hate each other".[67] Apparently, "scientists are coming to the same broad view" that the universe is made up of matter and we are all little "whirlpools of matter" within it.

> As spirit, it does not move or change: it is one unchangeable, unbroken homogenous atom. We must uphold the Upanishads and believe that I am the soul.... I am the Omnipotent; I am the Omniscient... Let us look upon every man and every woman as God... *We must give up the idea that by ruling over others, we can do them any good.*[68] (emphasis added)

Perhaps in response to those words of wisdom, the Labour Minister for Communities, Wendy Alexander, went "omniscient" and made considerable play with the phrase "small minds". She did not want Labour's plans for the regeneration of Glasgow's housing stock to be limited by "small solutions that come from small minds".[69] This was one of the biggest issues in Scottish politics as far as the ordinary voter was concerned. It was a problem of long standing and not confined to Glasgow. But Sturgeon intervened to move the discussion onto the more speculative subject of "the secret plans of the Glasgow City Council" to close a fifth of the city's primary schools. Alexander response was: "Small minds, small solutions."[70]

When another SNP member asked about rumours of the closure of the heart transplant unit as the Glasgow Royal Infirmary, Sturgeon herself began her reply by saying: "Let us not scare people, let us come to the nub: small solutions for small minds."[71]

---

[67] 17 May 2000, col. 647,8

[68] *Ibid.*, col. 648

[69] *Ibid.*, col. 651

[70] *Ibid.*, col. 652

[71] *Ibid.,* col. 653

Bill Aitken, a Tory, took Alexander to task for her condescension. It would have been more positive, he said,

> if, instead of berating people for having simple, small minds and small solutions to the problem, a small lady [Alexander is short] had been a bit more generous and had accepted that any minds and solutions that could ease the problems that Glasgow faces are to be welcomed.[72]

Alex Neil for the Nationalists did his best to be negative: "There is one thing about small minds—facts never confuse them."[73] But it was Sturgeon, the carthorse of the complaints department within the SNP, who hauled the discussion back to a really negative point, namely her unappeasable loathing of Tories who she could not, it seems, "look upon... as God":

> This has, in the main, been a good debate. However, as is so often the case, there have been some honourable, or not so honourable, exceptions. Let me start with the Tories, who thoroughly deserve today's award for bare-faced cheek. The Tory amendment "asks the Executive to address these problems in Glasgow as a matter of urgency". I would echo that sentiment—but let us ask ourselves why the problems in Glasgow are so urgent. I will tell members why the problems in Glasgow are so urgent: in the 18 long years that the Conservatives were in government, it slipped their minds to do anything at all about the problems in Glasgow.[74]

***

Before leaving Sturgeon's contribution to the parliament's first year, it is worth recalling the debate which must have had the highest concentration of platitudes of any that session. It is also a revealing vignette of the way the parliament worked in its early years. Still in Glasgow, the debate concerned the boxer Mike Tyson, whom the SNP wanted to prevent from coming to Scotland to fight a month hence.

In the middle of a comeback after serving three years of a six-year

---

[72] *Ibid.,* col. 663
[73] *Ibid.,* col. 674
[74] *Ibid.,* col. 743

sentence for rape, Tyson had been booked to fight at Hampden Park against Lou Savarese who, in the event, Tyson despatched in 38 seconds—one of the shortest title bouts in history. But it was not the fight that interested most parliamentarians; rather it was Tyson himself. Even more important were the "signals and messages we are sending out to young people," as Roseanna Cunningham put it when she opened the debate for the SNP.[75]

> With Tyson, the message is that no matter what the crime, the level of violence, the fact that your behaviour has included rape—a crime right up there with murder—you can go on, live your life, make megabucks, be a hero, be surrounded with all the trappings of success... It is therefore entirely proper that we should question the apparent adulation of an individual such as Mike Tyson and seek to address the problem of the message that that sends out.[76]

No SNP member disagreed with the view that the problem with Mike Tyson was that, having served his sentence, he was enjoying life and making money. Perhaps they saw a touch of the Tory in "Iron Mike".

The actual Tories took a different line altogether. David McLetchie, the Conservative leader, pointed out that this should be an issue for Westminster since immigration was a reserved matter under the Dewar Constitution. The debate had been initiated by the SNP, and was intended to "further its agenda of separation and division."[77] McLetchie reflected wider opinion when he went on to say:

> Far from wanting this Parliament to work in the interests of the Scottish people, the SNP wants to rip up the Scotland Act 1998 and start all over again. It ignores the fact that people in Scotland have had thirty years of debate about the constitution and made their decision in the devolution referendum. They voted for a Parliament that would improve housing, health and education in Scotland, not one that would continue to debate endlessly Scotland's constitutional position... The campaign to keep Mike Tyson out of Scotland is yet another bandwagon on which the SNP has jumped to further its political agenda... This debate is not about violence against women; the Parliament and its committees have had very important debates

---

[75] 24 May 2000, col. 916

[76] *Ibid.*, col. 917

[77] *Ibid.*, col. 921

on that subject. This debate is about an SNP motion that calls on the Executive to disrupt the constitutional settlement… That is irresponsible gesture politics of the worst kind and does no service whatsoever to people working to counter violence against women.[78]

The Deputy Minister of Justice, Angus MacKay, sided with McLetchie:

There is no SNP solidarity with Scottish women; there is only solidarity with the nationalist desire for separation… The SNP's agenda is less about domestic violence than it is about the nationalists' perpetual demand for the break-up of Britain.[79]

Maureen Macmillan, also Labour, talked of the "deep-rooted culture of violence in Scotland" and said that the debate was about the "values of Scottish society. What do we value more: footballers, film stars, pop stars and boxers—whether they be rapists or wife beaters—or the creation of a country free from abuse and violence, particularly violence against women?"[80]

This was the sort of occasion when everyone's favourite pharisaism was on display. Alex Salmond was concerned about violence towards women, but Jackie Baillie, the Deputy Minister for Communities, asked why he had not raised this matter at Westminster where it could be properly dealt with. In fact, the SNP MPs had taken very little interest in the matter. "Morality does not stop at the Scottish border," she said.[81]

Everyone knew that in his fight against Evander Holyfield, Tyson had bitten off a chunk of his opponent's ear, and that moved Jamie "Weedkiller" Stone of the Liberals to say he wanted to "hit Tyson hard" by means of humiliation and ridicule. He wanted to *bend* his ear, so to speak, not bite it.

Lord James Douglas Hamilton made one of the few speeches that do not read today like moralistic posturing. Unfortunately he was not able to combine that with relevance. He talked about his father, the Duke of

---

[78] *Ibid.,* cols. 921-3
[79] *Ibid.,* col. 927-8
[80] *Ibid.,* col. 946
[81] *Ibid.,* col. 955

Hamilton, who had been Scottish amateur middleweight boxing champion. He had trained with Tommy Milligan of Glasgow who "very nearly became world heavyweight champion, but came up against a Tyson-like figure called Mickey Walker." Lord James neatly deflected an intervention by John McAllion about the Socialist Workers Party without losing his flow:

> John McAllion's grandfather was in the Cameronians—an honour that I had—and connected with that regiment was the McGowan family. Walter McGowan was a world champion boxer who was smaller than Tyson, but a great deal more skilful. It is my considered opinion that Mr Tyson is not as great as boxer as our Mr Lennox Lewis, who has been totally underestimated and who is a very good ambassador for boxing. Lennox Lewis is a man who exercises self-control; he is an admirable example of the best of British sportsmanship. He is a genuine role model and would not dream of biting off his opponent's ear.[82]

Sturgeon, who had no boxers in her family, wound up the debate for the SNP. She said the real issue was "whether this Scottish parliament is prepared to allow that man [Tyson] to come to fight here in Glasgow." That was not relevant since the Scottish parliament had no *locus* in the matter, but it was a bold statement of her desire to take control of everything that happened in the country, right down to sport.

"The SNP believes that this Parliament should have all the powers of an independent Parliament," she said, before raising the issue of Tyson's success. She implied that only virtuous sportsmen should be allowed to be "glorified" in Scotland:

> I feel disgust at the prospect of a man who has been convicted of rape and other violent assaults, and who currently stands accused of violence against women... coming to Glasgow to be cheered, adored and glorified in our national stadium.[83]

More substantially, she said that "domestic violence is a public health issue." She explained just how violent some Scots can be when they have someone weaker than Mike Tyson to hit. "Here in Glasgow the annual

---

[82] *Ibid.*, cols. 950-1

[83] *Ibid.*, col. 956

cost to the national health service of treating health problems related to domestic violence is £12 million."[84]

She went on to say confidently that "two thirds of the people of this country do not want Mike Tyson to come to Scotland." However, that point was rather devalued by the Glasgow City Council, the authority responsible for granting the safety certificate necessary for the fight to go ahead at Hampden Park. It voted 10-1 in favour of Tyson.

A less determined character than Sturgeon would have reflected on that vote and thought twice about the mountain she still had to climb if she were to get the whole country behind her campaign to destroy the United Kingdom. But she never wavered.

***

The first serious political shock Sturgeon received came at the end of her first year in parliament when Alex Salmond resigned as party leader. She had been a strong supporter of his and later said, "I learned pretty much everything I know about the art of politics from him."[85] But once he said he was going she immediately moved to support his most likely successor, John Swinney, and got herself appointed campaign manager.

Swinney was to be a permanent feature of SNP politics, and is still, in 2022, Deputy First Minister. He is a controversial figure, despite his militantly dull manner, which has become more pronounced with time. He shaved his head and adopted a lean, skeletal look, which reflected his austere habits and somniloquent speaking style. He was addicted to facts and an outward show of rationality, which is rarely a successful recipe for electioneering in a democracy. It is hard to believe that he ever, when young, ran through a wheatfield or cut off a doll's plastic hair, much less tried to blow up a respectable school with weedkiller and sugar. He oozes conventionalism and never breaks a rule. Passionless repetition in tones of monkish sobriety is his parliamentary style. Gobson wonders if he "has ever had an iconoclasm".

Swinney's tolerance of tedium has been described by Douglas Fraser,

---

[84] *Ibid.*, col. 957

[85] *GQ Magazine, op. cit.*

BBC Scotland's Economics Editor. As an 18-year-old budding politician, he attended an SNP local area council meeting in the Mitchell Library in Glasgow "where Matters Arising from the Minutes of the previous meeting took *more than six hours.*"[86] (emphasis added)

As a result of this passive-aggressive dullness, Hamish Gobson and others took to calling him "Dr Death". He has had only one known brush with fun and that happened forty years ago, in 1983, just before the "Falklands War" election, when he appeared on a Channel Four programme about the minority parties standing. Despite the programme's being called "A Partly Satirical Broadcast", no warning bells seemed to have rung with the po-facers at Party HQ. The 19-year old Swinney was put up to represent them.

With a full head of hair, he announced himself as "John Swinney, national secretary of the Young Scottish Nationalists". He gave a plucky opening speech over apocalyptic shots of council-estate hell in Edinburgh (his home town): "Scotland is being attacked and viciously decimated by London government," he said. "The SNP believes that it is of paramount importance that for the entire survival of Scottish people and for the survival of Scotland and the beautiful scenery of Edinburgh today"—at which point he gestured over a rain-soaked townscape from Calton Hill—"the only way we'll have a decent future will be if we establish a Scottish parliament because if London is insistent on using us as a target in the event of nuclear war and a nuclear missile happens to hit Edinburgh all this will be gone. There'll be nothing left."[87]

Swinney was followed by a more empathetic lady from the Young Communist League and after that by Screaming Lord Sutch, of the "Raving Monster Loony Party", who was filmed being rowed about the Serpentine in a boat flying the skull and crossbones for Radio Sutch in its sternsheets. Next up was Jonathan King, the crooner and paedophile who represented the Royalty Party. He was followed by the National Front, the Socialist Workers Party ("We can construct a world in which people come before profit") and the Green Party (then called the Ecology Party). It was represented by a man standing on a pillar, like St.

---

[86] *SNP Leaders, op. cit.,* p. 306

[87] The programme can be seen in full on YouTube. Swinney appears 9 minutes in.

Simeon of Stylites, except that Simeon, being more "sustainable" than modern eco-saints, spent 37 years up his pillar in the Egyptian desert, rather than a few minutes while the cameras rolled.

All this was, so to speak, good clean fun, but the SNP was not amused. They thought it was beneath them to appear on the same programme as the other guests. The Party made an official complaint to the Independent Broadcasting Authority about what was, in effect, *lèse-majesté*.[88]

Seventeen years later, Swinney had still not learned to laugh at himself. He was not alone. The Party as a whole projected an image of querulous nerdiness which showed little had changed since the six-hour meeting in the Mitchell Library. Swinney's public speaking style reflected this. After he won the contest to succeed Salmond as leader of the party, he said in his "victory speech":

> I stand here as the first leader in the history of the SNP who has a hard-headed opportunity to lead our party into government and our country to independence.[89]

There was not a hint of salesmanship, style or even elegant English. An "opportunity" cannot be "hard-headed", or soft-headed for that matter. Opportunities do not have heads, John.

Words may have seemed unimportant to Swinney and his colleagues, but *titles* were critical. He was not to be "leader" of the party, as his predecessors had been. He was going to be "National Convener". Not much salesmanship there either, just inverse status display.

***

After a year of parliamentary debate, it was clear that Sturgeon's humourless, po-faced steeliness was in harmony with her Party's general approach to business. This was a change from the fringe party of cranks,

---

[88] *Glasgow Herald,* 11 May 1983

[89] *Guardian,* 25 March 2001. The article called him "the child-prodigy of Scottish nationalism." He beat the only other contestant, Alex Neil, by a significant margin. This was the election when Ian Blackford was defeated as Treasurer. Roseanna Cunningham beat Kenny MacAskill for Deputy Leader. Electors were 700-odd branch delegates.

xenophobes and dreamers which the SNP had been for most of the time since its foundation in 1933. Sturgeon was free of those vices, being neither a crank, nor a xenophobe nor a dreamer. Her only relevant vice was obsession. But even that, like her clannishness and inverted snobbery, was considered a virtue by most within the SNP.

From the age of 16 she had the simple goal of breaking up her own country. To maintain such an attitude in the face of an apparently irremovable Labour (i.e. Unionist) majority in an openly gerrymandered parliament, she needed a hard shell and a touch of obsessiveness. Not only did Sturgeon's world-historical ambition call for "grit and determination", it also required that she be, in Mandy Rhodes's phrase, an "authentic Scot". Whether that necessarily includes being rude to almost everyone in your workplace is debatable. But in a clannish society, you have to show *attitude* to outsiders as evidence of your "loyalty" to the group. Sturgeon was learning how a natural introvert could play the role of "nippy Nationalist" in the main opposition party within a subordinate parliament. Rather like Mr Putin in the Kremlin, with his "authentic" *Russian* nationalism, she benefitted from the fact that the politer the opponent, the better this approach works.

Chapter 3

Talking the Talk

The parliament had disappointed many, both MSPs and members of the public, in its first year of operation. But Sturgeon had risen rapidly, partly because she took her work seriously. Lacking a sense of institutional history, many parliamentarians approached their job as if they were civil servants. They had well-paid jobs and seemed content with that. Some clearly enjoyed being in the limelight but, unlike Sturgeon, few had an original act to offer.

However, Sturgeon's almost sectarian approach to Tories presented a long-term threat to the institution if it were ever to mature. Parliamentary democracy cannot work when parliamentarians consider loyalty to party, or "clan", more important than their duty to act rationally and responsively in the interests of all their *constituents*. But that is in the nature of "list" politics, in which the member's job depends more on keeping party managers happy than helping constituents. Between the jobsworths and the clansmen (of both sexes) there was already too little flexibility for measured disagreement and constructive debate. This was not to change. That was the first reason for the parliament's disappointing performance. The second one was the skills shortage. This, too, was to become a permanent feature and requires some explanation.

The Dewar Constitution provided for a parliament of 129 members, within which it was always going to be hard to find enough capable, informed and acceptably socialised individuals who could cover the range of issues modern government has to deal with. The pool of talent is too shallow. It is also comparatively stagnant. As will be seen below, many names from the first parliament—indeed from Sturgeon's university days—still dominate the Scottish political news, thirty years later. This variant on the "old boy network" increased the tendency to "clan up"— i.e. form a "clan" and refuse to interact candidly and constructively with members of other "clans". This trend was noticeable right from the start. Scots rarely need an excuse to adopt a defensive posture against outsiders. Openness and transparency, the shibboleths of political correctness today, are alien habits, despite their being universally "embraced".

In Sturgeon's defence it should be noted that she had the disadvantage of a short training period. She had gone into politics before establishing a significant reputation for lawyering. She lacked both professional authority and a political hinterland. In that, she was unusual in the first parliament as several members had served in the House of Commons—in Dennis Canavan's case, for 26 years. As will be seen in volumes 2 and 3, the concentration of MSPs who have no significant interests or occupations outside politics has increased steadily. In this, Sturgeon was ahead of the pack.

***

Overall, the young SNP spitfire represented the anti-UK clan effectively as a *clan*. She was rarely at a loss for a pluckily insolent retort when she faced an opponent from a different clan. Early in the second year of the parliament, she was speaking in a debate about long-term care provision when Iain Grey, the Deputy Health Minister (who had been promoted to that role without any previous parliamentary experience at all), stood up to intervene.

"Just sit down and listen for once in your life, Mr Gray," Sturgeon said.[90]

Two months later, Sturgeon dismissed a point made by Hugh Henry, a Labour MSP, saying: "He should acquaint himself with parliamentary procedure."

To Ben Wallace, a Tory who is now the UK's Secretary of State for Defence, she said, "I remind Mr Wallace that patience is a virtue."[91]

---

[90] 20 September 2000, col. 770

[91] 16 November 2000, col. 78, 79

A few months after that, she blank-faced a question from David Davidson, another Tory, by saying only "Patience is a virtue" then returning to her text.[92] She even said to Tommy Sheridan, who was a far more substantial political figure than she: "If the member listens, he will shortly hear..."[93]

Hardly ever did she make a productive point after the arrogant put-down. Politics is full of *amusing* put-downs but they become both mannerless and pointless if they do not have some positive idea behind them. But the average "kale and ceilidh" MSP who was trying to look like a "smart successful" bureaucrat seems, at least to this reader of the *Official Report*, to have been almost entirely devoid of a sense of humour, or even of fun. That was the gallery which Sturgeon played to so well.

By the time the summer recess was looming, Sturgeon had begun speaking disrespectfully to ministers as well as ordinary members. One victim was Malcolm Chisholm, Iain Grey's successor as Deputy Minister for Health and Community Care. In a debate on child poverty, she interrupted him to say, "I am sure that Malcolm Chisholm's misunderstanding of my point about dental checks was deliberate."[94]

Sturgeon had no respect for the political fiction in Westminster that "we are all honourable Members." Was that arrogance or calculated rudeness? Or was it just "a new way of doing politics"? She never seemed willing to try to *persuade* non-Nationalist MSPs of her case, only to browbeat, humiliate or ignore them, as if her prejudices were "matters of principle". She adopted this tone right from the start. Gobson thinks it was a way of asserting her inherited class status as "authentic" and therefore "disadvantaged", and therefore with a licence to be rude to Tories. Though she evolved a full-spectrum "grievance strategy" with time, she understood guerrilla "grievance tactics" from the start.

***

After his death, Donald Dewar was succeeded as First Minister by

---

[92] 1 March 2001, col. 87

[93] 12 December 2001, col. 4711

[94] 3 May 2001, col. 440

Henry McLeish, who took office on 26 October 2000. But he was cut from different cloth than the lanky tribune of the people. McLeish was an ex-professional footballer and urban planner who had been an MP since 1987. Unlike Sturgeon, McLeish was accustomed to treating fellow parliamentarisms with respect as "honourable Members". He used courteous language in debate and, once in office in Edinburgh, introduced generous measures like taxpayer-funded personal care for the elderly. The main criticism of him was that he was almost as uncharismatic as Swinney.

But at least he was civil—in public anyway. In private, he could be less inhibited. He was discovered by accident to have a habit of plain speaking about his colleagues when he thought the microphones were turned off. He called the bullet-headed ex-Communist Cabinet minister, John Reid, a "patronising bastard" and described the anti-lairdist agitator-turned-government minister, Brian Wilson, as a "liability" because he spent so much time in Dublin.[95] In short, McLeish was human. So it was particularly unfortunate that he was to be the victim of the first financial scandal in the new parliament.

This teacup storm came to be known as "Officegate". It involved no impropriety beyond failure to notify the House of Commons authorities about income received by his Westminster constituency Labour Party— i.e. not McLeish himself. There was not a whiff of personal dishonesty, and the case had no direct connection with the Scottish parliament. Even Alex Salmond said he saw no evidence of impropriety. Nobody but the pharisees, fanatics and all-weather haters seemed bothered. McLeish himself emerged untarnished, going on to become a much sought-after public speaker, especially in the United States where he was a visiting professor at the University of Arkansas Law School, specialising in European institutional culture.

However, Sturgeon and her colleagues decided they would try to destroy this man's career over Officegate. It was a bold strategy, not least as the SNP itself had so many skeletons in its own cupboard, from World War II Nazis to a bitter hostility to the European Economic Community in the 1970s which had suddenly to be hidden when "independence in

---

[95] BBC, 8 June 2001

Europe" became policy in the 1980s.[96] Perhaps the Party's most embarrassing "sin" from Sturgeon's point of view was the fact that it was the SNP which had smoothed the path of Mrs Thatcher into government in 1979.[97]

The new way of doing politics required old-fashioned thuggery from time to time and McLeish was the parliamentary SNP's first important scalp. He resigned out of respect for a principle that Sturgeon, when she was in a similar position two decades later, simply ignored. Gobson maintains that it was McLeish's decency that offended the SNP enforcers. If anyone could have made the parliament work constructively at this stage, it was probably McLeish. Certainly, his replacement, Jack McConnell (once a schoolmaster in Alloa and now Lord McConnell of Glenscorrodale), was a less experienced figure, never having served in the House of Commons for example. To the SNP, he presented an easier target.

McConnell took over on 21 November 2001, just thirteen months after McLeish had come to power. The new First Minister had spent his whole political life in Scotland and was vulnerable to the charge of "cronyism" due to the semi-"Soviet" way in which the local Labour Party worked. That presented Sturgeon with a tempting target on McConnell's first appearance as First Minister.

"The Government that Jack McConnell assembled yesterday has

---

[96] It is widely forgotten today just how strongly opposed to the European Economic Community the SNP was in the 1970s. The leader in the House of Commons, Donald Stewart (Western Isles, 1970-87), was the first SNP MP to have won his seat in a general election (in which surprise results are less likely). He wrote in his autobiography: "It seemed illogical (to put it mildly) for a nationalist striving to regain power for the people of Scotland, to hand over power to a faceless European bureaucracy." (*A Scot at Westminster* (1994), p. 50) The SNP's trajectory on Europe was similar to that of Sinn Féin in Ireland. They first saw the democratic limitations, then became supporters of the EU once they realised how much harm it could do Britain.

[97] After the failure of the 1979 referendum on the establishment of a Scottish Assembly, the SNP took revenge on the Labour Party because it had stipulated a 40% threshold for "yes" votes from the electorate as a whole. The SNP retaliated by introducing a vote of no confidence in the Labour government, which by then had a wafer-thin majority. The Tories joined in and managed to defeat the government by 311 votes to 310, thus forcing Callaghan's resignation and provoking a general election. Mrs Thatcher won that, to the fury of the SNP which had made that outcome almost certain. Callaghan said that the SNP were "turkeys voting for an early Christmas."

been almost universally described as a Cabinet of cronies," she said, before making the startling claim that Scotland had "the unhappiest nursing profession in the whole wide world." She used this as a pretext to attack Malcolm Chisholm once again, but in a novel way.

> That brings us back neatly to the crony Cabinet. The big question is: what did Malcolm Chisholm do for Jack? The one thing that unites all the ministers in Jack's Cabinet is that at some point they have all done a favour for Jack. What was the favour that Malcolm Chisholm did for Jack McConnell?[98]

Despite her unapologetic lack of respect for people outside the SNP, Sturgeon demanded respect for herself from everybody in all parties. In a health debate she picked out a Labour member who was whispering to a colleague while she was talking. "He may want to share what he is saying with the rest of the chamber... If Mr Fitzpatrick listens instead of muttering to his colleagues...."[99] There may have been something personal in all this—they had both been Glasgow lawyers—because after berating Malcolm Chisholm again—"if the minister had listened..."— she broke off from her argument and said:

> It appears that Brian Fitzpatrick has a problem with his hands—I am sure that it is not the first time that he has had a problem controlling his hands or other parts of his anatomy.[100]

This was certainly a new way of "doing debate". But Sturgeon had judged the mood of the new parliament to a tee. Manners, she seemed to say, are so Tory. The same applied to language. Sturgeon understood early on that the parliament was filled with people who wanted most of all to have somebody *listen* to them. This insight was to have some surprising consequences.

***

MSPs' desire for an audience raises the tricky question of

---

[98] 28 November 2001, cols. 4173-4
[99] 13 December 2001, col. 4778
[100] *Ibid.*

communication in public life generally. "Aspiranto" is the universal language spoken by aspiring—hence the name—possessors of power, influence and wealth. In a knowledge-based economy, the kings of the keyboard set the standard. Aspiranto-speakers stand in relation to ordinary citizens much as "the Establishment" used to stand in relation to deferential Britain in a different age. Like the old-boy network, the inner circle of government has not changed much, only the people who are admitted to it have. The structural story in Scotland goes back to the eighteenth century.

In the wake of the Jacobite rebellion of 1745, Scotland was "punished" by the abolition of the original Scottish Office. Administration was left in the hands of the Lord Advocate. The result was that the country enjoyed a long period of almost complete abandonment by central government. That was when the Scottish Enlightenment transformed the world, and Scottish industry transformed Scotland. By 1914, the country was the wealthiest in Europe, having a higher GDP per head than England, which was its nearest competitor. The "punishment" after Culloden proved to be the best tonic Scotland ever enjoyed. Decline from that peak was contemporaneous with the intrusion of national government, starting with the re-founding of the Scottish Office on a tiny, almost experimental, basis in 1885. The institutional results were disastrous. They included the stimulation of local separationism.[101]

The First World War necessitated restrictions on personal freedom due to the unity of national effort required to win it, and the centralisation that implied. The result for Scotland has been that it has not had an independent business/political elite of international importance since the 1920s. Bonar Law, who grew up in Helensburgh, was the last Prime Minister of Great Britain to think of himself throughout his life as based psychologically in Scotland, in his case in Glasgow where he had become a millionaire iron broker. As Scotland's economy declined to a "regional branch" of larger structures, bureaucratic management took root. With the arrival of the welfare state after the Second World War, the civil

---

[101] I use the word "separationism" rather than "separatism" because the SNP's aim is separation, not independence. For that it would need to be outside the European Union too, which is *not* its stated aim.

service started to assert its ascendency over the productive economy. Civic values became more important than value creation. A layer of "untouchables" at the top of the administrative tree began to evolve. Today they act as an informal, unstructured and shadowy "establishment" which agglomerates power, stays out of the limelight, and moves in mysterious ways its wonders to perform.

The new establishment's language is Aspiranto. It is not compulsory, but the aspiring public sector careerist needs to master it if he or she wants to get on. This is the case in any bureaucracy. Without a bottom line in the form of profit or something measured externally, keywords become the main discriminators internally. It is a short step from keywords to insiderish euphemisms, and not much further to coded language generally.

The attraction of a code which can sound like plain English is that it enables politicians and others to say one thing to monoglot English-speakers while being understood by Aspirantists to have said, or at least *meant*, something different. Fluency in the language separates those who are "on the inside track" from the general public, which relies on its mother tongue. Language and status go together, as they always do in hierarchical systems, whether the old British Establishment or the new world of trans-national Aspirantists.

Aspiranto is not "Newspeak", as described by George Orwell in *1984*. It is important not to confuse the two. Orwell's dystopian language echoes the sloganeering and attempted mind-control of the Soviet Union, and in that sense amounts to an attempt to *force* thought into new tramlines. Aspiranto, by contrast, does not force anybody to change their habits of thinking, if they do not want to. It exists to allow modern elites to look "open and transparent" when they are not.

Those who wish to confine themselves to plain English and private life are entirely free to do so. What such people do not realise is that they are condemning themselves to a life of civic below-the-saltery. They might as well forget about high public office. Better to move to Great Todday and start enjoying themselves as political nobodies, with all the personal freedom that implies.

Whereas Newspeak was a technique appropriate to a totalitarian age, Aspiranto evolved to style-fence power in an apparently democratic one—and thereby covertly undermine the formal equality on which democracy depends. It does that by making it almost impossible to choose between alternative policy peddlers on the basis of what they *say* since they all use the same misleading words and phrases. To the citizen voter, simple choices between apparently competing alternatives end up, on closer inspection, to be more than differently flavoured varieties of the same policy chewing-gum. Shades of Disraeli's Tadpole and Taper, with their "Tory men and Whig measures"—or was it the other way round? Does it matter?[102]

If the unwritten contract behind political reciprocity is the basis of the rule of law, that contract is vitiated when the rulers use either force or fraud to get the answers they want from the public. Newspeak is an example of force, and Aspiranto one of fraud. Both evolved from the root which Orwell describes in his Appendix to *1984*: "Newspeak was designed not to extend but to *diminish* the range of thought." (emphasis in original)

The Aspiranto-speakers who form the new, post-Big Brother elite are what Gobson refers to as the "bureaugarchs". They operate within a "bureaugarchy", which sits on top of the ordinary clerical bureaucracy. But the group is not limited to senior civil servants as it is a cross-competence status level which includes politicians, media people, "opinion formers" in the non-government organisations (NGOs), pressure groups and other bodies in which "attitude"—i.e. keyword consciousness—is king. They all speak Aspiranto, operate internationally while using the shifting sands of "attitude fashion" to stay opaque while still appearing "open and transparent" to the ordinary citizen.

The ultimate goal of bureaugarchy is the creation of a closed system in which the only options for the citizenish hoi polloi are those already specified in a multiple-choice framework which the bureaugarchs themselves have devised. The digitalisation of decision-making and population control presents another opportunity create a closed system. But life is an open, or analogue, system, in which surprises, creativity, emotions, happy accidents and irrational passions also feature—especially passions,

---

[102] The language issue will be discussed in more detail in chapter 9, in connection with party manifestos for the 2007 election.

the motive for action, which are *entirely* analogue. As David Hume argued, without passion there can be no creative action, and without that, there can be no human evolution.[103]

The more life is digitalised, the more people have to think within the confines of the bureaugarchs' priorities. If you ignore their logic, you find you cannot click on "Next" in order to progress to the following page in the website of daily life. Where open-ended answers are forbidden, it is impossible to "Add to cart" without having chosen one of the pre-specified range of allowable responses. That is how multiple-choice questions impoverish human interaction and destroy reciprocity. They work well for simple commerce, but are disastrous in politics where the bureaugarchs specify both the questions *and the allowable answers*. That puts them in an unassailable position *vis à vis* the citizen. The role of Aspiranto is to conceal their victory from their victims, who are ordinary monoglots speaking only their own language.

✳✳✳

Sturgeon appears to have picked up a certain amount of Aspiranto before arriving in parliament. Once there, she quickly became fluent. But right from the start, she could utter without embarrassment certain basic phrases like: "make Scotland a better place"; "how our politicians can better reflect the Scottish people's aspirations"; and "public services of which we can be proud".

Some MSPs used Aspiranto apparently without realising it. Bill Butler, a teacher-turned-MSP who had taken over Donald Dewar's seat of Anniesland, interrupted Sturgeon in a health debate to say in flawless Aspiranto: "Democracy, accountability and transparency are very important." But he lapsed into plain English when asking about the

---

[103] Though it is beyond the scope of this story, it might be mentioned in passing that the same applies to judgement, whether of qualities, as in connoisseurship, or of actions, as in court. A fully closed system implies a form of computer justice. But computers cannot have empathy, sympathy, flexibility or compassion, much less emotional intelligence or social memory. Only humans can have that. The ideal of a value-free computer-style "justice" system operated by bureaucrats trying to imitate computers has been deconstructed by Ian Hamilton QC, as discussed in *The Justice Factory* (*op. cit.,* pp. 151-2). "Civil servants are trained mice. Judges are human," he wrote.

publication of "death-rate league tables for individual surgeons." Mixing his languages into an opaque soup, he said, "We would be comparing apples with oranges. How will that help transparency?"[104]

Sturgeon reacted to that in plain English as it better expressed her condescension: "I am glad that Bill Butler managed to read the intervention notes that were provided by his party bosses."[105]

Plain English is the language for real arguments. Sturgeon has always been able to speak it with exceptional facility. In a debate about school meals, she talked in high Aspiranto of her desire "to change our culture".[106] Then a competitive nipping match broke out, in old-fashioned English, about lavatory visiting:

> **Shona Robison (North-East Scotland) (SNP)**: For the record, the Health and Community Care Committee took evidence on 8 May and 15 May. Both Nicola Sturgeon and I were present for all the oral evidence during those meetings. Perhaps the convener of the Health and Community Care Committee would like to take the opportunity to withdraw her remarks.
>
> **Mrs Margaret Smith (Edinburgh West) (LD)**: I will not withdraw the remark, because I know for a fact that Nicola Sturgeon was not in her seat on that occasion.
>
> **Nicola Sturgeon:** I was at the toilet.
>
> **Mrs Smith:** I remember thinking at the time that she had been away long enough to send a press release. That is what I thought that she was doing—
>   [*Interruption.*]
>
> **The Deputy Presiding Officer:** Order.
>
> **Shona Robison:** Perhaps Margaret Smith should check the Official Report before making such comments in the chamber. I have the Official Report here and it says that Nicola Sturgeon and I were present for all that evidence.
>
> **Mrs Smith:** On a point of order. As far as I am aware, the minutes of any meeting simply say that someone was present at a meeting. I did not say that Nicola Sturgeon was not present at the meeting. I said that Nicola Sturgeon was not there to hear all the evidence that was given. That is not the same thing.

---

[104] 16 May 2002, col. 8941

[105] *Ibid.*

[106] 20 June 2002, col. 9990

Nicola Sturgeon: What about you?

Mrs Smith: I was there actually, apart from going to the toilet once. I did not say—

[*Interruption.*]

The Deputy Presiding Officer: Order. I do not regard that as a point of order. I suggest that Ms Robison continues and talks to the substance of the issue that is before the Parliament.[107]

As Gobson points out, the Aspirantist phrase for "going to the toilet" is "taking a comfort break", while the older expression, "going to powder my nose", is no longer an acceptable euphemism for ladies with political or bureaugarchic ambitions.

Are we all on the same page with that?

---

[107] *Ibid.*, col 10003

Chapter 4

The Second Parliament

The first couple of years of the parliament had not provided the route to stardom that a lesser politician than Sturgeon might have preferred. She had scored many small successes in debate but not achieved the level of public name-recognition that a pure careerist might have hoped for. Mandy Rhodes has written of the transformation of the "gauche, un-smiling teenager" into "a powerhouse politician, beloved by the masses."[108] But that took time. Sturgeon was still the "introvert" who had "few lifelong friends", and they tended to be long-time members of the Party—"cronies", McConnell could have said. For all "the selfies, the informality on Twitter, the public shows of affection and so forth, when it comes down to actually talking about herself or sharing intimacies, even with close associates, she is much less comfortable."[109]

The SNP had not done well in elections thus far, so it is worth asking what provoked Sturgeon's single-issue focus. It cannot have come from ordinary political ambition or she would have joined the Labour Party when she was 16. Perhaps there was another factor. "What played on me then," Sturgeon said in the run-up to the 2014 independence referendum, speaking of her feelings in the 1980s, "is that we had a right-wing, uncaring Tory government that *we did not vote for*, doing significant damage to the fabric of our society."[110] (emphasis added)

---

[108] *SNP Leaders, op. cit.,* p. 352

[109] *Ibid.,* p. 355

[110] *Daily Record,* 6 July 2014. She was forgetting the SNP's role in putting Mrs Thatcher into 10 Downing Street (see above).

This was an old theme, but a popular one. As early as 1980, before Mrs Thatcher had been in power for a full year, Alex Salmond was already writing in his local press: "Scotland is now totally helpless against a government *we did not elect* but was forced upon us…"[111] Examples of this line of argument could be multiplied endlessly. It rests on a misunderstanding of democracy in a free society. Sentient human beings will always disagree, sometimes strongly, so that without what is known as "losers' consent" democracy cannot function. If those who are outvoted do not accept the result, anything short of unanimity becomes a threat to civic peace. Non-violent government is impossible when only the majority accepts the result of any vote. Otherwise, every election must provoke civil war. Democracy is a system for choosing between alternative policies so that disagreements can be resolved without recourse to violence.

Intransigent losing is the modern equivalent of feuding, which all medieval monarchs had to suppress before they could think of trying to establish law and order through the idea of "the king's peace". Few succeeded. The English monarchy managed it—and only partially—after the Tudor revolution, which started in 1485 with Henry VII's victory over Richard III at the battle of Bosworth Field. In Scotland the equivalent moment was the battle of Culloden in 1746.

The internal pre-requisite for sovereignty is the state's monopoly on armed force. That is legitimately used when sections of the population do not accept the results of the generally accepted method of taking decisions. It is *not* legitimately used when the mass of the population does not accept the major decisions by government, yet they are nevertheless enforced in defiance of the principle of reciprocity. That becomes a problem of losers' consent *on the part of the state*. One example might clarify the point at this stage.

The Northern Isles—Orkney and Shetland—have long had an ambivalent attitude to Scotland, which colonised them after 1468, when they were transferred from Danish to Scottish control. For example, in the 1650s they were the only part of Scotland which "gave any positive signs that they wished to make the Union [with England] work or

---

[111] Quoted in *Salmond*, Torrance, *op. cit.*, p. 60

facilitate the establishment of English rule in Scotland."[112] Little has changed in that respect since. What would happen if they decided they would prefer to stay out of an independent Scotland today, and remain in some association with the United Kingdom? Would the Scottish government allow them a vote on this? And if the islanders chose a different path from mainland Scotland, would a government in Edinburgh feel it right to try to take back the islands by force, on the Putin-Ukraine model? Does the SNP accept the principle that if Scotland has the right to destroy the United Kingdom, the Northern Isles should have a corresponding right to destroy Scotland?

If that ever happened, Hamish Gobson and I would start campaigning for a referendum in Kintyre and the Hebrides for "Hexit", which would mean the revival, in a modern form, of the Lordship of the Isles. We would be governed by a low-cost, carbon-free, wind-powered, hyper-decentralised, anti-bureaucratic "dáil" on the shores of Loch Finlaggan on Islay. There would be whisky in the bar, and Aspiranto strictly barred.

***

Despite the replacement of McLeish by the wooden figure of Jack McConnell, Swinney was not a success as the SNP's National Convener, either in parliament or within the Party. It went into the Scottish general election in 2003 with massive debts and no ringing slogan or charismatic figurehead.[113] Dr Death was incapable of motivating the masses. Not only that, he made some decisions which were to have long-term consequences that many have come to regret.

For example, Swinney was responsible for hiring Peter Murrell as Chief Executive of the Party. Murrell replaced Michael Russell, the lazy-eyed litterateur with the mandarin air who had graced the position with loose suits and tight stubble since the late twentieth century. Whereas Russell was known as "the SNP intelligent member", Murrell presented

---

[112] *Cromwellian Scotland*, Frances Dow (1999), p. 44

[113] The Scotland Act imposed a strict 4-year cycle of general elections, on a "fixed term" basis.

himself as a clean-cut but colourless, Euro-style functionary, complete with databases, algorithms and cliquish enigmatisms. He stayed out of the sales side of the business as his role was behind the scenes and managerial. He has been called "the most powerful Scot nobody has heard of."

Murrell made an illuminating contrast to the old, unbiddable individualists that once made up the SNP. Curiously, he started professional life as a press officer for the Church of Scotland, like Alasdair Allan, the future Western Isles MSP. But unlike Allan, he did not have the benefit of a university education. Michael Russell did and, curiously, he too started adult life studying theology.

In the UK general election of 2001, the SNP had lost ground, going from 6 to 5 MPs, so the omens for the general election in 2003 in Scotland were not good. The parliament itself had been a disappointment, and the nationalist campaign was a failure. Alex Neil's 1991 slogan "Free by '93" was re-treaded as "Free by 2007", which did not have quite the same ring. It called to mind what Salmond had said at the start of his career: "I'll give it ten years and if Scotland isn't independent, I'll pass the torch."[114] "Passing the torch" in this context is Aspiranto for "getting back out on the golf course."

Before the election, which was held on 1 May 2003, Swinney smiled out at discontented voters from a thousand posters and a million leaflets. But all to no avail. Scotland was not interested. The party went sharply backward. The SNP dropped from 35 to 27 MSPs, and was equally embarrassed in the last first-past-the-post local government elections which were held on the same day.[115]

---

[114] In 1992 at least one opinion poll showed support for independence at close to 50%, which is almost exactly what it is in 2022. Thirty years of work and sacrifice has made no difference whatsoever. The Macdonalds *still* do not trust the Campbells.

[115] Henceforth local elections were to be by proportional representation, but on a different system from the parliamentary "list" seats. There were to be no more colourful personal contests. Local authority government was to be by faceless coalitions, European-style, and the ability of the voter to influence the result was compromised by yet another electoral system which may have been understood by those who devised it but was not by the electorate. Proponents of the new system claimed it would result in "greater efficiency", which is Aspiranto for "more cheaply". The march of the bureaugarchy continued unseen.

This led to calls for a more inspiring National Convenor—someone more *leader*-like. What was wanted was someone who appeared to be *enthusiastic* about independence. Swinney looked too rational to be enthusiastic about anything. His time was running out.

Before the election, Sturgeon played a characteristically canny game. She put her hatred of Mrs Thatcher in her back pocket and campaigned on the dull subject of Labour's inefficiencies in government. Perhaps that is why, once again, she lost to Gordon Jackson QC in the democratic vote in Govan. Everyone knows that governments everywhere are inefficient. Nothing new there. Her speeches are barely readable today now that the passions of that moment have subsided, and the policies been forgotten.

However, Sturgeon was beginning to develop the important non-verbal communication skills that Swinney lacked. She could leave unspoken words hanging in the constituency office air, after the single-use plastic tea-cups had been dumped, along with the agenda and sederunt sheets, in a sustainable waste-paper basket. She could, without saying so explicitly, give party workers a plausible reason for believing that it was all in the spirit of Robert the Bruce that they had forgone watching the football that evening to come out and be bored with political trivia.

2003 turned out to be the "election of freaks", as some journalists put it. Tommy Sheridan's Scottish Socialist Party jumped from one seat to six, and the Greens, led by Robin Harper, a cheerful schoolmaster who wore brightly-coloured scarves, went from a single seat (his) to seven, though that was achieved by gaming the system. The Greens *did not stand in a single constituency for democratic election.* Instead they put up candidates in "list" seats only, where they were compensated for not having won (as if they had stood and lost) any democratic seats. That was the rule and theirs was a triumph of bureaucratic manipulation. They were the first party to realise the possibilities of misusing the Dewar Constitution in this anti-democratic way. Others soon followed, further undermining the democratic legitimacy of the new parliament.

Labour lost almost as many seats as the SNP (6 to the Nationalists' 8). Only the Tories and the Liberals held firm. But the public's lack of interest in the new parliament was evident in the low turnout. That point was made by the ubiquitous psephologist from Strathclyde University,

Professor (now Sir John) Curtice, in a report for the Electoral Commission. In his summary findings, he wrote: "The Scottish parliament is failing to motivate the electorate... with 57% of the electorate (and 67% of non-voters) saying that it has made no difference to the way Scotland is governed."[116]

Overall turnout was slightly less than 50%. Inner-city Glasgow, one of the core areas of "authentic" Scotland, was even worse. There, only 40% voted and in Shettleston, a sink suburb which was the only part of the United Kingdom where the life expectancy was falling, just 35% did so.

Shettleston was one of the constituencies Sturgeon herself had stood for, in 1992, when she was trying to find an electorate that would put her in a parliament or council. It had not always been a dying community, having been the home of several high achievers in the past. Among them was the first Lord Wheatley, a socialist lawyer of Irish descent who rose to become the Lord Justice Clerk.[117] Others were Alistair MacLean, the author of *HMS Ulysses* and *The Guns of Navarone*, Beaumont Neilson, the nineteenth century inventor of hot blast iron smelting, and Junior Campbell, who wrote the music to *Thomas the Tank Engine*.

Gobson thinks that the SNP manifesto for that election was principally responsible for the low turnout. It carried the Aspirantish title: "Releasing our Potential", and was a document of such head-banging tedium that it is hard to believe even Dr Death could have seen it as a vote-winner. The first concrete commitment was "to sort out the problems in our public services that Labour and the Liberal Democrats have created." If that didn't get the party faithful roaring for blood, it went on to say that the SNP would "fix" the health service, "improve" education, "tackle" crime and "stimulate" the economy—adding patronisingly that these are "the things that concern you in your daily lives." How did they

---

[116] "Scottish Elections Research May-June 2003", p. 4

[117] He was also one of the first Roman Catholic judges in Scotland. It was for the sin of attending his funeral that Lord Mackay of Clashfern, one of the most distinguished judges Scotland has produced (Margaret Thatcher appointed him Lord Chancellor), was expelled from the Free Presbyterian Church. It was Lord Wheatley, an ex-player and life-long fan of football, who produced the Wheatley Report into the Ibrox disaster of 1971, in which 66 Rangers supporters were crushed to death when railings failed on the exit steps.

know? In any case, the logic was flawed. Apparently Lord Wheatley, Beaumont Neilson, Alastair MacLean and Junior Campbell had *not* "released their potential" because they had clearly had non-political concerns in their "daily lives". The whole pitch was nonsense, and condescending too. No wonder voters preferred the football. The document's introduction ended with a classic flat-footed Swinneyism: "By being honest, we'll persuade you that only with Independence can we release Scotland's potential."[118]

The disappointing result of the election showed that neither the National Convenor's inverse charm, nor Murrell's power-point enigmagraphs could make any dent on the people of Scotland. Inevitably, there were calls for Swinney's resignation. The Party's membership in December 2002 had been 16,000 and a year later was 9,450. Half-way through that period, the title "National Convenor" was dropped and replaced by "Party Leader". Soon afterwards, Swinney was dropped too.

After the initial euphoria of 1999, the SNP now seemed in danger of splitting into two opposing factions: the "fundamentalists", who wanted "independence now" irrespective of legal restraint, and the "gradualists" who wanted to work for independence within the confines and conventions of the rule of law. Swinney was so strongly identified with the latter group that he could not appeal to the former in the way Sturgeon and Salmond could with their cultivated ambiguity. Being natural Aspirantists, they both had appeal beyond their precise words. Swinney had not. He did not seem to realise that electoral politics is a game of hope rather than fact. Facts may be important for governing, but electioneering depends on hope, however false or fraudulent.

***

At 9.30 a.m. on 7 May, a week after the 2003 election, the Presiding

---

[118] *The Complete Case for a Better Scotland*, SNP, 2003, p. 3. Where clichés failed them, statements of the obvious filled the gaps. Thus: "We'll keep what works in government and change what doesn't"; or "We will deliver [*sic*] continuity where needed and change where it matters." Defying categorisation was this mysterious boast: "What we want, we can deliver." To the sentient citizen, that should have been "What *you* want, *we* can deliver."

Officer, Sir David Steel, invited all members to take their oath of allegiance to the Queen, or to make an affirmation to the same effect in non-religious form. Leading off was Jack McConnell, as First Minister, and he was followed by the leader of the opposition, John Swinney. That was where the fun started, as he objected to any form of allegiance.

At the beginning of the first session in 1999, few had minded having to declare allegiance to the Queen. Suddenly, in 2003, there was widespread resistance to the idea that members of a parliament within the United Kingdom should have to declare their loyalty to the head of state. In 1999, only Alex Salmond, Dennis Canavan, Robin Harper, Tommy Sheridan and Roseanna Cunningham bridled at the idea. The other 124 members, including Sturgeon, accepted the constitutional structure of the state in whose higher councils they were about to participate. Something appeared to have changed in the intervening four years. Now, 23 members wanted to make personal statements about the constitution. Since most of them had essentially the same objection, and one of those was now Nicola Sturgeon, it will be useful to describe briefly the point she wished to make.

Sturgeon's statement was one of the simpler ones, but the point was central to the issue of governance in a devolved parliament: "Before making the affirmation, I wish to declare my belief in the sovereignty of the Scottish people."[119] She had glided smoothly from acceptance of the affirmation without reservation in 1999 to this statement of the new SNP orthodoxy. When most of her Party colleagues accepted the *status quo*, she accepted it; when they did not, she did not. When the issue dropped out of parliamentary fashion, she dropped it too. After the next election, in 2007, she made no objection to swearing allegiance to the Queen.

Was she a trimmer? Possibly, but an effective leader can lead only in a direction the troops are willing to go. Being still a trooper in 2003, she had been shown the way by Swinney's opening:

> On behalf of my colleagues, I reaffirm that the Scottish National Party's primary loyalty is to the people of Scotland, in the constitutional tradition

---

[119] All quotes about the oath taking come from 7 May 2003, cols. 2-8

of the sovereignty of the people.

This went beyond Sturgeon's cautious point, which was only that sovereignty lay with the Scottish people. She made no mention of Scottish constitutional tradition, one hopes because she knew it was nonsense. The idea that "sovereignty lies with the people" in Scotland is a populist conceit which has no basis in historical fact—as Sturgeon must also have known from her studies of public international law.

"Sovereign" states are those whose ultimate freedom of action is in principle unconstrained except by voluntary agreements or contracts. A sovereign state is one that has the will and the means to act independently of other sovereign states, should it so choose. Sturgeon's statement was either not serious in a legal sense or, if it was intended to be political, it was an impertinent attack on a serious ceremony. Maybe the Scottish people *should* be sovereign, as many believed. That is a perfectly legitimate proposition for the future, but the fact is that on 7 May 2003, it was the *British* people who were sovereign.

The way Sturgeon followed the Nationalist herd while aspiring to lead it showed how cleverly she was able to camouflage her ambition. The idea that Scottish constitutional law has always been different in this respect from English law is a historical fiction *invented by the SNP* in the 1930s, at a time when populist nationalism was all the go in Germany, Italy, Spain, Portugal, Ireland etc., indeed most countries of the pre-1991 EU. The SNP claimed then, as it still does, that there is a distinction to be made between "popular sovereignty" and "parliamentary sovereignty". This is such an important delusion, but at the same time so appealing to people unversed in Scottish history, that I have explained it at some length in the Appendix. Spoiler alert: they are essentially the same thing in a representative democracy. The British electorate as a whole is the ultimate sovereign within the United Kingdom. The Crown (today) is the symbol of that.[120]

The oath, or affirmation, which members had to swear or affirm before they were allowed to take their seats in the new parliament was very

---

[120] It is perhaps relevant that a plausible but misleading book on this subject was first published in 2003. Called *For Freedom Alone*, it is discussed in the film "The Declaration of Arbroath" as noted below.

short. It merely asked the prospective MSP to confirm that he or she "will be faithful and bear true allegiance to Her Majesty Queen Elizabeth, Her heirs and successors, according to Law." It is hard to understand why that should be objectionable, except as a demonstration of unwillingness to co-operate with existing institutions, perhaps in the hope of undermining them. It was not as if the unbiddables represented popular opinion outside "authentic" Scotland. That was still overwhelmingly in favour of the state of which the Queen was the monarch.

In 2003, the majority of the SNP members followed Swinney and tried to disrupt the ceremony by making their affirmations of loyalty to the Queen only under protest. None turned their principles into action and actually refused to express loyalty. Hamish Gobson wonders if that might have had anything to do with the fact that salaries, pensions, expense allowances and other "top table" privileges were at stake. They were not prepared, he said, "to put their money where their oath was— in the bin."

Bruce McFee said: "Before performing this ritual, I would like to say that my loyalty and affirmation are to the people of Scotland and not to the British state or any of its institutions." That was odd as the Scottish parliament itself was an institution of the British state.

Christine Grahame said: "I wish to make a statement that I make the affirmation under duress, believing as I do in the sovereignty of the Scottish people and the Scottish people alone." That was puzzling on different grounds. What "duress"? The only duress was the "package" offered: salary, pension, expense allowance, parliamentary facilities, etc. Was she trying to hold herself out as some sort of *victim* because she had been elected? Alternatively, she might not have understood the difference between accepting something "under protest", which in this context was quite reasonable, and accepting it under "duress". As Annabel Goldie, Lord James Douglas Hamilton or David McLetchie—or even her own Fergus Ewing or Nicola Sturgeon—could have explained to her, any contract formed under duress is void, but one signed under protest is valid since it is a free decision, however uncomfortable to the signatory. Why was Grahame trying to make her own free choice sound like one controlled by implied violence?

No Tories or Liberals objected to the idea of the Queen as head of state, and only one Labour member, Elaine Smith, did so. Most of Tommy Sheridan's Scottish Socialists followed the SNP objectors, though some of them made statements which indicated that they had actually thought about the issue. Sheridan himself made a coherent point that was original and reasonable in its own terms since it omitted all mention of the SNP's myth about Scottish constitutional superiority to the British state.

> Before making the affirmation, I would like to state that I and my party colleagues were elected on a clear and honest commitment to an independent socialist Scotland—a socialist republic—and a Scotland of citizens, not a Scotland of subjects. We will continue to fight for such a society.

Rosemary Byrne, another Socialist, amplified Sheridan's point but in terms which echoed Grahame's claim to victimhood:

> Before I make the affirmation, I would like to make a short statement that I do so under duress. I was elected by the people of the South of Scotland as their representative in the Scottish Parliament. I am a socialist. I believe in equality. We are all Jock Tamson's bairns—we are all equal and we should not need to take an oath. However, it is a means to an end: an independent socialist republic.

For the SNP, Sandra White echoed Tommy Sheridan more closely than she did her National Convenor. Also, she appeared to understand the difference between "under protest" and "under duress":

> Before I make the affirmation, I would like to state that I believe in a free and independent Scotland in which the Scottish people would be independent citizens rather than subjects. Therefore, I make the affirmation under protest.

A more personal tone was adopted to make a similar point by Carolyn Leckie of the Scottish Socialists:

> I would like to make a statement. Like all my comrades, I think that the Parliament should be accountable and loyal only to the people. I believe in an independent socialist republic, so I take the oath, which is to a woman who has inherited privilege, under strong protest. Apart from anything else, I do not even know the woman. I apologise to my mother, who is actually a great fan of hers, but that is not for me, thank you.

This appeared to irritate the Presiding Officer, who said, "Will you proceed to the oath, please." Perhaps he found it absurd that someone would imply that they were unwilling to swear an oath to someone they do not "know", as if the state should be no larger than anyone's circle of friends and family—in other words, a clan.

Rob Gibson, an SNP "list" member for the Highlands and Islands, had a different way of throwing sand in the machinery. He asked to be allowed to take the oath in Gaelic. However, he was forced to say it in English first, which rather knocked the arse out of his bucket, as Hamish Gobson would say.

The best fun was provided by Colin Fox, another of Sheridan's new intake. He was one of the more personable and intelligent of the new intake, and he decided to entertain the chamber with a song:

Colin Fox (Lothians) (SSP): Before reading the affirmation, I wish to make a short statement. As a socialist, I make the affirmation to the Crown under protest. I would like to offer some words of the national poet, Robert Burns:

"A prince can mak a belted knight"—

The Presiding Officer: I am sorry, but there is no singing in Parliament—

Colin Fox:

"A marquis, duke, and a' that;
But an honest man's aboon his might,
Gude faith he mauna fa' that!"

The Presiding Officer: I am sorry, but if you are not prepared to take the oath, you will have to wait until the end of the queue—

Colin Fox:

"For a' that, and a' that,
His ribband, star and a' that,
The man of independent mind,
He looks and laughs at a' that.—"

The Presiding Officer: I am sorry—

Colin Fox:

"Then let us pray that come it may,
As come it will for a' that, ...
That Man to Man the warld o'er,
Shall brothers be for a' that.—"

The Presiding Officer: You will have to go to the end of the queue. You cannot take up other people's time.

***

A month later, undaunted by her Party's electoral reverse, Sturgeon swung back into parliamentary action. She moved a motion on British adoption of the Euro. In future, I will precis most such motions, but the full text of this one will illustrate their style and language:

> That the Parliament supports the European Union as a confederation that collectively exercises certain sovereign rights pooled by states but in which each state retains its own sovereignty in respect of constitutional, fiscal and other matters of national importance; believes that decisions about pooled and retained sovereignty should always be taken in Scotland's national interest; therefore welcomes the development of a European constitution but opposes the conferral of exclusive European Union competence over the conservation of marine biological resources under the common fisheries policy; considers that the terms of the final draft constitution should be subject to the approval of the Scottish people in a referendum prior to ratification; regrets that the decision by Her Majesty's Government to delay entry to the single currency does not take account of Scotland's economic interests, and believes that Scotland's interests would best be represented in the European Union as an independent member state.[121]

The first point to make is the scope of the motion. After the overture about sovereignty, Sturgeon mentioned European fishing policy, a Scottish referendum on the European constitution, the British adoption of the Euro and, of course, independence. Every one of those issues was worth a debate in itself, except that each was a matter reserved to the United Kingdom parliament under the Scotland Act. The mystery is why the new Presiding Officer, George Reid, who had been elected by MSPs to succeed Sir David Steel, permitted discussion of matters outwith the competence of the parliament.[122]

---

[121] Motion S2M-124 "in the name of Nicola Sturgeon on Europe." 12 June 2003, col. 641. Note the words "each state retains its own sovereignty". This appears to contradict the new SNP idea that sovereignty lies with populations rather than states.

[122] George (now Sir George) Reid came from Clackmannanshire, which he represented for the SNP in the Westminster parliament 1974-9. He was educated at Dollar

Did the Dewar Constitution give him no control over the use of time in the chamber? Debates were regularly aborted for lack of it, and almost all speeches time-limited for the same reason. Why waste precious time on matters which could have no outcome of any sort as their subject was *ultra vires*? The Standing Orders are published on the Scottish parliament website. Rules 5.4-5.8 set out how the Business Programme is allocated, while Rule 8.2 describes the limit on Motions. It is so broad as to be meaningless. The House of Commons gives the Speaker much more power to enforce reasonable behaviour.

Once again, the finger points back to Dewar and his "new way of doing politics". It was he who insisted that the parliament be allowed to debate any subject it chose. That was supposed to be the mark of a "parliament" as opposed to an "assembly". Dewar wanted to avoid the charge that he was creating "a glorified town council" and so permitted discussion on any subject, thinking that would make it look like a "sovereign" body when he well knew that it wasn't one. That was an attempt to deceive by sleight of word. The cost of his Aspirantish dishonesty has been considerable.[123]

Sturgeon's opportunism in using the parliament for purposes it was not designed for was the mark of a goal-orientated politician who was confident—rightly, as it turned out—that her support-base would never get tired of destructive rhetoric. For example, she objected to Britain's having a united view on European policy:

> Our distinctive economic conditions demanded a separate Scottish assessment of the five tests [the Chancellor's tests for joining the Euro], but that was never going to happen because, as we know, Scotland's interests were

---

Academy and St Andrews University, where he took a first in history. He has held many distinguished posts including serving on the pre-parliament Consultative Steering Group, and overseeing the construction of the parliament building. He was elected for "Ochil" (i.e. Clackmannanshire) in 2003, stepping down in 2007. Subsequently, he was appointed the Queen's representative, as Lord High Commissioner, to the General Assembly of the Church of Scotland.

[123] Such a distinction once had a practical purpose. In his history of the old Scottish parliament Robert Rait points out that the reason why James VI and Charles I tried to avoid calling *parliaments,* as opposed to functionally similar "Conventions", was partly because in a consultative body not officially a parliament "business was limited to topics authorised in royal letters." (*Parliaments,* Rait, *op. cit.*, p. 163)

never a factor. The decision was based solely on the economic needs of London and the south-east, and on the pathetic powerplay between Tony Blair and Gordon Brown.[124]

What are the "distinctive economic characteristics" of what the SNP so often said was potentially "the wealthiest country in Europe"? According to Sturgeon: "As we have heard many times in the chamber, we have a chronic and long-term problem of low growth."[125]

Likewise, she said: "The Scottish National Party is passionately pro-European. We believe in an enlarged, confederal Europe". But she added: "We oppose a European superstate." So how might that work? The SNP, she said, would approach "each development on the European stage" and consider "whether, on any given matter, sovereignty should be pooled or retained." SNP policy "will be governed by a simple test: is it in Scotland's national interest or not?"[126]

It was clever of Sturgeon to be able to present cherry-picking as a matter of coherent principle, knowing that few in the chamber had a detailed grasp of European institutional politics. The SNP may have been sinking electorally, but she was rising within the Party, due largely to her ability to "pick the cherries" in almost any debate.

Occasionally, a member would try to probe the principles on which she selected her parliamentary cherries. She did not appear to like that and could respond capriciously. George Lyon, a Liberal, wanted to intervene in this debate, but she refused to let him. Nonetheless, she allowed Alex Johnstone, a *Tory*, to do so. When Lyon asked a second time, she refused again. But she did allow Keith Raffan, another Liberal, to interject. He asked her to comment on Alex Neil's statement that "A Scottish economy run from Frankfurt will be no more successful than one run from London." Sturgeon responded by saying that Neil could speak for himself, as if they were not members of the same Party. She added rather patronisingly, "If Mr Raffan listens, he might learn something." She then resumed her prepared speech without answering his objection or saying what he might have learned.

---

[124] 12 June 2003, col. 642

[125] *Ibid.*, col. 641

[126] *Ibid.*, col. 643

Her superior tone with Raffan did not discourage Lyon. He stood up again:

George Lyon: Will the member give way on that point?
Nicola Sturgeon: The member should be patient. If he keeps asking, he might get somewhere.

That was toying with the man. She carried on for another half a minute or so, till Lyon stood up again.

George Lyon: Will the member give way on that point?
Nicola Sturgeon: God loves a trier.
George Lyon: We have noticed—the member is trying.... [127]

The killer blow to Sturgeon's argument about Scottish cherry-picking should have been landed by Margo MacDonald, who was one of the "old stars" of the SNP. She had been deputy leader of the Party from 1974-79, serving briefly as the MP for Govan, Sturgeon's desired seat. MacDonald's victory in 1974 was one of the biggest upsets in post-war political history. It paved the way for the revival of the SNP in the later 1970s and led indirectly to the referendum on an independent Scottish Assembly in 1979. MacDonald had achieved something which Sturgeon still dreamt of.

MacDonald was a charismatic figure and an independent-minded woman. But independent minds are not tolerated in the independence clan. MacDonald had been "disciplined" by the party for expressing views in the press without having them cleared beforehand by the centre. Furious, the party bureaucrats contrived to ease her out of a winnable position on the Party "list" for 2003. She was busted down to fifth position. She could not win from there. The aim was clearly to exclude her from parliament, but without openly saying so. However, MacDonald confounded them by standing as an Independent. She was re-elected in defiance of the unseen manipulators of the party "list", one of the few ever able to do so. The SNP anger at her presence in the second parliament was palpable.

MacDonald intervened to ask this key question:

---

[127] *Ibid.*

Margo MacDonald (Lothians) (Ind): On the matter of the constitution, I absolutely agree with what the member [Sturgeon] has just said about steadfastly opposing a federal constitution, but what will she do if Germany, France and Italy say yes to federalism?

Nicola Sturgeon: As Margo MacDonald is, *I believe*, a nationalist, she would agree that Scotland should be independent in Europe so that we can influence those decisions in a way that we simply cannot do at present.[128] (emphasis added)

The idea that Scotland would put up a more effective fight against Franco-German federalism than the United Kingdom would was unrealistic, to put it at its mildest, even then. But more significant was a practice at which Sturgeon soon became adept: replying without answering the question she had been asked. In this case, there was more to her answer than that. To say MacDonald was "*I believe* a nationalist" was insolent coming from the novice who had failed to get elected for Govan three times and who knew full well that MacDonald's stature within the independence movement, and the contribution she made to it while Sturgeon was still in nursery school.

Etiquette let Sturgeon down again a minute later when she told Tavish Scott, a Liberal, that a point he had made was "singularly stupid". After MacDonald, Sturgeon had said that before the UK government ratified the new "constitution" under discussion (what became the Lisbon Treaty in 2007), it should "have the courage to seek support in a referendum" in order to give the EU "democratic legitimacy".[129] It would have been a perfectly acceptable point, if expressed courteously.

The Deputy Minister for Finance and Public Services (Tavish Scott): Would Nicola Sturgeon care to state at this stage what the referendum would be about? At this moment, the convention has not concluded its discussions, there is no agreement on its final proposals and we do not know whether the final proposal will include a single president of the European Council. It is ludicrous to suggest that we should have a referendum today until we know what the final outcome is.

Nicola Sturgeon: Tavish Scott should listen. I did not suggest that we

---

[128] *Ibid.,* col. 644

[129] *Ibid.,* col. 644

should have a referendum today and, if he does not mind my saying so, that is a singularly stupid point to make.[130]

The insult was uncalled for. Tavish Scott had not suggested that the referendum be *held* "today"—obviously, as it was already mid-morning. His point was that Sturgeon was suggesting "today" that a referendum be held once the treaty had been finalised. That is completely different. Did she not understand that, or was this an example of her developing habit of responding to almost any question from non-"authentic" members with either aggression or contempt?

Even Sheridan's hyper-authentic Scottish Socialists were able to tolerate agreement from "inauthentic" people. One of them managed to cut to the heart of the matter with the support of—wait for it!—a *Tory*!

> **Frances Curran (West of Scotland) (SSP)**: The European Union has no democracy... The commissioners are accountable to no one—not to the European Parliament and not to any national Parliament. Neil Kinnock, who could not win an election in Britain, has no problem being in charge of transport policy across Europe.
> **Keith Raffan**: Is Ms Curran aware that the European Parliament sacked a previous Commission? The European Parliament has the power to remove the Commission, so she is misinformed on that issue.
> **Murdo Fraser (Mid-Scotland and Fife) (Con)**: The commissioners were all reappointed, however.
> **Frances Curran**: I thank Murdo Fraser, who rightly points out that the commissioners were all reappointed, even though they were accused of fraud, corruption, expense claims irregularities—the lot.[131]

It is not every day that the most extreme socialists in Scotland are able to co-operate with the Tories in correcting facts. Curran was a college lecturer who had been a founder member of the Scottish Socialists, and was an ex-member of the Militant Tendency. Yet, unlike Sturgeon, she was capable of both courtesy and open-mindedness in debate.

The other "extreme" party, the Greens, supported Curran's view of the EU. Mark Ballard, an Englishman who had lived in India and Pakistan, really went tiger-shooting:

---

[130] *Ibid.*, col. 645
[131] *Ibid.*, col. 658-9

Mark Ballard (Lothian) (Greens): The EU is pushing the process of economic globalisation ever more ruthlessly through its role in the World Trade Organisation. Economic and monetary union is exacerbating economic centralisation and accelerating the removal of democratic control over the economic system. Enlargement, as it is currently designed, is little more than the export of the free-trade model eastwards with potentially devastating impacts on the economies of central and eastern Europe. Therefore, Her Majesty's Government's decision to delay entry into the single currency was in Scotland's interest… The drive is on to create one huge European economic superpower that is able to compete ever more fiercely in international markets with Japan and the US… People are therefore questioning the future role and direction of the European Union. There is a growing sense that the European institutions are disconnected from the people whom they are supposed to represent… If the European Union continues to put its corporate-led, deregulated, neo-liberal agenda above social justice and sustainable development, the result will be the further marginalisation and exclusion of growing numbers of its citizens. People will engage only with a European Union that is relevant to their everyday lives and that they feel is democratic and accountable.[132]

Though the debate lasted all morning, it did not get much further than that, especially after Maureen Macmillan, a Labour member, poked fun at the SNP's unrequited love for Europe.

I believe that the SNP leadership's attitude to Europe is moving inexorably to the right. Whatever happened to the SNP love affair with Europe? Was it broken on the rock of reality? In 1999, the SNP MSPs all rushed off to Brussels to say, "Here we are. Look at us; we are the SNP. Aren't we lovely?" Nobody was interested.[133]

Apart from repeating her point about a referendum, Sturgeon took no further part in the discussion, leaving Roseanna Cunningham to sum up for the SNP, which she did in a Sturgeon-like tone, saying of one Labour member who tried to intervene:

Irene Oldfather has been up and down all morning like a jack-in-the box.

---

[132] *Ibid.*, col. 665-6
[133] *Ibid.*, col. 671

Someone really should put a lid on her.[134]

***

After the election, Sturgeon had been upgraded by her Leader from the health portfolio to being the spokeswoman on justice. Despite her non-stellar career as a lawyer, Sturgeon was still one of the more experienced members the SNP had in this field. This is an example of the skills shortage, which I have already noted. The problem is compounded by the refusal of the SNP to tolerate creative but off-message comment from its brighter but more independent-minded members, as the expulsion of Margo MacDonald illustrated.

The competence problem was on display in the debate on a motion which, beneath the Aspiranto, was actually about the legal system.

> That the Parliament notes the commitment made in *A Partnership for a Better Scotland* to working for a safer Scotland, supporting safe communities and improving public services and supports the Scottish Executive in working to modernise the courts and criminal justice system for those who have to use them, including victims and witnesses, and in delivering modern laws to deal with the complexities of modern Scottish life.[135]

The proposer of that unfocussed portmanteau list of saloon bar grievances was the new Minister for Justice, Cathy Jamieson. She was an art therapist to trade but had been a social worker before going into parliament. She had no significant experience of jurisprudence—but then few in the Labour Party did. She did not say why "modern laws" could be assumed, as her motion did, to be superior to ancient ones like "Thou

---

[134] *Ibid.,* col. 709

[135] S2M-191, 25 June 2003. The *Partnership for a Better Scotland* is a 50-page document which has *nothing* in it except vaguely rallying, undefined, hyper-Aspirantist statements of intent which, in any field I know about, have not been carried out in the two decades since. It is impossible to work from such slippery material—e.g. "We will continue to support the establishment of youth cafes and other alcohol-free activities for young people" (p. 32), or "We will improve procedures, services and support for adoptive and foster parents." (p. 33) There are *no* recommendations for concrete action. It would be interesting to know why civil service time was wasted in this way, and how much it cost. Or was it really just tax-payer-funded advertising for a government trying to prolong its time in office by publishing meaningless feelgoodery?

shallt not kill" or, more appropriately for parliament, "Thou shallt not bear false witness against thy neighbour." This superficial approach was damaging to a field of endeavour which has been the pride of Scottish administrative culture for three hundred years.

In her opening speech, Jamieson covered her professional nakedness with teasing wisps of Aspirantist lace. She talked of: "supporting safer communities... an efficient, effective and fair justice system... accessible and user-friendly... honest, hard-working people in our communities... a new, transparent system... ordinary people... build on the work... modernisation is about efficiency... fairness is crucial... punishment fits the crime... people from every background, tradition and community... relevant and appropriate... abolish archaic laws... our beliefs, our values and our aspirations..."[136]

That was only from the first two columns of a five-column speech. She seemed to acknowledge an element of scepticism in the audience as she said: "Modernising justice is not just a slogan."

Her aim, Jamieson went on to say, was to reform the High Court and the sheriff courts, "bring forward new ideas on sentencing", invent a "new system for offender management", and introduce "an exciting agenda to reduce reoffending." In addition, she was going to "tackle anti-social behaviour" by spending £1 million on "community safety partnerships" which would give children more opportunity to participate in "sports and other constructive pursuits over the summer."[137]

As the new shadow minister for justice, it was Nicola Sturgeon's job to respond. She supported Jamieson, saying that, without the state organising their leisure, modern Scottish children would lapse into "disorder, antisocial behaviour and petty crime." That was an early statement of a principle which has become widely accepted in SNP circles, namely that families are not so much a social formation as an approach to communal accommodation provision. They have no independent cohesion or internal loyalty. Human love is so deficient in Scotland that it needs to be replaced by state care. That is why we have a "Chief Mammy" to supervise government regulation of amateur parenting.

---

[136] 25 June 2003, cols. 1045-6

[137] Jamieson is now Director of Kilmarnock Football Club.

Jamieson described what her government was going to do with civil justice, family law, bankruptcy law, a Scottish human rights commission, a sentencing commission and many other measures designed to produce "a justice system of which Scotland can be proud." I doubt that Scotland is, in general, prouder of its justice system now than it was before Jamieson began to tinker with it. The interesting point that emerged from this debate was how it avoided reference to the principle of the rule of law, which ought to have been the basis for all legislation from a minister of justice.

Sturgeon began her reply to Jamieson's proposals generally by "welcoming" the White Paper (a consultative document prepared by government on legislative proposals), which had been published some days before, outlining plans to reform the court system. I will not go into those proposals in detail as they have been covered elsewhere.[138] She completely avoided—or perhaps was unaware of—the threats to the rule of law contained in that wide-ranging document. Instead, she adopted her usual "small picture" approach and concentrated on a single aspect of the whole avalanche of proposals. This was that the "110-day rule" should be extended to 140 days. That refers to the period within which a trial has to start after the accused has been remanded in custody, failing which the case must be abandoned. Sturgeon was in favour of Jamieson's proposal. Apparently justice delayed did not mean justice denied.

The change to 140 days was made in 2005, with the result that people accused of serious crimes could spend up to five months in jail awaiting trials in which *they might be acquitted*. They were, in practical effect, guilty until proved innocent, which violates one of the foundational principles of the rule of law. That is what happens in Russia and China, and it was one of the abuses referred to in the Magna Carta. The case of Sergei Magnitsky, who served 358 days in the Butyrka prison in Moscow before he died there, still untried, illustrated what happens when the state has unlimited power over its citizens. None of this seemed to trouble the SNP.

I stress this to illustrate Sturgeon's approach to her new role as justice

---

[138] See *The Justice Factory, op. cit.*, especially pp. 322-332

spokeswoman. She supported an authoritarian measure without seeing the broader picture. She fixed on an issue which was important in itself but which was secondary to the underlying problem of the justice system as a whole. That was—and is—*resources* (i.e. money). Hamish Gobson pointed out that the total salary bill for all the Court of Session/High Court judges was of the order of £5 million per annum, while the parliament was at that time spending over £400 million on a new building in which to hold its own debates. There was no absolute shortage of resources, just an unwillingness to channel them to places where they might help the country generally rather than the emerging establishment in Edinburgh.

The structural resource problem was stated unambiguously by the Tory justice spokeswoman, Annabel Goldie. She was a partner in a substantial Glasgow law firm (having also, like Sturgeon, once worked at McClure Naismith). She knew a lot more about legal practicalities than her SNP counterpart, and probably a lot more law. She was emphatic on the biggest point Sturgeon had ignored:

> I now come to two issues of profound concern, which—the minister will be disappointed to hear this—concern *resourcing*. They are the overall resourcing of the police and the Crown Office and Procurator Fiscal Service.
>
> The availability and swift provision of evidence to the prosecution depends upon the police being able to do their job timeously. The appalling recent disclosure that, due to time bar and delay by police or reporting agency, more than 17,000 cases were marked "no proceedings" [i.e. charges dropped] in 2002-03 is the measure of the problem. Unless we resource the police properly, we can reform the High Court until the cows come home, but there will be no improvement. My party, as the minister is aware, supports a significant increase in resources for the police—an extra £45 million per annum.
>
> The Lord Advocate described the Crown Office and Procurator Fiscal Service as a Cinderella department due to a great lack of resources. If lack of resources is masquerading as a catalyst for changes in procedure, that is not acceptable. That brings me to the nub of my concerns—the proposal to extend the 110-day rule, whereby an accused may spend an extra 30 days in custody before coming to trial. A fundamental precept of Scots criminal law is that an accused person must not be allowed to languish in jail for an unreasonable time and that the prosecution should be given a reasonable time

to prepare the case. That principle has reigned supreme for three centuries. The period was 100 days, and the Criminal Procedure (Scotland) Act 1887 increased it to 110 days. I find it remarkable that, in the days of Sir Walter Scott and the quill pen—before telephone, fax, e-mail and the internet had ever been heard of—prosecution and defence agents could bring cases to trial within 100 days, but in 2003, with communications technology undreamt of 300 years ago, we need 140 days to get a case ready for trial.

The reality is that an under-resourced police force and an under-resourced Crown Office and Procurator Fiscal Service are not being given the tools to do the job quickly. That is no excuse for sweeping away the 100-day rule. It is no justification for denying an accused, who may be innocent, his or her liberty for a further 30 days. *That is not modernisation. It is repression and it is illiberal.*[139] (emphasis added)

Colin "the singer" Fox for the Socialists made a timeless but important point which put Sturgeon's selective focus to shame:

It seems to me that fewer professions in Scotland are held in lower regard than are lawyers and perhaps journalists. Here we are as politicians talking about lawyers in the company of journalists—perhaps that is why nobody is in the public gallery to my right.

Then he added his voice to Annabel Goldie's, saying:

The issue for the Parliament to consider is the shortage of resources that are available in both the High Court and the sheriff courts. Public services need more money—this one as much as any. It is time that we found more money for the legal aid budget as well.

He ended by letting a rare shaft of cultural light into the prosaic atmosphere of the parliament. Though educated as a mathematician, Fox revealed broader knowledge:

We must pay attention to the widespread belief in Scotland that, although everyone is equal under the law, some are more equal than others, and that the rich are powerful, above the law and the ones who are getting off scot free. I finish by offering members a quote from the Greek philosopher

---

[139] 25 June 2003, col. 1056. One of the reforms the parliament made in 1690 after it established its independence from the Crown in 1689 was to provide for bail within 24 hours (on application to a judge) on all charges other than capital ones, which had to be brought to court within *sixty* days.

Anacharsis, no less. He might have been Scottish, for he once remarked:
"The laws appear to be like cobwebs—strong enough to catch the weak,
but insufficient to hold the strong."[140]

Much of the rest of the debate seemed more appropriate for discussion in the common room at the Drumchapel Law Centre. The principles of legal policy seemed to be above the competence ceiling of most members. An exception was Bill Aitken, a Glasgow Conservative who made a point that was to be borne out by the legislation which resulted from Jamieson's proposals:

In the lexicon of Labour Newspeak, the words "modernising" and "modernisation" have a particular resonance. Labour is always seeking to modernise. It does not necessarily seek to improve things—it seeks just to modernise.[141]

Donald Gorrie for the Liberals reinforced that point when he said:
"In this country, we suffer from a disease in which we incessantly introduce new projects instead of continuing to fund existing successful projects."[142]

There was speech after speech in which a member "welcomed" this proposal, or "warmly welcomed" another, while "also welcoming" a third one. It was a display of personal attitudes as much as a debate about public policy on law in one of the world's oldest and, in times past, most respected jurisdictions. All they were really saying was: "Can I be in your gang?" Margo MacDonald, by contrast, actually contributed to the discussion.

"I find myself in agreement with much of what Donald Gorrie and Colin Fox said," she began, going on to raise another important point about Scots law, namely the issue of whether civil litigation should be dealt with at its final stage in Scotland rather than in the House of Lords (later the Supreme Court), as had been done for three centuries. This point was much discussed outside parliament and was entirely appropriate to a debate such as this one.

---

[140] *Ibid.*, cols. 1061-3

[141] *Ibid.*, col. 1067

[142] *Ibid.*, col. 1073

Lord James Douglas Hamilton spoke next and agreed with MacDonald, from the opposite end of the political spectrum. Lord James was a QC and knew his law. He said the issue of civil appeals to London had been questioned in Scottish legal circles since the first case was taken there in 1711, in arguable violation of the Treaty of Union.[143]

That was pre-eminently a "practical nationalist" issue, and one of the few on which Sturgeon would have had friends on all sides of the political debate if she had been interested in political friendship. But she completely ignored this important matter. So did the rest of the chamber. MacDonald and Douglas Hamilton were alone in seeing the importance of the House of Lords issue. The independence firebrand and the stately peer were the only ones able to lift up their eyes to the larger issues of Anglo-Scottish relations. Sturgeon, by contrast, looked more at home with second-order issues which she could pursue with single-minded focus and self-righteous abrasiveness.

The debate highlighted the problem of a parliament which lacked the breadth of experience and depth of learning that a mature legislature needs if it to work for the citizen rather than elected dilettantes. This collective amateurism reflected a point which Jim Sillars, the prominent nationalist and sometime MP for Sturgeon's desired seat, Govan, has made in connection with the institution he campaigned so long to establish. Devolution, he says today, has "provincialized" Scotland.[144]

---

[143] Criminal appeals have always ended in the Court of Appeal in Edinburgh, and still do. Civil appeals are different. The 1711 case Lord James mentioned, *Greenshields* v *Provost and Magistrates of Edinburgh*, concerned an episcopalian minister in Edinburgh who was convicted and imprisoned in Edinburgh for using the Book of Common Prayer—an Anglican rather than a Presbyterian text—in a private service. This amounted to "introducing a form of worship contrary to the purity and uniformity of the Church established by law." He appealed to the House of Lords. They found for him, establishing religious toleration in Scotland for the first time. This case established a legal route beyond the Court of Session. This was arguably contrary to the Treaty of Union but, as Professor Walker says, "the right of the House of Lords to continue to hear appeals from England and to hear appeals from Scotland was simply evaded by the Treaty, since the House of Lords was not another 'court in Westminster Hall", which courts were specifically precluded from hearing Scottish appeals. (*The Scottish Legal System*, David Walker (2001), p. 155)

[144] See *A Difference of Opinion; my Political Journey*, Jim Sillars (2021), p. 168. Sillars is not the only one to have made this point: "[Holyrood] has turned Scottish public discourse inward. The media's coverage of politics has become more parochial." (*Natural and*

Chapter 5

The Talking Shop

Part of the process of provincialisation was the generation of the "talking shop" atmosphere in the chamber. This was well illustrated by a debate on 2 October 2003 on the subject of "Anti-Social Behaviour". It started at 9.30 a.m. and, apart from short intervals for minsters' questions and lunch, it lasted till 5 p.m. That was unusually long for a single debate, yet the day began with this announcement from the Presiding Officer: "The first item of business is a debate on antisocial behaviour, which will be concluded without any question being put."[145]

This meant there was no motion to agree or disagree with, no legislative measure to oppose or support, and no specific policy proposal to commend, criticise or comment on. The entire day amounted to little more than a display of attitude. What was the point of that? Most members appear to have thought that it was part of the parliament's function to give vent to their opinions on matters which are widely debated in the media—parliament as focus group.

The medieval Scottish parliament had a comparable tradition of "result-free" debate. What later were called parliaments were at first, in the thirteenth century, referred to as "colloquia". The modern form of this word implies exactly what the parliament was doing. Then it was less pretentious. They were discussing matters of common interest but without a specific end in view beyond co-ordinating the views and actions of the ruling clique—the king and the leading nobles, barons and burgesses.

Necessary Unions: Britain, Europe and the Scottish Question, D.H. Robinson (2020) p. 88)
[145] 2 October 2003, col. 2269

Hamish Gobson, who has knocked about the world a bit, compares Scotland's unfocussed exchanges of opinion with the more business-like equivalent used by the East Nguni people in Africa—Zulus, Xhosas, etc. Their version is called an "indaba". In tribal society, policy is formed by a general assessment of the "vibe" rather than through the "consultation" which modern governments pretend to conduct if they need bureaucratic cover with the public for their intentions. The African approach is at once more inclusive and more business-like.

The word indaba became fashionable at COP17, the climate change conference held in Durban (in what was originally Zululand) in 2011. Indabas were held to reconcile 195 countries' views on how to tackle the problem, and the procedure was ultimately productive. The main feature in the context of the Scottish parliament was that there was a "presiding officer" who imposed the strict rules of East Nguni political debate. They tended to be more mature than the those of the Dewar Constitution. The most important one in this context was that it was *forbidden to repeat yourself.* You make your point on behalf of your sept of the tribe, state your "red lines" and leave the decision to the paramount chief who tries, like any good chairman, to reconcile all stands of legitimate opinion (i.e. excluding class war, personal detestation, inverse snobbery, inherited class privilege, teenage hatreds, etc.). Only the main "clans" are invited, but everybody may observe the proceedings. A similar process was adopted at COP 21 in Paris in 2015.[146]

The indaba worked as a policy formulation mechanism, and it seemed to Gobson to represent a civilisational advance on the Scottish parliament, in which too many members are gifted with the rhetoric of contempt for those who disagree with them and burdened with an inner need to repeat themselves endlessly. Gobson doubts such egotists would last long in Zululand.

The aim of the indaba is to achieve *consensus* which the chief then enforces. That is what Donald Dewar wanted Scotland to revert to, after three centuries of increasingly plausible democracy. However, things have moved on since the Zulu invasion of south-east Africa at the end

---

[146] See, e.g: "Climate talks turn to South African indaba process to unlock deal", Bate Felix, *Reuters*, 10 December 2015

of the eighteenth century. The essence of democracy is that voters have a *choice*. The electorate votes and the winning group rules in conformity with what we call the rule of law, a central point of which is that those who win allow those who lose to live as fellow citizens and to challenge the result at the next election. That is the basis of both "losers' consent" and minority rights.

This is not so peaceful a process as the indaba/consensus method, but it allows for unusual, oppositional and eccentric people to find a place in the life of the community, and for unpopular suggestions to be made about routes forward. The problem with consensus politics is that it marginalises Tommy Sheridan as much as it does Lord James Douglas Hamilton. The Dewar Constitution gave Scotland a bureaugarch's dream and a democrat's nightmare.

The effect is reinforced by the seating arrangement in the new chamber. The government sits in the middle and the opposition is split in two, to the left and right of it. It is *physically* marginalised. That helps prevent the opposition uniting against the government of the day. "Consensual" politics without indaba etiquette becomes colourless, conventional, uncreative, managerial, centrist, repetitive and ultimately sclerotic—as it did in the Soviet Union under Brezhnev and his successors. An obsession with consensus leaves politics to what Gobson calls "the halt, the lame and the bland."

Though arguably colourless, Scottish politics is *un*arguably expensive. The question rarely asked is this: how much does the parliament cost *as an institution*? I will deal with the cost of the *building* below, after it was finished in 2004. Here I refer to the *running* costs which, according to the accounts published by the Scottish Parliamentary Corporate Body (SPCB), amounted to £109 million in 2020-21. The parliament sits for about 107 days a year, so it costs the country about £1 million per working day.[147]

---

[147] The Annual Report and Accounts of the SPCB are available on the parliament's website. Though the cost figure is exact, the sitting days and hours vary slightly from year to year, so I have taken a rounded average. Also I have quoted the most recent accounts available as of this writing (see: Accounts: pp. 12, 56, 62, 68). The actual figures would have been less in former years, though due to inflation in reverse, they would have been similar in relative terms.

Since the hours in the chamber vary considerably—sometimes afternoons only; other times the whole day—I have taken a rough average that seems fair, which is 5 hours a day. That represents about £200,000 per hour as the global cost to the Scottish taxpayer for "indaba services". This omits committee meetings and other ancillary business, but that all happens only because of the chamber, and would not happen if there were no chamber. So I will use the £200,000/hour as a working, global, rounded figure below.

Democracy does not come cheap, unlike traditional indabas which, as Gobson emphasises, needed no fixed capital beyond trees for shade, and little in the way of running costs beyond a few teenage boys with sticks to keep the hippos out of the pumpkin beds while the elders were debating. With MSPs' less sustainable approach to their own comfort, prestige and importance, the issue for Scotland's taxpayers is whether they get value for their millions.

***

Margaret Curran, as Minister for Communities, started the day's colloquium by saying that anti-social behaviour is "one of the first issues we should debate" because it is "one of the real problems facing real people." Disorder, vandalism and graffiti were the features of "anti-social" behaviour that she highlighted. When challenged, she started talking about

> the mother with a three-year old daughter who has to climb over vomit, blood and urine every day, and has to live with threatening intimidation in the evening if she complains... I have met that woman. What about the family who are under constant bombardment from the family next door because they had the temerity to ask them to stop the noise from an all-night party and who have had their car tyres slashed, their children threatened and their teenagers assaulted?[148]

The picture Curran painted was of a degenerate Scotland which had lost its self-respect, but also of a country which abused liberty, in part

---

[148] 2 October 2003, col. 2270

because it did not have a functioning police force in the heart of the community. But, as Annabel Goldie and others had already argued, that is a question of inadequate resourcing. Curran said "discussions" had been held about police *powers*, but without result. The reason was that it might provoke worse behaviour. "We do not want to undermine good [*sic*] relations between police and communities. We do not want to reinvent the wheel."[149]

That last sentence was Aspiranto for "we intend to do nothing" so, when Curran turned to solutions, more Aspiranto was needed to conceal the absence of action. She said she recognised "three simple, fundamental truths." These were: "First, there are no miracle solutions or overnight cures." Secondly, "an effective solution will require more effective joined-up working by a range of agencies." And thirdly, "we recognise that there will be resource implications." Curran was proposing to spend £30 million for "community wardens" and the like and "an extra £30 million… to strengthen action on the ground", whatever that meant (it was not explained). Another £35 million was set aside for "action that falls within Cathy Jamieson's portfolio," which was not explained either. Shortly after that, she stopped, saying it would take hours to explain the details, but her measures would "provide a sound platform for delivery".[150]

The context for these huge sums was that, as Annabel Goldie had noted in the Jamieson debate, the police resource problem could be fixed for about £45 million—less than half the sum that Curran's ill-defined proposals amounted to. Yet that was not discussed. Curran had announced £95 million of new spending without saying what it would be spent on. A whole day's debate was too short to discuss actual policy, only attitudes. Before 1999, undiscussed administration would have been called, with some justification, an aspect of the "democratic deficit" that Scotland suffered from due to rule from Westminster. But the establishment of the parliament had not so much cured that deficit as concealed it. The resourceful elitists in the bureaugarchy now had an "open and transparent" way of being opaque and secretive.

---

[149] *Ibid.,* col. 2276
[150] *Ibid.,* col. 2277

Most of the rest of Curran's contribution to the day's proceedings was like that: full of empty clichés or statements of the obvious delivered in slippery Aspirantist language to a half-empty chamber at a cost of £200,000 per hour, without any conclusion being arrived at. Her own contribution lasted 20 minutes and therefore cost the country about £65,000.

Sturgeon spoke next, saying: "We all know that anti-social behaviour is a problem." Reading her speech as a whole, the impression comes across of a person not fully engaged with the subject. She seemed to be going through the motions, without passion or commitment.

> If kids [*sic*] are committing offences, drinking, shouting, swearing and being abusive, the police already have the power to move them on. The police should have no hesitation in using that power. If the power is not being used, we should want to know why. If the kids are committing no offence, having the police on their backs might serve only to alienate them from the police and from society as a whole.[151]

Much of the rest of what she said consisted of cod wisdom dressed up as earthy principle. "Not all people who display anti-social behaviour are young."[152] "If we limit our wrath to kids, the many adults who cause misery will also escape responsibility."[153] "If we are to get anywhere, we must understand the problem in all its complexity."[154] "There are no excuses for making other people's lives a misery."[155]

Sturgeon was equally weak on possible remedies. "Effort must be directed at tackling those underlying causes as well as the effects of antisocial behaviour."[156] Measures she singled out for individual mention included:

> community reparation orders, acceptable behaviour contracts, the greater involvement of communities in the development of strategies, banning the sale of spray paint to under-16s and tougher action against landlords.

---

[151] *Ibid.*, col. 2279

[152] *Ibid.*

[153] *Ibid.*, col. 2280

[154] *Ibid.*

[155] *Ibid.*

[156] *Ibid.*, col 2281

Other measures merit more discussion, although that is not to say that we will not support them. I am not opposed to the idea of extending anti-social behaviour orders to under-16s because it could be a useful part of a bigger package of measures.[157]

Perhaps because she was only an armchair parent herself, the "Chief Mammy" appeared to discount any influence on children other than the state. That means the law. Which healthily adventurous adolescent would have any respect for an "acceptable behaviour contract" (whatever that is) drawn up by the *government*?[158] Like Jamieson, Sturgeon appeared to think that the bonds of family were inadequate, and the police were needed as auxiliary parents. But police cost money, so we are back to the budget issue. That was rendered slightly more acute due to the cost of all these speeches. Sturgeon's came to about £50,000, or a penny per citizen. "Was it really worth as much as that?" Gobson asks. "After all, every mickle wasted on pointless debate maks a muckle o' 'vomit, blood and urine'."

In her speech Sturgeon supported the expenditure of the £20 million that was budgeted for "community wardens" or "the 400 extra police officers that that money would fund."[159] That implies a cost for the provision of one police officer for a whole year—a "police officer year", or POY—of £50,000. That seems cheap today, though it was more reasonable in 2003.

Was the debate really worth the cost, especially when it included this exchange in salaried time?

> **Ms Curran:** I will ask the member the same question that I asked her earlier but, for the record, I have to say that her insulting behaviour is no substitute for argument. What specifically does the member think that we are doing to stigmatise young people?
>
> **Nicola Sturgeon:** I bow to the master of insulting behaviour. I have answered her question. The rhetoric of the minister and her colleagues during

---

[157] *Ibid.*

[158] The phrase itself is not English. A "contract" is an agreement between equal parties, entered into freely without force or fraud, which binds both sides to future action. Policing by contract is a contradiction in terms in a free society.

[159] *Ibid.*, col. 2283

the past few weeks is a specific action that has stigmatised young people. I am sorry if she does not understand that, but maybe she can go away and think about it.

Ms Curran: Will the member give way?

Nicola Sturgeon: No. If the minister would just sit down and listen, she might find that the debate is a bit more instructive.

Ms Curran: Answer the question.

Nicola Sturgeon: I have answered the question. The minister's rhetoric stigmatises young people. What part of my answer does she not understand?[160]

Annabel Goldie made an important point about "consensus debates" in general.

This debate is aptly entitled. Can there be many more antisocial, anti-fruitful or anti-functional forms of parliamentary proceedings than occupying MSPs for a whole day with no motion to address, no opportunity to lodge amendments reflecting different views and no vote to decide anything anyway? That is not a snide pop at you, Presiding Officer, because the topic is hugely important. It is a genuine comment on whether time in the chamber is being used for qualitative purposes or simply just *to pass the time*.

On the matter of antisocial behaviour and the current consultation process, the public may want to ask why the Scottish Executive seeks views on 21 proposals to deal with antisocial behaviour when we lack adequate policing and prosecuting resource to enforce existing laws. *The public will certainly want to ask why politicians are wasting time talking instead of using time to do something.*[161] (emphasis added)

Goldie's allegation was that unfocussed colloquia of this sort amounted to little more than recreational politics—"just to pass the time." Gobson would go further and say they were a way of virtue signalling by people who wanted someone to listen to them in decision-free discussions at public expense.[162]

Goldie was right to draw attention to the cost of this wasted

---

[160] *Ibid.*, cols. 2282-3

[161] *Ibid.*, col. 2285

[162] The Presiding Officer said: "I should also make it clear that this is the second of the looser debates that should *encourage more conversation and more dialogue between members* of this Parliament, and we should judge it as such." (col. 2285) (emphasis added)

parliamentary time. The colloquium lasted for 2½ hours in the morning (9.30 to 12.00) and another two hours in the afternoon (3.00 to 5.00). At £200,000 per hour, the whole show cost the Scottish taxpayer about £900,000—or eighteen Police Officer Years (POYs). Indeed, the parliament as an institution costs the country 22 POYs per day to run, or 2,640 POYs per annum. If, as most MSPs seemed to accept, low police numbers cause vandalism, a lavish but futile indaba of this sort must have contributed directly to the anti-social behaviour MSPs were lamenting.

***

An institution substantially devoted to recreational politics was ideal habitat for a breaker of nations since Sturgeon, unlike many MSPs, took her personal mission seriously. The British government had provided a platform—the parliament—and she used it, less to diminish the democratic deficit than to foment constitutional subversion by repeating endlessly her detestation of Tories. The only direct pressure the Nationalists could bring to bear on Westminster was through electoral success, but that had so far eluded them. *Indirect* pressure, however, could be exerted in debates on matters properly reserved for the House of Commons. By wasting their own time, MSPs could demonstrate "attitude" to matters with which they were supposed to have no professional concern. One such issue was the European Union.

Since May, Sturgeon had been SNP spokeswoman for "Europe and External Relations", as well as for justice. In October, she had introduced a Proposed EU Constitution Referendum Bill, which never came to anything. In November, the SNP rekindled the fire when it lodged a motion complaining that Scotland was not adequately represented in Europe by the British government. The occasion for the debate was a proposed reduction in the UK's representation in the European Parliament in order to give votes to the new members expected to join in 2004.[163]

---

[163] They were the Czech Republic, Estonia, Hungary, Latvia, Lithuania, Poland, Slovakia, Slovenia, Cyprus and Malta. Sturgeon's first point was that since Malta, which had a smaller population than Edinburgh, was an independent state and soon to be represented in the EU, there was no reason why Scotland as a whole should not be. She omitted to mention the curious fact that in 1956 Malta sought to *join the United*

The point was made explicitly in the motion proposed by Sturgeon:

> That the Parliament notes the reduction of UK seats in the European Parliament from 87 to 78 to accommodate enlargement of the EU; welcomes the accession of 10 new countries in 2004; believes, however, that Scotland, with no seat on the Council of Europe, no Commissioners and fewer MEPs than comparably-sized independent member states, has little enough influence in the EU, and therefore believes that the Scottish Executive should resist the reduction in Scotland's MEPs from eight to seven.

The essence of Sturgeon's argument was that Scotland is a special case:

> Scotland should not share the burden of that reduction and agree to a reduction in its MEPs from eight to seven. The reason for that is simple: Scotland is not the same as every other electoral region in the United Kingdom—in fact, Scotland is not a region at all—but, in deciding where the axe will fall, the Electoral Commission has treated Scotland as if it were a region that is the same in character as every other electoral region in the United Kingdom, which is manifestly not the case.[164]

It is hard for someone who believes in democracy, referendums etc., in which all votes are equal *in principle* to argue that in some circumstances all votes should *not* be equal. But Sturgeon was unabashed. Scottish exceptionalism has been a core belief of the SNP since competitive national self-righteousness became fashionable throughout Europe in the 1930s (see Appendix). But democracy is another core SNP belief, at least at election times. Exceptionalism and egalitarianism are logically incompatible. That seemed to make no impression on Sturgeon, who repeated her point in different terms:

> I do not oppose the reduction in the number of the UK's seats in the European Parliament. I am asking members to recognise that Scotland has a distinctive position in the UK and that, unlike the other regions that will

---

Kingdom, on a similar basis to Northern Ireland. A referendum was held, and the proposal approved by 75%. However, it was never implemented mainly due to British government reluctance to finance an equivalent level of social expenditure there, but also due to aggressive opposition to the socialist government on the part of the powerful Catholic hierarchy. The Archbishop of Malta, Sir Michael Gonzi, consulted God, one presumes, and declared voting Labour a mortal sin.

[164] 26 November 2003, col. 3658

have their numbers of seats cut, Scotland has a Parliament with legislative powers in the same areas in which the European Parliament has legislative powers. That means that we have more of a case to have our voice heard loudly and clearly where those decisions are taken.[165]

The idea appears to have been that because Scotland had more democracy at home (two parliaments), it deserved more "democracy" (i.e. special treatment) abroad. Provincialized Scotland was superior to provincial England. That was an ingenious answer to a tricky logical problem. As Gobson argued, it is on a par with arguing that people who are born rich should be entitled to special welfare provision in later life *because* they had always been rich.

The next SNP speaker, Richard Lochhead, translated the current grievance into a historical one.

During the past 300 years, many people south of the border complained that Scotland was over-represented in the Westminster Parliament. The whole of Scotland united in opposing that view and said that we are distinctive, that we have to protect our cultural identity, and that Scotland is not simply a region but an ancient nation... I hope that the whole Parliament is united in agreeing that Scotland is not simply one of the UK's regions. It is a nation, which has been recognised in the past and should continue to be recognised in the future. That means retention of 8 MEPs.[166]

It was left to a Liberal, Nora Radcliffe, to raise the obvious practical difficulty, despite the fact that she came from "north of the border":

The impact of seven Scots in a Parliament of over 700 members will not be significantly less than was the impact of eight.[167]

Phil Gallie for the Conservatives amplified this argument while also pointing to one of the common complaints about the Scottish parliament:

As Nora Radcliffe suggested, it is perhaps not all that important if we drop from eight to seven MEPs, recognising the total number of members of the

---

[165] *Ibid.*, col. 3660

[166] *Ibid.*, cols. 3661-2. Lochhead's phrase "people south of the border" was necessary Aspiranto in a party claiming to be anti-British but not anti-English.

[167] *Ibid.*, col. 3663

European Parliament and the fact that the length of time for which they are allowed to speak is less than the length of time that we are allowed here in the Scottish Parliament.[168]

Alex Neil tried to justify the SNP's exceptionalism on grounds that could have been risky:

> What Nicola Sturgeon is asking for is not just about a numbers game but a matter of principle. The principle is that nations within member states should be recognised as such. They should not be regarded as merely another electoral region. Therefore, they should not get just proportional representation in relation to population. As happens at the European level itself, *representation should be a combination of population and constitutional status*. That is why, in addition to the numbers game, it is important that we ensure that we maintain eight representatives, rather than have only seven.[169] (emphasis added)

The idea of "nations within states" was problematic in this context. What about former states like Brandenburg, Bavaria, Sicily, Venice, Castille, Tuscany etc? Europe has dozens of them. Neil appeared to be suggesting that they should enjoy special status within either their "host" countries or the EU. Would he make a similar argument about Zululand, Matabeleland or Biafra, or about Chechnya, Tatarstan or Bashkortostan? *Scottish* exceptionalism is not the only form that such elitism can take. Is it wise to encourage it? After all, it was frustrated exceptionalism that caused Germany to start the Second World War and Mr Putin to order his invasion of Ukraine.

Sturgeon was clever enough not to get lured into this logical bog, unlike some of her less calculating co-Nationalists. Stewart Stevenson offered a different, but equally problematic, definition of Scotland's constitutional superiority to lesser breeds:

> Can the member tell us of any other legislature in an incorporating state that has an entirely different legal system with a different tradition and origins?[170]

So Scots *law* was the key to Scottish superiority over Brandenburg,

---

[168] *Ibid.*, col. 3664. The "other" debate will be considered next.

[169] *Ibid.*, col. 3668

[170] *Ibid.*, col. 3669

Zululand, Bashkortostan, etc? That was another dead end. Was Wales not really a nation as it did not have "an entirely different legal system"? All states are different, just as all nations, and all people, are.

For Labour, Christine May rejected the idea that

> as Scotland has a Parliament with significant legislative powers, it is therefore not the same as other regions. I do not think that that argument stands up. Among the regions with legislative powers… there are regions that have similar and sometimes greater legislative powers [than Scotland].[171]

It took Tavish Scott for the Liberals to make the point that: "This debate is about a reserved matter."[172] He said that it was really about nationalism, meaning that it was only secondarily concerned with Europe. This is where Sturgeon's skill would have been noticeable had there been anyone present with the sensitivity to appreciate it. The whole point of raising reserved matters was to unsettle what is settled in the hope that the results might benefit the Nationalists. The use of debating time for reserved matters is a sand-in-the-machinery tactic. The main beneficiary on this occasion was the SNP. It got free advertising for its position on Europe and its prejudice against "people south of the border" at a cost to the taxpayer of about £150,000.

***

A week later, a second session of what Gobson calls "listen-to-me therapy" was organised on the same theme. Once again, it was Sturgeon who proposed the motion. It was shorter this time, but essentially the same as the last one: "That the Parliament supports the European and External Relations Committee's unanimous call for Scotland to retain eight Members of the European Parliament."[173]

I will not examine the Nationalist argument because it was the same as on the previous occasion. However, one exchange is worth rescuing from the obscurity of parliamentary history:

---

[171] *Ibid.*, col. 3668

[172] *Ibid.*, col. 3672

[173] S2M-694, 4 December 2003

Nicola Sturgeon: In arriving at the recommendation to reduce the number of Scotland's MEPs from eight to seven, the Electoral Commission has treated Scotland as though it were just the same as every other electoral region in the UK. That approach is fundamentally flawed. Scotland is not the same as every other electoral region in the UK. Scotland is not a region at all, electoral or otherwise. Scotland is a nation with a Parliament that has extensive legislative powers in areas such as health, education, justice and fishing.

Irene Oldfather (Cunninghame South) (Lab): Does the member accept that many other regions and nations in Europe, such as the German Länder, have far greater powers than the Scottish Parliament? Is she recommending that we should increase the number of seats for those? Would that not take us back to where we started?

Nicola Sturgeon: Some of those regions have far more power than we do. For example, the Belgian regions have the opportunity to lead debates and discussions in the Council of Ministers. A similar ability would be in the interests of our fishing communities right now—

Irene Oldfather: Answer the question.

Nicola Sturgeon: Rather than shouting at me from a sedentary position, the member should perhaps reflect on what I have said.[174]

The logic of Sturgeon's point about Scotland's being a "nation" because it has been given a parliament is that before July 1999, it was *not* a nation, and little more than a "region". That is as ludicrous as the exceptionalist idea that, after the parliament opened in Edinburgh, Scotland suddenly deserved preferential treatment abroad. That was an elitist argument which had nothing to do with the egalitarian idea around which the SNP's policy of "independence in Europe" was built, namely that in Europe Scots can escape the world of privilege and smart, self-confident Londoners because, once across the Channel, we are all Jock Tamson's *enfants, kinder, bambinos*, etc.

The debate was short, undistinguished, self-referential and dull, enlivened only by Tavish Scott's rising irritation with Sturgeon's clamant approach to debate.

Tavish Scott: I will not take sniping from Ms Sturgeon or anyone else on the sidelines about what we do or do not do.

---

[174] 4 December 2004, cols. 3952-3

Nicola Sturgeon: Will the minister take an intervention?

Tavish Scott: No, I will not.

[*Interruption.*]

The Deputy Presiding Officer: Order.

Tavish Scott: I have two minutes in which to try to deal with the points and SNP members just scream and shout like a bunch of wee bairns.[175]

Once again, all the shouting and "bairning" was to no avail. Sturgeon's motion was predictably defeated, at a cost to the public of another £70,000.

***

Sturgeon's singleness of mind was impressive in its relentlessness and consistency. The downside was that she made little contribution to debates which had no potential for constitutional sniping. This was less the case in the early years, but by 2003, she seems to have managed to organise her time in such a way as to make few contributions on a purely constructive basis. One example of that, which is so important it has to be mentioned, was the debate held on the same day as the first European parliamentary seat-numbers "colloquium".

The subject was the "Scottish Parliament Founding Principles", as considered in a report by the Procedures Committee of the parliament. Sturgeon did not contribute in any way. Was this because she was not interested in the parliament beyond its potential as a nationalist platform, or was the explanation simpler: this was a Labour debate and the SNP were no longer on "talkers" with their main electoral competitor?

Karen Gillon, the Labour member for Clydesdale, opened the debate with a speech in which she made a point that ought to have interested Sturgeon:

> The Parliament has achieved a great deal in its four years, yet the public has become disillusioned with us and with what we do.[176]

Hamish Gobson attempted to answer this point in a blog post in

---

[175] *Ibid.,* col. 3958-9

[176] 26 November 2003, col. 3598

which he argued that few MSPs have any idea of what the real purpose
of a parliament in a representative democracy is. Most think that the idea
of "representing the people" means that 129 MSPs gather in Edinburgh
and tell the *Official Report*—few others are listening—what they think
about the issues of the day. That is, he says, *not* what most Scots thought
they were voting for in the 1997 referendum. How many envisaged em-
ploying 129 people to "emote" for five hours a day, three days a week,
on a listen-to-me basis at the taxpayers' expense? Many wanted some
work to be done dismantling central government's more grossly insensi-
tive intrusions into Scottish daily life. That is, after all, a core function of
most devolved legislatures.[177]

The motion that day was that the parliament "endorse the four principles of access and participation, equal opportunities, accountability and
power-sharing as the guiding principles for the Parliament."[178] These are
all good ideas, and few Scots would oppose them. But, as *founding principles,* they are of secondary importance. Really, the purpose of any parliament should be simple: translate the general will of the whole people
into a ruling government and, once that is appointed, keep a close eye
on its operations until the election of the next parliament. That has been
the generally accepted view at least since, to take one important yardstick
connected with Edinburgh, David Hume published the seventeenth century volumes of his *History of England* a few years after Culloden. There
is nothing new in it.

Hume's focus on public opinion in the broadest sense, and therefore
on reciprocity, was what Dewar sacrificed when he decided to allow
nearly half the seats in his new parliament to be allocated by party managers to candidates who had either been rejected by the voters as individuals or who had not even stood for democratic election (e.g. the
Greens). The power of patronage over individual careers emasculates
the interrogating power of any parliament. Ask the wrong question and
you'll be busted down to the unelectable last place on the party's "list",

---

[177] See for example the Prologue, "A Bedroom in Bremanger", to my *Isles of the North: a
Voyage to the Realms of the Norse* (2004) concerning the ludicrously damaging effects of
the London-based planning system on housing development on the isle of Barra, and
the comparison with Norwegian practice. (pp. 1-4)

[178] Motion S2M-603, *op. cit.*

and off the gravy train. Margo MacDonald's fate illustrated this well.

Allied to this was the problem of rigid whipping which deprives in-duvial MSPs of an individual voice, or at least vote. Given all that, Gob-son suggests that the quorum for debate could be reduced to a single representative for each party. They would carry a national vote-weighted mandate from the whole electorate, instead of a constituency, rather as block voting in Trades Union Congresses used to work. Since reasoned argument seems to change no MSP's view, one delegate from each party could meet in a conference room somewhere, forgo the charade of de-bate and take decisions in minutes based on the numbers they each rep-resent. The cost to the public would be trivial and the parliament build-ing itself could be released for more productive use, perhaps as a luxury hotel or a high-end casino.

"Accountability" is one of the main purposes of any non-delegate parliament, but the other three founding principles reflect second order aims. If the Scottish parliament were to rescue its reputation from the decline Karen Gillon mentioned in her speech, it needed to return to its two basic functions—choosing governments on the basis of broad pub-lic preference, then controlling them in the broad public interst. One important step in that direction would be to stop debating "reserved matters". That, it transpired, was to be one of the subjects which was picked up in the course of this debate.

The second speaker was Ken Macintosh, a future Presiding Officer. He had been Deputy Convenor of the Procedures Committee, and it was that body's report on founding principles which provided the text for the debate. Macintosh is a man of unarguable public-spiritedness, which is perhaps why he took on the thankless task of trying to restore the tarnished reputation of the parliament he so clearly valued:

> The Scottish Parliament was founded on great expectations. For many peo-ple, it was the vehicle for restoring their faith in democracy. I feel, and I hope that everyone in the chamber shares the feeling, that although some of the gloss might have rubbed off, we still carry those hopes in everything that we do and in the institution that we are helping to shape. The Parlia-ment was founded on a set of principles and our inquiry was set up to ex-amine whether we have been true to those principles and whether they were

the right ones.[179]

The context was that, though few people voted against establishing the parliament in 1997, fewer still were happy with its work in 2003. That at least was Gillon's point in opening. Macintosh was asking why the parliament as a body has gone from hero to zero in one session. He raised a number of points in his description of the Committee's findings. These included the organisation of First Minister's questions, the "themed approach" to question time generally, the length of members' speeches, the activity of the Public Petitions Committee and the futility of longer debates without a vote at the end. Macintosh said of this and similar procedural experiments,

> It is fair to say that [they] have not, so far, been an unqualified success, and I will not pretend that I agree with the thinking behind them at all.[180]

By far the most often repeated complaint in this debate concerned the use of scarce parliamentary time. Partly this was due to having time-limited speeches and partly to the habit of allocating time to fringe issues as if they were as important as the central tasks of government. Both were the result of what Gobson calls the "Dr Spock approach" of giving as many people as possible time for "listen-to-me therapy". The Spock principle applied to this context is that just as children are more important than the family unit, so MSPs are more important than the parliament (and parliament is more important than Scotland; and Scotland is more important than the UK). The institution must therefore be bent—out of shape if necessary—to accommodate the attitudes of people who have volunteered to accept its salaries, expenses, etc.[181]

---

[179] *Ibid.*, col. 3599. Macintosh is also unusual amongst MSPs, many of whom are childless, in that he has no fewer than six children. Gobson suggests he should be called "Chief Pappy". His father, a Gaelic-speaker from Skye, was Rector of the Royal High School in Edinburgh.

[180] *Ibid.*, col. 3603

[181] Strictly speaking, Gobson goes beyond what Benjamin Spock actually prescribed. But it is the way his ideas have been applied by many of the 50 million people who bought his book, *Baby and Child Care* (1946). Spock also promoted vegetarianism, which he had been forced to adopt as a sickly child. Many people consider that equally faddish, but Spock was an athlete. He won a Gold Medal at the Paris Olympics in 1924 as a member of the US men's rowing eight (a Yale crew).

Apart from Ken Macintosh, many others raised the "time" point, including Alex Neil, John Home Robertson, Robin Harper, Mike Watson and James Douglas Hamilton.[182] This was more than any other single issue. Their criticism was that time-limited speeches (as they have in the European Parliament and the Russian Duma) make it impossible to develop an important and complex point fully. This is an important manifestation of bureaugarchy, which must trivialise democratic expression if it is to protect elite control.

The opposite of time-limited control is portrayed in the classic film *Mr Smith Goes to Washington* (1939). The climax occurs when a passionately committed outsider/newcomer in the US Senate talks until he drops, literally, in order to prevent corruption succeeding. Filibustering is an obvious abuse of etiquette in debate, but the fact that it was even possible in theory is evidence of an underlying attitude to freedom which does not exist in official Moscow, Brussels or Edinburgh etc., but which still does to some extent in Westminster and in Washington.

Related to this was the problem of time wasted on second-order issues. That was demeaning to the dignity of an institution which believed it was there to *govern*. But, once again, the spirit of Dr Spock was flitting through the rafters. It was more important to allow members to let off steam than it was to give full consideration to important matters of national priority. Parliament was there for the parliamentarians more than for the voters. Government by a body thinking more about itself than the country is precisely what the Scottish Parliament Founding Principles were designed to prevent.

Ken Macintosh illustrated the silliness of the time limits when he said, "There has been a dramatic improvement with the move from four to five or six minutes per speech." The problem was illustrated shortly afterwards:

> **Mr Macintosh:** In the early days, the Public Petitions Committee had trouble discriminating between petitions on which the Parliament could act and petitions that, to be frank, were a waste of time. If we are to be truly participative, we should embrace the ability of individual citizens to petition the Parliament. Presiding Officer, do I have time to continue?

---

[182] Respectively: cols. 3603, 3619, 3624, 3629, 3631 and 3640

The Deputy Presiding Officer: I would certainly appreciate it if you would bring your remarks to a close fairly quickly.

Mr Macintosh: All right—I will miss out a part of my speech.[183]

***

One other important general issue was mentioned in this debate. It was not explored in depth, but it was an early airing of a theme that will recur below, namely the relationship of the executive to the legislature.

Stewart Stevenson, the SNP member for Banff and Buchan, echoed Karen Gillon when he said, "praise for this Parliament from outside the Parliament is a pretty rare commodity."[184] Being one of the more public-spirited Nationalists, Stevenson tried to explain this. He described the three meetings which the Procedures Committee, of which he was also a member, had held in public, in Hawick, Paisley and Ullapool, in order to gauge public reaction to the performance of the new institution. After noting that the Paisley meeting highlighted the view that parliamentary answers provided for ministers by the executive "were often obfuscating", he said:

> A more difficult point was raised in Ullapool, where it was observed that, on issues such as genetically modified crops and fish farming, *the Executive has appeared to ignore the Parliament's view.*[185] (emphasis added)

Power struggles between the legislature and the executive are a constant feature of democratic government everywhere, so it should have been at the core of this debate. But it was dealt with only in passing, even though it represented an early warning of the possibility that it is not the parliament which is in charge of the executive in Scotland, as it should be in a democracy, but the other way round, as is the case in Russia or the EU.

Support for the creation of a Scottish parliament came originally from people who believed it would rectify the "democratic deficit" in an

---

183 *Ibid.*, col. 3603-4

184 *Ibid.*, col. 3605

185 *Ibid.*, col. 3606

over-centralised state. Dewar's idea was not only that democracy could be operated on the basis of consensus but also that the bureaugarchs would respect that. Neither has turned out to be the case.

Brian Adam, also SNP, followed Stevenson by giving an important and sinister example of the way the bureaugarchy manipulates the parliament. Members would get a Bill through consultation and the early stages of legislation, but civil servants would change it *after* it had undergone line-by-line scrutiny by parliament.

> My particular disappointment was the fact that, in a number of cases, the Executive felt it necessary to lodge major amendments at stage 3, some of which introduced new material that had not passed through the pre-legislative consultation stage in any way. We will have to address that weakness in the system and the Executive will have to give serious thought to the practice.[186]

Adam was on firm ground here. Stage 3 of a Bill is the last before getting Royal Assent. Section 9 of the Standing Orders lists the rules in full, but a convenient summary is given on the Scottish Parliament website, which explains: "Only amendments that were referred back for consideration at stage 2 are debated now. The Parliament then votes on the bill." This means that amendments introduced at stage 3 cannot normally be debated. Parliament's only option if it disagrees strongly with what the bureaucrats have inserted into the Bill is to reject it in its entirety, and throw the parliamentary baby out with the bureaucratic bathwater. No other course of action was open to them. Naturally, in an aggressively whipped body, that almost never happens. That was Adam's complaint and, if correct, constitutes serious anti-democratic malfeasance on the part of the Scottish civil service. It amounts to tricking members into voting for legislation they had not fully approved. Not one member took up Adam's point.[187]

Fergus Ewing, the SNP member for Inverness East, Nairn and

---

[186] *Ibid.*, col. 3642.

[187] That was roughly how the old Scottish parliament worked, at least until 1690. For most of its life, it was under the control of an appointed sub-committee, called the Lords of the Articles, which proposed and drafted all legislation. The parliament could do no more than accept or reject Crown proposals as they were explicitly forbidden from debating them. This is dealt with more fully in the Appendix.

Lochaber, made a related point about the way in which ministerial answers, provided by the civil service, were sometimes more than merely obfuscating, to the point of being intentionally time-wasting.

> The report's recommendation on ultra-long ministerial answers has been dismissed rather casually by the Executive, which says that there is no need to alter standing orders. Time and again, we have heard the Presiding Officer say that he has no power over the answers that are given. Time and again, members... are cut off by the Presiding Officer because they go on for too long. That is to keep order, but why is it that ministers can ramble on and on, taking up inordinate amounts of time and not actually revealing a great deal?[188]

This combined the "bureaugarchic ascendency" point with the time problem. If the Scottish parliament has to limit speeches to a few minutes, then the obvious way to find more time would be to omit the pointless debates, like those on reserved matters or the whole day devoted to off-topic lamentation and hand-wringing on the subject of "vomit, blood and urine".

It is noticeable that those members who drew attention to ministerial time-wasting and the subversive influence of the civil service on parliamentary voting were overwhelmingly Nationalists impatient with the bureaucratic style of the Labour-Liberal government that ran Scotland from 1999-2007. Phil Gallie was a Conservative exception, perhaps because he understood House of Commons procedures, having been MP for Ayr from 1992 to 1997:

> One issue that I feel strongly about is that the Presiding Officer should be able to some extent to control responses from ministers. Ministers should stick to the point of the question. Members are obliged to do that and Presiding Officers ensure that they do. There should be no exceptions for ministers in those circumstances.[189]

Ken Macintosh said his committee's inquiry had been about parliamentary principles "and whether they were the right ones". He appeared

---

[188] *Ibid.,* col. 3632

[189] *Ibid.,* col. 3635. Ayr is close to Dreghorn, yet Gallie's constituency was one of those in which Sturgeon said "nobody I knew in my entire life" had voted Tory.

to be one of the few to understand the question. Either that or most of the contributors to the debate were not interested in fundamental principles, only in trivia concerning what they appeared to think of as life "at the top table". Most of the contributions other than those I have mentioned were self-referential. They focussed on issues like the TV viewing figures for First Minister's Questions, the recommendation that "reports should be concise and easy to read", or the fact that the standard of debate was so low. That last point provoked this exchange:

> **Alex Neil (SNP):** Since the election [in May], the Parliament's agenda has been dumbed down. When the Parliament was set up, many people said that they were worried that it would be another Strathclyde Regional Council. There are days in which we do not even reach its standard in the substance of chamber debates.
>
> **Des McNulty (Lab):** I can confirm that members, especially on the SNP benches, do not reach the standards of Strathclyde Regional Council.
>
> **Alex Neil:** That was an exceptionally helpful intervention. Des McNulty must have been up all night thinking about it, as usual. I have to say that there were exceptions in Strathclyde Regional Council.[190]

McNulty, a sociology lecturer from Lancashire who had himself served on the Strathclyde Regional Council in the 1990s, had the last laugh because he spoke after Neil. Even so, he raised an important point:

> I enjoyed Alex Neil's speech, even if it did not quite reach the standards of Strathclyde Regional Council. *Debates in the council were generally about matters for which the council was responsible and were therefore meaningful.*[191] (emphasis added)

There was a host of issues which could have been discussed under "Founding Principles"—for example, the consequences of the unicameral structure of the parliament; the fact that nearly half the members are selected by unelected party managers and represent meaningless "super-constituencies" with half a million voters; or the anti-democratic attempt

---

[190] *Ibid.*, col. 3620. Neil was complaining of the six-minute limit to speeches which made it impossible to "put forward an argument and articulate a case". He said he had been reading a biography of Iain Macleod (Chancellor of the Exchequer, 1970), whose maiden speech in the House of Commons had lasted an hour and a half.

[191] *Ibid.*, col. 3635

to make consensus rather than choice amongst competing policies the basis for parliamentary discussion. Instead, most contributors preferred to talk about trivial operational matters, which concerned members more than voters. That must have been one reason for the public's growing indifference. It was a "corporals" debate, rather than an officer-level one. Few seemed interested in the institution as a whole. Fewer still were prepared to take any personal responsibility for its failure to develop. Ken Macintosh was an honourable exception.

Tommy Sheridan was one of the few other contributors who exhibited some officer qualities. He talked at length about a Bill which he had piloted through the previous parliament. It abolished the brutally authoritarian practice of poindings and warrant sales for poor people fallen into debt who had to endure sheriff officers smashing their front doors in, valuing their possessions for later sale, and in some cases taking them out onto the street and auctioning them then and there to the highest bidder. This was one of the less attractive relics of the sacred edifice of Scots Law.

Sheridan's success with his Bill was a rare victory for a single member against the unseen, and therefore unaccountable, influence of the civil service.[192] He hit the bureaugarchic nail firmly on its flat head when he said:

> What happened then was that the *Parliament imposed itself on the Executive instead of the Executive imposing itself on the Parliament.* I worry about whether that will happen again. I hope that there will be independence of thought…
>
> We seem to be saying that it is *wrong to allow heated or strong debate* at committee level… The suggestion seems to be that we should not do that in public *because it will appear not to be consensual.*[193] (emphasis added)

Dewar's socialist idea that consensus can co-exist with its conceptual opposite, independence of thought, was not one that appealed even to the leader of the Scottish *Socialist* Party. Sheridan's point was that the

---

[192] In the previous parliament, when the Abolition of Poindings and Warrant Sales Act (2001) was passed, Sheridan had been the only SSP member.

[193] *Ibid.,* cols. 3617,8

bureaugarchy was manipulating the parliament. His plea for independence of thought raised once again Jim Sillars's argument that the effect of devolution has been to provincialize Scotland.

***

It was to be another five months before Sturgeon made an important contribution in the chamber. The debate she initiated was about a reserved matter, so once again no action was possible. The subject was the European Constitution again, this time as it related to fishing. She proposed this motion:

> That the Parliament calls on Her Majesty's Government to negotiate out of the draft EU Constitution the clause stipulating that the European Union shall have competence over the conservation of marine biological resources under the common fisheries policy, and ensure that the final draft of the Constitution is not detrimental to Scottish interests.[194]

Sturgeon was far from being an unalloyed enthusiast for EU government during her early years in parliament. Pre-Brexit, the formula was to state a general pro-EU stance and then to criticise the institution in detail, in this case the Common Fisheries Policy (CFP). After the semi-polite preliminaries, including a jealous reference to other small EU nations now "at the top table", she got down to the SNP position:

> When the Scottish National Party says that it cannot and will not support a constitution that sells out our fishing industry, that does not make us anti-Europe; it means that we will not sign up to something that is fundamentally anti-Scotland. The clause in the constitution that stipulates that the EU shall have exclusive competence over the conservation of marine biological resources under the common fisheries policy is anti-Scotland. Even Jack McConnell thought so before he was called to heel by his masters in London.[195]

Leaving aside her cheap jibe at McConnell, it is noticeable that Sturgeon confused being "anti-Europe" with being "anti-EU". That would

---

[194] 29 April 2004, S2M-1218
[195] 29 April 2004, col. 7848

be a trivial point but for the fact, which Hamish Gobson laughed about in *Todday Today*, that it is exactly the sort of confusion which irritates Scottish Nationalists when "England" is substituted for "Britain". Sturgeon was making a comparable mistake about those who "begin at Calais".

More substantially, the idea that control of fishing should be referred to as "conservation of marine biological resources" is pure Aspiranto. If you can conceal resource extraction behind euphemisms about "saving the planet", then you are half-way to fooling the public about the intent of the measure. Sturgeon, however, was not deceived:

> Jack McConnell should be ashamed of himself. How can any self-respecting First Minister of Scotland defend the status quo on fishing when the status quo, in the form of the common fisheries policy, has brought the fishing industry in Scotland to its knees? ... The EU has total control over fishing, as it has had for the past 30 years, but it does so only under secondary law. If such control were to be put into the constitution, it would be entrenched in primary legislation, which would make it impossible to change. It would set the position in stone, which would amount to our handing control over fishing to Brussels in perpetuity. That would be the death knell for the industry in Scotland. That is why it would be anti-Scotland to do so.[196]

Sturgeon was dismissive not only of Jack McConnell but also of George Lyon (again), and Irene Oldfather (again). To Lyon she suggested that he should "read carefully" the terms of her motion, as "A bit of principle from the Liberal Democrats would go a long way."[197] To Oldfather she refused two requests to intervene, but took the third, saying: "I will take one more intervention, after which the member can sit down for a while."[198]

That was not helpful as Oldfather had an important point to make. Alex Salmond had said an EU pre-legislative proposal (a "green paper") on fisheries policy, tabled three years earlier, was well received in Scotland. Now Sturgeon was claiming the opposite. Oldfather wanted to know what had changed between then and now? Sturgeon was not about

---

[196] *Ibid.*

[197] *Ibid.*, col. 7409

[198] *Ibid.*

to tell her:

> It would not have been hard for any green paper to be better than anything
> that had gone before. The few steps closer to destruction that our fishing
> industry has taken because of the common fisheries policy are what has
> changed things over the past few months. Perhaps Irène Oldfather should
> go and talk to a few fishermen before she comes to the chamber to pontif-
> icate.[199]

Sturgeon added to the effect by talking sarcastically about the First
Minister:

> A few months back, Jack McConnell, in what must have been one of his
> less waffly and more insightful contributions to the debate, made the star-
> tling revelation to the Parliament that fish can swim across borders.[200]

She then dismissed a Tory intervention by saying:

> Being part of Europe is about compromising, but it is also about standing
> up for the national interest. If we had a blank sheet of paper, I am sure that
> we would change some things about the draft constitution. Our red line is
> fishing; perhaps it is about time that the Tories decided what theirs is and
> stood up for fishing.[201]

Then it was back to abuse, this time for the Minister for Finance and
Public Services, Andy Kerr. He had said that the real question was about
EU decision-making. Sturgeon repeated her perfectly reasonable point
about Scottish fisheries, but in terms which precluded the possibility of
co-operating with the government in the interests of fishermen:

> The question that the minister must answer is why Scotland should be the
> only country in the whole of the European Union that does not stand up
> and fight to protect its national interest. Why does he not address that ques-
> tion, instead of waffling in a manner that would make his First Minister
> proud?[202]

Kerr retaliated by pointing to the SNP's long history of

---

[199] *Ibid.*, col. 7850

[200] *Ibid.*

[201] *Ibid.*, col. 7852

[202] *Ibid.*, col. 7853

Euroscepticism, stretching back to the 1970s and its campaign against the EEC in the 1975 referendum:

> The motion has a lot to do with the upcoming election and divisions in the SNP. The Euroscepticism that Nicola Sturgeon's party displayed in relation to independence in Europe is simply outrageous. That was a long time ago, but the anti-Europe position of the SNP is now becoming clear. The SNP has to decide whether it is for or against Europe, whether it will stand up for all Scotland or part of Scotland and whether it is prepared to stay in bed with the Tories and the Trots to campaign against the treaty.[203]

Not for the first time, it fell to Tommy Sheridan to bring a higher sense of responsibility to the pointless bickering. Not only could he tell the difference between a geographical entity and a political one, but he also seemed to have a broader view than most of his fellow MSPs:

> Being an internationalist and being pro-European has nothing to do with the European Union. The European Union is an undemocratic, corrupt and insatiable monster that seeks greater powers from the EU constitution to allow it to devour more jobs, more communities and the democratic rights of nations. It is a monster that many on the left had hoped could be tamed and dispatched for progressive purposes, but as most people now recognise, it is out of control and is a real and present danger to social welfare and public services...
>
> The EU is not just an undemocratic, corrupt and insatiable monster, it is a big-business monster whose desire is to plunder and privatise in search of maximum profits for the few, regardless of the consequences in lost jobs and broken communities for the many. The EU constitution would confer the necessary powers on the EU monster that would allow it to destroy democracy within nations and promote a big-business, privatisation agenda throughout Europe.
>
> I call on those who believe in democracy, socialism and independence to oppose this dangerous constitution and to begin the process of renegotiating our membership of and relationship with the European Union, based on greater readiness to defy the diktats of EU bureaucrats and put Scottish workers and communities first...
>
> The debate is riven with contradictions. The rump of socialists who are left in the Labour Party oppose the constitution. The Tories are divided

---

[203] *Ibid.*, col. 7856

between the far-sighted big-business wing that supports such expansion, and the neanderthal bulldog wing that opposes it for its own flag-waving reasons. The biggest contradiction is within the ranks of the Scottish National Party.[204]

After that, the rest of the debate seemed trivial and futile, especially as it could not lead to any action. The only interest from the point of view of Sturgeon's future was the language used by Kenny MacAskill in summing-up for the SNP. He first criticised Sheridan's language, saying:

Mr Sheridan described the European Union as undemocratic, corrupt and an insatiable monster. Such language is better, and more frequently, used in connection with the Soviet Union rather than the European Union.[205]

But his own language failed him when he wanted to describe the fact that fishermen in the north-east of Scotland were dissatisfied with Europe more generally. He said of the Green Party member, Robin Harper:

He should remember that the perception in the northeast is not that Europe has created a free-for-all, but that Europe has given F-all. That is the major cause of controversy on the streets.[206]

This called for comment by the Deputy Presiding Officer when closing the debate a minute later.

I wish to make what is effectively a point of order of my own. In the course of his remarks, Mr MacAskill used an expression that is a commonly known euphemism for an obscenity. That language is not acceptable and it will not be tolerated in the chamber from now on.[207]

***

Two months later, on Thursday 10 June 2004, elections were held for the European Parliament. Across the continent, they revealed the intelligence of the average voter. The majority had better things to do than

---

[204] *Ibid.,* col. 7864
[205] *Ibid.,* col. 7900
[206] *Ibid.,* col. 7901
[207] *Ibid.,* col. 7902

vote for a powerless parliament that was essentially a cover for bureau-cratic control of the member states through the unelected Commission. Turnout sank to 45%. In Britain an increasingly Eurosceptic electorate reduced turnout to 38%. Scotland proved even less interested than the rest of the UK, contrary to what has been said by the SNP since the Brexit referendum. Turnout was just 31%. Less than 1 Scot in 3 could be bothered to vote for a project which is now one of the mainstays of SNP policy. In the next European election, in 2009, turnout in Scotland sank to 28%.

The SNP manifesto for the 2004 European election included this re-statement of much of what Sturgeon argued in the previous debate:

> The draft [European] constitution gives a framework for the kind of EU the SNP wishes to see and to participate in - a more effective and democratic confederation of states choosing to share sovereignty over defined policy areas for mutual benefit. But for Scotland it has a major flaw. It entrenches an exclusive power over fishing in the hands of the EU institutions. We have seen far too many of our great, national industries destroyed. We cannot sit back and watch another one - fishing - go the same way. If Scotland were independent, we would use the power of veto to remove the proposal to make fishing an exclusive EU competence.[208]

Scotland, then, is in favour of "shared sovereignty" so long as it does not include commodities which in Scotland are plentiful, e.g. fish. Scotland was happy to share resources in sectors in which it has a deficit but *not* to share those of which it has a surplus. Scotia does not, so to speak, "stand its round."

There was recent precedent for such selfishness. The SNP had ar-gued in the 1970s that "It's Scotland's oil." Britain, they said, was obliged to support Scottish unemployment and other problems when Scotland was poorer than England, but if Scotland found it had a valuable re-source in its own territory, the sharing should stop. Social democratic levelling up within the United Kingdom applied only when Scotland needed helping, not when it was in a position to help others less well off than itself. "Scotland's oil" should be used for Scotland's benefit *only*.

---

[208] Ascription: "Published by Peter Murrell on behalf of the Scottish National Party, both at 107 McDonald Road, Edinburgh EH7 4NW" (undated)

More than that, Scotland should be granted independence so that it could put a complete stop to ideas of resource-sharing. This is a theme which will recur below, especially in connection with the 2014 independence referendum, the Brexit referendum, the Covid pandemic and the war in Ukraine.

Hamish Gobson guyed this selfishness in a blog post in which he pointed to the "manly chauvinism of applying to Jimmy Foreigner the paternalistic principle behind old Scots matrimonial law: 'What's yours is mine, and what's mine's ma oan.'"

The electorate did not buy the SNP's mean-spirited argument. The Party's share of the vote in the 2004 Euro-election sank from 27% to 20%, leaving it even further behind "the auld enemy", Labour, which sank from 29% to 26%. The main winners were the Liberals and, perhaps surprisingly in Scotland, UKIP (the United Kingdom Independence Party), which won a significant share for the first time (7%). It even beat the Scottish Socialists, who got 5%. Swinney had predicted before the vote that the SNP would overtake Labour into first place. In fact, without UKIP, which took votes mainly from the Tories, the Nationalists might have sunk from second to third place. It was a humiliating rejection by the people they imagined shared their new vision of "Scotland in Europe—with red lines (underwater)."

But Scotland's loss turned out to be Sturgeon's gain. After putting a brave face on defeat, John Swinney fell on his sword and announced his resignation as Party leader. He made a statement:

> "It has become clear to me over the last few days that the constant and relentless speculation over my position is obscuring - and crucially in my judgment, will continue to obscure - the political objectives of the MSPs.
>
> "I have come to the view that the SNP cannot make the electoral progress I believe is possible, if our vital political message is communicated through an endless debate of [*sic*] my leadership.
>
> "As someone who has devoted all of my adult life to the cause of Scottish independence that is something I cannot allow to happen."[209]

It is hard not to feel sorry for a man who spent his teenage years sitting in cranky Party meetings in the Mitchell Library, where Any Other

---

[209] *Guardian*, 22 June 2004

Business lasted six hours, and who has devoted all his life since to "the cause of the people", only to find that the people were not particularly interested. Worse still, his closest colleagues fought like hungry hyenas to get his job. Michael Russell, one of the hyenas, came up with the only witty comment from this debacle. He had warned that the result of Swinney's lack of electoral success would be that "the men in grey kilts" would be coming for him. This is almost the only memorable witticism ever recorded by an SNP politician about their Party.

The grey kilts had a word with the grey man, and on 22 June 2004, just 12 days after the election, Dr Death admitted defeat and resigned. Gobson points out the irony of his choice of date: the anniversary of both Napoleon's fall in 1815 and the Nazi invasion of the Soviet Union in 1941. Like Swinney, both Napoleon and Hitler worked towards a united Europe and a broken Britain. In Scotland, it was the anniversary of the battle of Bothwell Bridge at which, in 1679, the Presbyterian Covenanters were smashed by the Scottish parliament's army in the name of religious intolerance, and all survivors hunted down as traitors, and murdered during what was known as "the killing time".

Though his leadership had been a failure, Swinney had one major success at a personal level. He is one of the few SNP MSPs about whom there has never been a hint of the squalid personal scandals which have tarnished so many other reputations. Outside politics, he gives the impression of being an honest and decent man, which is probably why there was "constant and relentless" pressure for him to get out of the hot seat and make way for someone more suited to the carnivorous world of minority politics in a constitutional backwater.

***

Immediately after Swinney's resignation, Salmond said, "If nominated [to the leadership] I'll decline. If drafted I'll defer. And if elected I'll resign." He was MP for Banff and Buchan, and without a seat in the Holyrood parliament. Such an unambiguous disclaimer left four contenders for the job, each of whom recurs in the story below and therefore might be briefly sketched here, in descending order of likelihood of winning. The favourite was Roseanna Cunningham.

Cunningham had found national fame in in 1995 when she won Perth and Kinross in a by-election after the colourful and talented but bibulous Conservative MP, Sir Nicholas Fairbairn, had died of drink.[210] The seat had once been held by Sir Alec Douglas Home and was far from being the natural habitat of the angry nationalist. It was a major upset. But Cunningham lost her seat in the Labour landslide of 1997 and entered the Scottish parliament in 1999 instead. She was a left-wing thinker but without the sleep-inducing manner of the outgoing leader. She was strongly anti-royalist and anti-nuclear, but she was bright and cheerful, and already deputy leader of the party. Some questioned her level of industry, and it was true that she was not so hard-working and po-faced as the "little engine that could". But, unlike Sturgeon, who had stumbled at the solicitor stage of a legal career, Cunningham had gone on to become an advocate in Parliament House, though she soon gave up law in favour of politics.

Cunningham had the distinction of having been involved in an affair with a married party member, which involved the Ewing family. Winnie Ewing, the *grande dame* of the nationalist "movement", was the censorious exposer of Cunningham's "misdeed". It is not a pretty story, and I do not propose to go further into it. At any rate, Cunningham was the only one of the contenders with any name recognition outside Scotland. Within it, or at least within the SNP, both her professional and her amorous achievements made Sturgeon look a little provincial, which undoubtedly had an effect in later years, when Cunningham was quietly side-lined by her "friend".

Second favourite in the race was the subject of this study, and in third place was Michael Russell, the "romantic Hebridean" author, film-maker and Gaelic campaigner who seems to have spent much of his political life trying to suppress a sense of humour, latterly with considerable success. He attracted long odds in this race as he was not, at that time, an MSP, having been a victim himself of the men in grey kilts. Russell lives

---

[210] Fairbairn could use plain English about his own Party. "The Honourable Lady herself was once an egg," he once said of Edwina Currie, also a Tory, in the House of Commons during the salmonella panic, "and many on both sides of the House regret its fertilisation."

on the edge of the Highlands in the Cowal peninsula, and seems to want to have one foot in the "top table" world of long meetings, urgent phone calls and insiderish memos, with the other in the altogether more congenial and cultured world of Highland Teuchteria. It is a mystery why someone with his broad interests—he was the only contestant who was not a lawyer—had chosen to waste his life fighting with the other hyenas who make up the "politburo" in the SNP.

Finally, the rank outsider was Kenny "F-all" MacAskill, who stood as "running mate", American-style, to Sturgeon. MacAskill is a forthright lawyer with a straight back. He was the only one of the four to have run his own business, a successful firm of solicitors in Glasgow. He had a reputation for sometimes reckless "fundamentalism"—hence perhaps his "euphemism for an obscenity"—and a love of football. He has the high distinction of being almost the only SNP politician ever to have actually *liberalised* something, in his case by ending the ban on alcohol sales at rugby matches in Scotland. Cheers, Kenny!

The race was open to either of the ladies to win. But as it developed, some began to worry that Cunningham might edge Sturgeon. It has been said that when it became clear to Salmond that Sturgeon, his protégé, might lose, he decided to stand. His categorical denial three weeks earlier turned out to be meaningless. He did a hand-brake turn and started cosying up to Sturgeon as a possible "partner". Since few members of the public read the *Official Report*, she could be presented to the voters as a more middle-of-the-road figure than Cunningham, one who might appeal to the more cautious Scot. Without the backing of "that demographic", the SNP would struggle to win power. There was also the fact that, as early as 2004, Salmond was thought for some reason to have been off-putting to female voters.

Salmond's retrospective telling of the story suggests that it was others who persuaded him to renege on his commitment not to stand again. In his referendum diaries, he had this to say on 18 July 2014:

> Back in 2004, *after I was persuaded to come back to lead the party*, I approached Nicola to run on a joint ticket. She was losing the contest, not through lack of talent but through lack of years… Our partnership has proved successful,

indeed unstoppable, for ten years.[211] (emphasis added)

It was not quite like that. Before announcing his *volte face*, Salmond had dinner with Sturgeon and asked her if she would abandon her own leadership bid and support his by standing as his deputy. She made a coy request for 48 hours to consider the matter. But that must have been for effect. She was being offered the job of her life, since it was unlikely that she and MacAskill would have the appeal of Salmond and herself. As Salmond was sixteen years older than she, the likelihood was that the deputy would succeed the leader one day. Salmond was offering her a leg-up that might clear her path forward for the eventual break-up the United Kingdom. Accordingly, after pondering for just 24 hours, she abandoned her own leadership bid and threw herself into the political arms of the man with the smooth manner and the meaningless disclaimers.

Salmond-Sturgeon's main problem was that by 2004 the Party was dying on its feet. As the main Glasgow newspaper commented: "The truth of the matter is that the SNP is desperate. After years of infighting and electoral decline, it is desperate for repair, and before the [UK] general election [due in 2005]."[212]

Jim Sillars criticised Salmond's decision to stand, saying that under his "continued manipulative dominance… [the SNP] has been turned into a poisonous cabal, operating with one controller."[213]

Cunningham's lack of "binge" (as Field Marshal Montgomery used to call it) meant that she did not learn of all this manoeuvring at the time because she was on holiday with her brother in Ireland—on *holiday* in the middle of an election to become *leader of the Party*! For a committed socialist, it was surprising that she had not learned Trotsky's lesson that to stay out of town when Lenin is dying is not the way to beat Stalin to the job of replacing him. Even Napoleon was clear that during a revolution you must be *in the capital.* Perhaps she really was lazy—which makes her, at a human level, rather more attractive, but proportionately less

[211] *The Dream Shall Never Die: 100 Days that Changed Scotland Forever*, Alex Salmond (2015), p. 106
[212] *The Herald*, 16 July 2004
[213] *Scotsman*, 16 July 2004

suitable to a world in which the hyenas laugh in Aspiranto. Sturgeon was cut from more industrious cloth and took the gap in what was, with hindsight, one of the most important decisions of her life.

When the result was announced, on 3 September, Salmond-Sturgeon won hands down. He received 76% of the vote for leader, while Cunningham got just 15%. Russell cantered home gamely with 9%.[214] The contest for deputy was closer. Sturgeon got 54%, beating Fergus Ewing on 25% and a third starter, Christine "under duress" Grahame, who got 21%.

Most of the comment was predictable and dull. Tommy Sheridan was the exception. He raised the issue of Salmond's U-turn and therefore his trustworthiness, a matter which Sturgeon appeared to ignore.

"Clearly, Alex Salmond agrees with me that there is no talent on the SNP benches in Holyrood," Sheridan said. "This is a man who not only takes his party for granted but has consistently taken the people of Scotland for granted. How can you trust a man who changes his mind this often?"[215]

---

[214] MacAskill had pulled out by then. One journalist said unkindly of Russell that "he came third in a two-horse race." Chris Deerin, *New Statesman*, 8 July 2021

[215] *The Herald*, 16 July 2004

Chapter 6

Holyrood

Salmond's first job after being elected Leader was to find some constituents to represent so he could walk into parliament through the top
tablers' entrance. In 2004, he was still sitting in the House of Commons,
an arrangement which, before he was elected Leader, had led to tear-
jerking references to "the king over the water" and afterwards provoked
jibes about the "absentee laird". That was all to the good for Sturgeon
as she was now the *de facto* leader of the Party in the Scottish parliament.
For a 34-year old with no significant achievements to her credit outside
politics, this was another testament to her dedication and singleness of
mind. At 16 she had joined the SNP; 18 years later she was Deputy
Leader. What next?

Salmond could not simply return to his old seat of Banff and Buchan
as that was now occupied by an SNP colleague, Stewart Stevenson. So
the men in grey kilts parachuted him into Gordon (in north-west Aberdeenshire). The logic of Salmond's choice of Gordon as the constituency
on which to bestow his presumed majority says much about his approach to politics. The sitting MSP was the Liberal, Nora Radcliffe, and
the seat was considered the twentieth most winnable for the SNP in
Scotland. Since the Party needed an additional twenty seats if it were to
take power, Salmond calculated that if he failed to win that seat, his party
would have failed to win the election. His priority was to become *First
Minister*, not a mere MSP representing the electors of Gordon.

"Back-benching" is a much more amusing activity in the dramatic
atmosphere of Westminster than amongst the po-facers in Edinburgh.
If he lost in Gordon he could abandon it to Nora Radcliffe and slip back

into the comfortable routine of the House of Commons, of which he was still a member, with his salary and expenses uncompromised. It was death or glory, except that the "death" part would take him back to the expense-account existence he had been enjoying since 1987.

It was much the same for Sturgeon, who had yet to come first in a public election in a straight fight anywhere. Despite this, she was the leader of the Opposition in the country's parliament at least until 2007 which was the earliest Gordon could be de-Radcliffed. Not only that, Sturgeon had "found love", as the press put it, with the head kilt, Peter Morrell. He had started as manager of Salmond's constituency office in Peterhead, and was now Chief Executive of the Party, another record-breaking ascent. As a political couple, they were "living over the shop."

According to the media, Sturgeon and Murrell had first met as a Party youth training summer camp when Sturgeon was 18. She is said to have been fascinated with the gadgets that Murrell had dangling below his belt, including one called a "Psion organiser". He was referred to as "Mr Gadget Man". But love did not blossom at the gadget stage. It was not until the 2003 election that that happened. Once Murrell was Chief Executive, they had to work together, and people in the Party "began to talk". That autumn, they "came out" as a couple at the Party conference in Inverness. It was a fairy-tale romance, at least from a political point of view. Everything beyond that I will leave to "lace curtain" biographers.

***

Four days after the results of the SNP leadership race were announced, parliament reconvened for the autumn season, beginning the parliamentary year 2004-5. But it was not the usual commencement. Since the parliament had last sat, it had a acquired a new home, in the irregular shape of the Holyrood parliament building at the bottom of the Canongate in Edinburgh. This was controversial because of the final cost: £414 million, which was close to £90 for every man, woman and child in the country. The estimated cost at the start was £40 million, so a 900% increase indicated a level of project mismanagement which was not to be matched until the Ferguson ferry contract blew up in the government's face in the early 2020s.

The idea of spending lavishly on a "signature" building was one taken in London before the Scottish parliament had been officially decided on. The story gives important clues to the problem of government by bureaugarchy rather than by a semi-elected parliament. That at least is Gobson's theory. He adduces Brian Adam's point about civil service trickery with Bill drafting (when amendments were introduced after parliamentary debate had concluded—see above), and argues that not only has devolution provincialized Scotland, as Jim Sillars first noted, but it has also damaged democracy and compromised the rule of law. The story of the relationship between the parliament as an institution and as a building illustrates this. It reveals some startling facts about devolved Scottish "democracy", and the careless waste of citizens' money by the bureaugarchy and its fellow travellers in the parliament itself.

Before MSPs moved into their expensive new "indaba hut" in 2004, there were four debates on the project and its progress, and afterwards another one on the report of the inquiry into the mismanagement of the project, which was carried out by Lord Fraser of Carmyllie QC. For some reason, Sturgeon did not speak in any of them. However, the new Holyrood building was to be such an important part of her political backstory, and its construction so clearly illustrates the way the Dewar Constitution has failed Scotland, that it is worth recalling how the project was viewed by MSPs at the time. The opening debate took place on 17 June 1999, even before the first sod had been turned on the chosen site. Some context is necessary.

In May 1997, the Labour Party won a landslide victory in a general election with a manifesto commitment to Scottish devolution. On 11 September in the same year, a referendum was held in Scotland on the question: "I agree/do not agree there should be a Scottish parliament". The "agrees" won by 74% to 26%. The historian, Professor Tom Devine, said this "was the most significant development in Scottish political history since the Union of 1707."[216] That was probably true. Tony

---

[216] BBC, 8 September 2017. He also wrote that it was "the single most important constitutional change in the relations between the nations of the United Kingdom since the emergence [*sic*] of the Irish Free State in 1922." (*Dewar*, Alexander, *op. cit.*, p. 196)

Blair, by contrast, celebrated the result by paying one of his rare visits to the city where he grew up and saying: "The era of big, centralised government is over." That was not true.[217]

The respectable (but not high) turnout (60%) added force to the result although, curiously, the lowest *turnout* figures were in the places where Nationalists get their strongest support today. Glasgow, Dundee and Aberdeen had the smallest percentage of electors who bothered to cast a vote—that is, if you leave out Orkney and Shetland where Edinburgh-scepticism has run high for centuries. The highest *percentage* "yes" votes were in Glasgow City and it neighbour, East Dunbartonshire. The combination of the lowest turnout with the strongest support for devolution moved Gobson to make the cynical generalisation that, in Scotland, it is the laziest individuals who are the most hostile to "people south of the border".

Since Sturgeon tends to base so many arguments on the results of opinion polls, it is worth pointing out that, of the nine polls leading up to the vote which have been analysed by most academics, *not one* came within a mile of the correct result. Even the one published the day before the vote—for ICM, in *The Scotsman*—put the Yes vote at 63%, when next day the result was 74%. The other polls were also inaccurate, most even more so.[218]

Controversy started early. By January 1998, *eighteen months before the parliament first met*, the Holyrood site had already been selected, even though it was known that this was likely to be the most expensive to build on. Alarm bells were already ringing in certain quarters, not least on Great Todday where "Grafter" Gobson had discovered that the site had been known in medieval times as "the Watergate". It was the gate at the bottom of the High Street where the city's sewage arrived after washing down the High Street, assisted by the rain and gravity, before it oozed into a noisome marsh outside the Royal Palace. In effect, the site had been a medieval midden.

More seriously, David Black, the only person to have written a book

---

[217] BBC, 11 September 2017

[218] The other polls were by MORI, NOP and System Three, published by *The Herald*, STV and *The Sunday Times*.

about the construction of the new parliament, criticised Donald Dewar for having decided on the site before allowing parliament to discuss it. He wrote to Dewar in March that year saying, "[This] building cannot be a symbol of devolution simply because it is, in essence, a *monument to centralised decision making*... I personally don't see this as a matter of money; rather it's about a lack of accountability, and the contradiction of a devolution decision which was not devolved."[219] (emphasis added)

The main alternative site was the old Royal High School, a dignified classical building on Calton Hill, which had become a symbol of the fight for devolution after the failed 1979 referendum. Black wrote to ask why it had been excluded from consideration since it was cheaper, as well as having an elegant building already on it. "Perhaps it fails the 'rebranding of Britain' test as advanced by what I believe is called Labour's 'River Café' set, who would seem to be nostalgic for the old 'white heat of technology' stuff and the '60s 'rebranding' of Glasgow, Newcastle, etc." He ended by saying all this would be a red rag to the Nationalist bull.[220]

Dewar's reply was very short, and ended with this: "I do not accept that the Nationalists will gain the substantial electoral advantage you fear. The matter rests with the electorate and I do not believe that the people of Scotland will endorse a party whose only reason for existence is the break-up of Britain."[221]

A year later, in June 1999, construction began. By then, MSPs were settling into their temporary premises in the Church of Scotland's Assembly Halls on the Mound. But even before the official opening of parliament there by the Queen in July, the first of the four "Holyrood" debates had taken place.

***

Donald Dewar, as First Minister, opened the proceedings on 17 July 1999 by discussing the various site and design options. I will not go into

---

[219] 12 March 1998. From *The Holyrood Inquiry*, Lord Fraser of Carmyllie QC (2004), document MS/10/4

[220] *Ibid.*, 2 April 1998, MS/10/7

[221] *Ibid.*, 18 April 1998, MS/10/9

the details, but simply note that Lord Fraser, in his Report (called *The Holyrood Inquiry*), echoed Black in criticising the haste with which the choice of site was narrowed down to the most expensive option, which is the one in use today. However, to the citizen inquirer the most astonishing aspect of this was that through the summer of 1997 Dewar was investigating possible sites for the parliament.[222] That was *before the devolution referendum had been held*. Was the outcome certain? And if so, what did Dewar know that the voters did not? Or did he intend to go ahead anyway, whatever the electorate decided?

Once Calton Hill had been rejected, the main alternative was a site in Leith near Victoria Quay, where the bulk of the Scottish workaday bureaucracy is employed. But, as Lord Fraser noted, there was resistance in Edinburgh to a site not in the centre, where senior bureaugarchs toil in "ocean liner" style at St Andrew's House (opened in September 1939). As Gobson pointed out, the serious bureaugarch does not, so to speak, live in Leith. For some unexplained reason, Fraser did not discuss the source of this "resistance".

In the debate, several speakers supported a more imaginative alternative, namely Donaldson's School for the Deaf and Dumb, a magnificent, vast and vacant building in West Coates, which is semi-central. Brian Monteith went so far as to identify a European dimension to this possibility:

> The school is a majestic building and features a quadrangle in which the chamber could be located in a way that would bring the old together with the new, similar to what Germany has recently done with the Reichstag— although that was rather more expensive. Donaldson's has a connection with the Reichstag, of course: the Kaiser's zeppelin blew out the windows of the school in 1916. To that extent, there is a European link.[223]

---

[222] See, for example, a memo by Dewar's Private Secretary, Michael Lugton, which discussed a visit to the Old Royal High School and mentioned Leith as a possible alternative. Lugton correctly notes: "that the Parliament itself… would have views on how it wishes to operate." This was dated 2 June 1997 which was less than a month after Dewar came into office as Secretary of State for Scotland, and *three months* before the referendum was held. After that was won, Dewar did not in fact seek parliament's "views" on the choice of site. (Fraser document SE/2/151)

[223] 17 June 1999, col. 557

The Liberal, Donald Gorrie, once a champion athlete, now also a member of the House of Commons, was more typical of opinion in the chamber. He reacted angrily to Dewar's assumption of complete control over the site selection process:

> In all my time in politics, I do not remember anything that has caused me greater offence than the idea that one man should decide the site of a democratic Parliament. That is what has happened and it is absolutely unacceptable. There was no consultation on the Holyrood site. *There was consultation on other sites and then, somehow, the Holyrood site was invented.* The decision was widely condemned at the time. The timetable under which we are operating has no logical basis; it is driven by the former Secretary of State for Scotland who is now the First Minister.[224] (emphasis added)

The fact that consultations were held on "other sites" but not on the one ultimately selected reflected Bill Adam's point about bureaugarchic trickery with legislative amendments.

Annabel Goldie sounded a more restrained warning, but along similar lines:

> Unless the investigation of the other options is made, there is a grave risk that the new Parliament will be identified as a product of self-interested, self-indulgent and profligate MSPs, and *Dewar's folly* will become a reality.[225] (emphasis added)

Dewar's authoritarianism reared its head a second time when it came to selection of the building's design. This was dictated largely by the choice of architect: Enric Miralles. Miralles was a Spaniard who had designed, for example, an extension to the Utrecht Town Hall and the archery pavilions for the Barcelona Olympics. He had no special connection with Scotland yet was entrusted with production of a building that was expected to reflect "Scottish values" (undefined). Miralles had spent much of his life in academia, which perhaps explained a preference for broad concepts over tiresome detail. In the end, he came to resent the condescending way in which he was treated by what he saw as authoritarian Scottish bureaugarchs. According to one report, he told a friend

---

[224] *Ibid.,* col. 526
[225] *Ibid.,* col. 534

shortly before his untimely death in July 2000 that "he was disillusioned that the project had become so politicised. 'He was tired of their *bureaucratic approach*, saying they treated him like an engineer, not a creative person.'"[226] (emphasis added)

Dewar told parliament about the meetings of the committee, which he chaired, that chose the designer. In this connection, he made a startlingly "nerdish" claim: "I make no secret of it, [it] was one of the most exciting and satisfying processes of my 25 years in politics."[227] Shades of "six-hour Swinney".

Dewar said that Miralles's design "treated the site with sympathy" and afforded a "vision of a group of buildings rising from the site to mirror and merge with the sweep of the Canongate and the surrounding hills and buildings. The way in which the project grows out of the landscape is attractive."[228]

That was an unacknowledged reworking of Miralles's bizarre submission to the design competition:

> The land itself will be a material, a physical building material. We would like the qualities that the peat gives to the water and turf to be the basis for the new Parliament… We imagine that our proposal for the New Scottish Parliament as a subtle game of cross views and political implications. But the crucial idea that sustains it is that: the Parliament sits in the land because it belongs to the Scottish Land. This is our goal. Since the beginning we worked with the intuition that individual identification with land carries collective consciousness and sentiments… The building should originate from the sloping base of Arthur's Seat, and arrive in the city almost out of the rock.[229]

I have no idea what most of that paragraph means as I don't speak Aspiranto. Perhaps Dewar did. To the plain English speaker, the document as a whole is full of anti-inclusive, citizen-repellent mumbo-jumbo.

---

[226] *New York Times*, 7 July 2000. David Black concurs from personal knowledge of Miralles.

[227] *Op. cit.*, col. 522

[228] *Ibid.*

[229] The whole document can be read on the parliament website, under "visitor information" (Enric Miralles Moya).

The prize for the most impenetrable sentence must go to this one: "The Parliament is a fragment of a large gathering situation." Runner-up was this: "The Parliament is a form in people's mind [*sic*]. It is a mental place." Miralles's feel for Scottish culture cannot have been very deep for him to have said with a straight face that the parliament was "mental".

In the six pages of sketches, jumbled typography and joiner photographs (David Hockney-style), there is little specific design and no wit, except this: "There should be a clear atmosphere of concentration inside the debating chamber." (p. 4)

Miralles did not stop there: "We propose the image of a university campus for the area, and more precisely, ordering spaces like a monastery with a series of buildings that are connected round a cloister." However, when the building was finished, there was no obvious "cloister" or "campus"—that is, if we disregard Gobson's joke about the whole thing being a "concentration campus".

One professional journal commentated on the "cultural appropriation" that is the basis of the design:

> Miralles, like many other postmodern architects, has a preference for piling on the motifs and ideas: upturned boats, keel shapes, deep window reveals like a castle, crow-steps, prow shapes, diagonal gutters, 'bamboo bundles' and above all the dark granite gun-shape that repeats as an ornamental motif at a huge scale.[230]

Gobson thinks Miralles was trying to make the building look "Scottish" without the slightest idea of what that meant in context. One example will stand for the whole, namely the "upturned boats". They are the most advertised feature of his decorative scheme. Yet in the Hebrides a boat is "upturned" not for entertainment but when it is out of use, either due to stormy weather or because of the death or incapacity of the owner. There is a practical reason for this: open boats unattended soon fill with rain and, if clinker-built, eventually burst. Beyond that, upturned boats on a deserted shore have often been the only shroud for drowned sailors after sinkings at sea, especially in wartime. Even in Shetland, when

---

[230] *Architecture Today*, January 2005

Viking longboats are set on fire for the festival of Up Helly Aa, they are burned *the right way up* because it is a festival of light in the midwinter darkness. Miralles's ham-fisted attempt to be "artistic"—had he seen them on postcards?—worked in committee because the Edinburgh bureaugarchs who controlled the project clearly knew even less about rural Scotland than the Aspirantophone Spaniard.

All these motifs and symbols, however inappropriate or offensive, came at a price. In the debate, Dewar addressed the thorny issue of cost, which had already escalated from the initially suggested £40 million to £109 million, before a single cubic meter of concrete had been poured. But this was to be the limit. "I make it clear," he said, "that the £109 million that we now hold to—to the best of our ability—includes VAT, fees, site acquisition and preparation, information technology and fit-out."[231]

That sounded firm, fixed and manly, but in fact was as slippery as a Fergusons ferry price. I will not dwell on the cost increases as they are now part of history. The general atmosphere of financial incontinence provoked an article from Gobson in *Todday Today* which he headlined: "NERD AT SEA ON UPTURNED BOAT."

More relevant today was the emotion attached to the building by MSPs. The Greens' Robin Harper expressed what, taking it as a whole, seems to have been the dominating concern of the members, and certainly the only one of any general significance other than the escalating cost:

> The result of today's debate will echo down throughout the history of building and architecture in Scotland for a century—a century that will look to the new building as an example of all that should be aimed for in public building… It must be beyond excellent. It must be the best building we can possibly produce.[232]

Harper was the first to express a concern that "Scottish" materials be used. Two or three others made a similar point, focussing also on the importance of using "Kemnay granite" (from Aberdeenshire) rather

---

[231] *Op. cit.*, col. 523
[232] *Ibid.*, col. 535-6

than Portuguese granite which was much cheaper. Also proposed was "Scottish oak", which came with an even higher premium. Contemptuous of such mundane issues as cost, the "creative" architect had specified exotic materials rather than the "recycled" ones Harper said he preferred. Of course, if Dewar had allowed parliament to use the Old High School on Calton Hill, the entire building, minus the cobwebs, could have been "recycled" at very modest cost.

Michael Matheson, for the Nationalists, said,

> My concern is not so much about the materials or cost of the building, but that we ensure that we have a Parliament that is open and *accessible to all* members of our society.[233] (emphasis added)

That is a cruel joke when you go to the palace of democracy today and are met with flint-faced police in flak jackets, carrying machine guns.

Matheson's colleague, Fergus Ewing, introduced the inevitable when he said:

> I believe that any new Parliament building will hasten progress towards full independence for Scotland... I wish to echo your words, Sir David [Steel], about this Parliament being a kitten, which we want, without any genetic modification, to see transformed into a proud Scottish lion, independent and free.[234]

Cathie Craigie, for Labour, talked of a building for the "new millennium". She supported Dewar's idea of avoiding a government and opposition layout for the chamber, preferring the flat-crescent-shaped seating plan that was adopted in order to "encourage consensus" by avoiding having ministers see their critics too easily. But she was unable to support the crescent layout without sneering at those who wanted members facing each other, House of Commons-style.

> The points made by some members about the shape of the chamber show that those members are driven by self-interest. Their concern is not about what the building can do for the people of Scotland, but about what it can do for them, for their inflated egos, for their desire to display their debating

---

[233] *Ibid.,* col. 537
[234] *Ibid.,* col. 543

skills and to be seen by the press.[235]

From the same side of the chamber, Frank McAveety, who went on to lead the Glasgow City Council, took up this theme in a more creative way:

> Unfortunately, the Scottish cringe has emerged once more in this chamber... I say this to Mike Russell, as he believes in words of eloquence... You saw the crescent, Mike. We saw the whole of the moon.[236]

In summing up the debate for the government, Henry McLeish caught the half-nervous, half-boastful tone, laced with high-street materialism, that had been expressed by the chamber as a whole:

> This is about pride. We are right to say that we want this Parliament to be a shop window for the world. Colleagues have said that it is more than a Parliament. It is a place where we can exhibit Scotland. It is a place where people can come. Let us be proud of what we are doing and let us get on with it... this Parliament is about prosperity. We have a great capital city and a great country. The Parliament will be not only a place where parliamentarians or constituents can come and see us, but a shop window for the world.[237]

***

A second debate was held nearly a year later, on 5 April 2000. By then the cost of the shop window had escalated from £109 million to £195 million, producing widespread opposition. But it was rather incoherently expressed, as is natural in a "committee" of 129. Most members preferred either to talk in national generalities or to raise diversionary hobby-horses of their own.

The debate was opened by the Presiding Officer, Sir David Steel, who spoke *ex officio* as chairman of the Scottish Parliamentary Corporate Body (SPCB). That was a recently constituted committee whose responsibility was to administer the institution and manage the buildings and services necessary to make it work. The Labour government made the SPCB

---

[235] *Ibid.*, col. 549
[236] *Ibid.*, col. 556
[237] *Ibid.*, col. 567-8

responsible for finishing a project which others had specified. Costs
were the SPCB's main concern but were not really under its control—
hence the diversions. Sir David's hobby-horse was public art:

> **Sir David Steel:** I receive many letters suggesting that, in the new building,
> we should have memorials both to historic figures and to some of our dis-
> tinguished political contemporaries who are no longer with us.
>> [*Interruption.*]
>
> **The Deputy Presiding Officer:** Order.
> **Sir David Steel:** I would like the corporate body to consider developing an
> idea that we saw in the new Parliament building in The Hague. Rather than
> have plaques or statues, why do we not consider having meeting rooms
> named after such figures. We could—
> **Dennis Canavan (Falkirk West):** The Steel vaults. [*Laughter.*]
> **Sir David Steel:** Hang on. We could invite private sponsorship to commis-
> sion Scottish artists, woodworkers, furniture makers, tapestry and carpet de-
> signers to provide high-quality rooms, not at public expense. Why should
> we not have a John Smith room, an Allan McCartney room, a Jo Grimond
> room, a John Mackintosh room, an Alick Buchanan-Smith room and so
> on?[238]

The febrile atmosphere was not dispelled by subsequent speakers,
who added little of substance, and nothing memorable. Michael Russell
quoted Emperor Augustus in Latin, though he offered an English translation for those not so cultivated as he.[239]

Tommy Sheridan said he thought the parliament ought to have been
housed in Glasgow, perhaps in the Strathclyde Regional Council building, which was vacant and had four times the floor area that was planned
for the Holyrood one. Thinking more from first principles than the other
speakers, Sheridan made the point that Dewar seemed determined to
avoid, namely that the *parliament* should have been allowed to decide
where its building should be.

> After analysing that option for eight weeks, the Parliament might have de-
> cided that Glasgow was not the best option and that Holyrood or Calton
> Hill was the most suitable. The sad fact, however, is that the Parliament was

[238] 5 April 2000, col. 1296
[239] *Ibid.*, col. 1305

not even prepared to give consideration to Glasgow at all. That is anti-democratic and anti-Glasgow.[240]

Sheridan also brought the debate down to earth after all the broken cost promises:

> This Parliament made a grave mistake last year when it went ahead with a project that we were told would cost £109 million, a sum that is £9 million too much. Let us remember what £100 million means to the people of Scotland: it means 4,500 nurses, 4,500 teachers, 4,500 firefighters, or 60 new primary schools.[241]

On his figures, the final cost, which was over £400 million, could have employed 18,000 nurses, teachers or firefighters, or built 240 primary schools. He was making an important point about general taxation in the context of bureaugarchic extravagance. No-one took it up.

Next on was Mike Watson, for Labour, who dragged the debate back down to the *ad hominem* level so many of the members seemed to prefer.

> That was a quite deplorable speech by Tommy Sheridan—I say that as a Glasgow representative.... [It] was pure populist rhetoric, which was nonsense. I am a Glasgow MSP and I would love to see the Parliament in Glasgow—I am sorry, Tommy, but generations ago, Glasgow was not made the capital city of Scotland. We are in the capital city of Scotland and, in any country, the Parliament should be in the capital city. Having the Parliament in Glasgow is romantic nonsense. That is no disrespect to Glasgow; it is merely disrespect to you, Tommy.[242]

At the other end of the "crescent", but equally opposed to the consensus in the middle, was Brian Adam. He was concerned at the way the reputation of the parliament was already, after less than a year of existence, beginning to sink. He was right about the reasons for this:

> One of the things that has, to some extent, turned the people against us in recent times is the fact that we have ended up debating how much we are

---

[240] *Ibid.*, col. 1319

[241] *Ibid.*, col. 1320

[242] *Ibid.*

going to spend on ourselves, how much we will spend on the Parliament.[243]

Christine Grahame, also for the SNP, made an equally valid point about bureaugarchic camouflage:

> I know an elephant when I see one and I know a shambles when I see one. This is not an elephant—the Holyrood project is a shambles. Sir David Steel suggested named rooms—I know crisis management when I see it… Let us stop saving face and save some millions.[244]

***

A year after that, in May 2001, a third debate was held. By then, Dewar had died and the estimated cost had risen to more than £200 million. The overall tone was one of recrimination, presumably because it was only now becoming clear how expensive Dewar's autocratic approach was turning out to be.

The aim of the motion proposed by David McLetchie, the Conservative leader, was to put a lid on the cost explosion. The debate, which was squeezed between one on tourism and another on urban regeneration, was held on the day of publication of David Black's book, called *All the First Minister's Men: the Truth Behind Holyrood*. In it, Black notes: "Holyrood is the issue that, more than any other, blighted Donald Dewar's time as First Minister and brought him 'to the black depths of despair'. It exposed flaws in his character: obstinacy, a prescriptive approach to decision-making, a tendency to engage in intrigue. This is not the Donald Dewar that most Scots would care to remember."[245]

Black shocked the parliament, which was bracing itself for a bill of more than £230 million, by touting expert sources and insiders' views that the cost would rise to more than the then unmentionably extravagant figure of £300 million—in Edinburgh of all places, the city of

---

[243] *Ibid.*, col. 1323

[244] *Ibid.*, col. 1328, 1330

[245] *All the First Minister's Men: the Truth Behind Holyrood*, David Black (2001), p. 70. Black suggests that Dewar's despair arose from his dawning awareness that he had been used as a pawn by Blair *et al* in London to push a Millennium Dome-like scheme on Scotland (and Wales: for the Assembly) in the form of the Holyrood building.

pension plans and private thrift.

McLetchie opened the debate by invoking the ghouls of the bureaugarchy:

> The £40 million economical option was rejected by the Scottish Office in favour of a new Holyrood Palace and the desire to build a monument to the political egos of the architects of devolution. Ever since, the cost of the project has escalated out of control.[246]

Michael Russell referred to Black's book and laid the blame at Dewar's door.

> This is a farce. It is also a tragedy, and it would have been easy to avoid if, at the beginning, the Labour party had listened, instead of insisting on getting its own way because it wanted to dish the Nats. It could have been avoided if Labour and the Liberals had put reason and common sense to play [*sic*] instead of backing ministerial reputations and if this Parliament, not Westminster, had made the first decisions. As David Black convincingly argues, the root of the problem lies in the way in which the project was conceived and presented from Westminster by Westminster ministers... Reluctantly—and for the first time—I accept that Holyrood will have to be built. To misquote Macbeth, we are now so steeped in debt that to return would be as tedious as to go o'er.[247]

Unlike McLetchie, whose speech was intended to assert control of the public purse and cap expenditure at the last limit that had been presented, the Labour Party preferred the destructive caricaturing that it was beginning to copy from some of the less mannerly Nationalists:

> **David McLetchie:** The Executive controls the public purse. The motion simply says that the Executive should tell the corporate body that not a penny more than £195 million should be spent on the project. That is not a constitutional outrage; it is common sense.
>
> **Mr Home Robertson:** I am afraid that Mr McLetchie is wrong. The Parliament funds the Executive, not the other way around. However, why let the small matter of parliamentary supremacy get in the way of a good rant against Scotland's new Parliament building? The Tory party has reverted to

---

[246] 10 May 2001, col. 571

[247] *Ibid.*, col. 575, 6

type. It has always been the principal opponent of democratic devolution in the United Kingdom... Tory members told us that they were reformed characters when they took their seats here, but they were never very convincing. Now, they try to rubbish the Holyrood Parliament building project...

Scots in general—and Edinburgh people in particular—have an unfortunate habit of talking down their own successes. After 300 years we have at last achieved our Scottish Parliament. We commissioned one of the best architects in Europe to develop a magnificent new Parliament building that is generating hundreds of new jobs and adding to Edinburgh's prestige as a capital city and as a tourist attraction. In any other city on the face of the earth that would be a cause for celebration. Here in Edinburgh, David McLetchie, Margo MacDonald and the *Evening News* condemn the whole enterprise as a scandal, a conspiracy and a disgrace. I hate to spoil a good moan, but the Holyrood project is very good news for Edinburgh and for the whole of Scotland.[248]

Home Robertson's claim that jobs, municipal prestige and tourism were relevant to decisions about a *parliament* building sounded like deflection. He went on to dismiss the cost concerns just as airily:

I appreciate that it may be difficult for the Tory party to get anything into perspective nowadays, but I will put it this way: the Holyrood building will be a one-off, once-in-a-century cost of about £40 for every man, woman and child in Scotland. That is the sort of money that I spent at my local garden centre last weekend. It is the sort of price that most of our constituents regularly spend on a night out. For the benefit of David McLetchie, it is equivalent to the cost of two tickets for Scottish premier league games at Tynecastle—which must make Holyrood seem an absolutely excellent investment, not least because it is quite near to Easter Road.[249]

The squabbling about costs, and the petty, disrespectful attempts to trip opponents up by verbal quibbling—"Parliament funds the Executive"—brought the whole institution into disrepute. It amounted to saying that parliament should not question the way public money was spent by its bureaugarchic "betters". But questioning the executive is the

---

[248] *Ibid.*, col. 579

[249] *Ibid.*, col. 581. Tynecastle is the home of Heart of Midlothian, a (once "Protestant") football club, and Easter Road that of its (once "Catholic") rival Hibernian.

second most important task of any legislature, after choosing it to begin with. The ease with which it was possible to shut down financial discussion of the biggest project in the parliament's history served to emphasise one of the most damaging weaknesses in the Dewar Constitution.

Brian Monteith made a related point:

> Where is the new politics of Scotland now? Where is the moral high ground now? I will tell members: it is in opposing the growth of this monument to the vanity of the Scottish political establishment.[250]

It was not only vanity that was the problem with some MSPs, but also simple rudeness. Monteith was followed by a Labour member, Richard Simpson, who had recently had to resign as deputy minister of justice after allegedly calling firefighters "fascist bastards".[251] He did not answer either McLetchie's or Monteith's specific points but started to analyse their motives—he was a psychiatrist by profession. He referred to the Tories' "ludicrous motion", which he tried to belittle by saying "no one will be interested in it south of the border", and calling Black's comparison with the Millennium Dome "ridiculous." He called Historic Scotland, which had to be consulted on Queensberry House (now ministerial office accommodation), "hysteric Scotland", and accused it of "utter stupidities", without giving any detail. He called Monteith's criticism "carping" without saying why and ended by claiming: "We are creating something that Scotland can be proud of."[252]

The effusion of personal bile coarsens debate. It is a problem that, to the citizen observer, ought to have been controlled by the Presiding Officer under more tightly-drawn Standing Orders. It was a problem in the old parliament whose records contain an admonition in 1641 from the President (equivalent to the Presiding Officer) to the members "for eschewing of contest and heat" in debate.[253] The practical result of weakly-drafted Standing Orders and timid "chairmanship" has been to hand the floor to the least courteous MSPs. Nuanced debate became increasingly

---

[250] *Ibid.*, col. 585

[251] *The Herald*, 18 December 2002

[252] 10 May 2001, col., 587

[253] *Parliaments*, Rait, *op. cit.*, p. 400

difficult. But few of the listen-to-me MSPs seemed to appreciate the link between aggressive bluster and bureaugarchic lying. Margo MacDonald was different:

> I used to believe that the Parliament had been misled inadvertently. Having heard John Home Robertson, I believe that it is no longer inadvertent; I believe that *systematic deception is being practised on this Parliament by the people associated with the project team* and I am prepared to back up that claim if anyone asks me to…
>
> As this is probably the last chance that I will have to say this, I urge the Parliament, please, to do away with the lies, to do away with the people who have given misleading information to the chamber and to demand to know what the budget now is.[254] (emphasis added)

Sadly, MacDonald was unable to make a dent in the complacent group-think. It was beginning to dawn on a select few that the parliament might be a well-camouflaged front for the bureaugarchic "establishment".[255] Civil servants had been accustomed to running Scotland without serious supervision since the Scottish Office was founded in 1885. That was what the 1980s cry about the "democratic deficit" referred to. The parliament had been created, at great expense, in order to redress a genuine grievance, but had almost immediately been manoeuvred into a position where it was camouflaging the problem it was designed to solve. That was a major win for the unseen centralisers.

Irene McGugan seemed to be selling the camouflage for the SNP when she resurrected the shop window theme:

> [The building] should be an internationally recognised symbol of our new democracy and a source of pride for all the people of Scotland. I suggest that that could be achieved, to a large extent, by ensuring that the building becomes a showcase for the very best of Scottish materials, Scottish design and Scottish craftsmanship. I welcome the use of Scottish oak and Kemnay granite. I hope that we can go further. We have not even begun to have the debate about an arts strategy for the building, because we are still tied up in

---

[254] *Op. cit.*, cols. 588, 589

[255] See, for example I.G.C. Hutchison's essay "Legislative and Executive Autonomy in Modern Scotland", in *The Challenge to Westminster: Sovereignty, Devolution and Independence*, eds. H.T. Dickinson & Michael Lynch (2000), p. 133

discussion about revised costs, completion dates and the like. I understand that a consultant will be appointed soon to advise on the best use of public spaces in the Parliament and to suggest appropriate pieces of artwork…

The languages of Scotland also need their rightful place in the building. There should be Scots and Gaelic signage, plaques, poems and whatever would enhance our new Parliament.

I suggest that making outstanding examples of Scottish design and talent an integral feature of our new Parliament would have a lasting impact on the people of Scotland and our many visitors. That would give a clear message about our heritage, our identity and our future.[256]

If the building conveys a "clear message about our heritage, our identity and our future", then it is relevant that David Black later wrote a pamphlet saying just how *unScottish* the building actually is. "Scottish architects were studiously avoided," he wrote. "While all that Japanese steel, Welsh cement, African and Chinese granite, American wood, and German glass meant that not only is it not Scottish, but it is perhaps the least 'sustainable' building in the world as far as its materials are concerned."[257]

Jamie Stone, for the Liberals, *wanted* an expensive building. "What a miserable debate," he said, "with everyone carping and whingeing about money":

> One thing needs to be said loud and clear: I am damned if I will compromise on quality. There will be no rubbishy jerry-building coming from my direction, although that is what David McLetchie and his cowboy outfit on the Opposition benches want. "To be sure, we can do it on the cheap"—I can say that in an Irish accent without offending anyone, because I am quarter Irish.
>
> We can be like something out of "Fawlty Towers" and take the Monteith option of having a fresh-air roof, but if we build the Parliament on the cheap, all the walls will fall in at some stage…
>
> Once again, our Conservative friends have misjudged the mood of the country. As has been pointed out, were it not for the Scottish Parliament, David McLetchie would still be doing a bit of conveyancing down the bottom of the Corstorphine Road. He owes everything to the establishment of

---

[256] *Op. cit.*, col. 591

[257] *Holyrood, the Magick Kingdom* (2004), not paginated

this Parliament; without it, he would not exist.[258]

***

The final attempt by the parliamentarians to take some control over the construction of their own building was made a month later. It turned out to be equally futile. The motion, proposed by Des McNulty for Labour, wanted the SPCB to be compelled to be more accountable. This was important because the whole cost was to be "top sliced" from the Scottish block grant from Westminster (i.e. be taken before any other spending was allocated). As David Black pointed out in his book, there was an inherent injustice in Labour deciding on an extravagant project without any parliamentary input, then foisting the inflated cost on the parliament.

A Holyrood Progress Group was formed by a few backbenchers in an attempt to monitor the monitors. But ministers were not interested in this any more than Jamie Stone had been. No representative of the government was prepared to sit on it, so it failed to achieve anything. The main issue was money and the Finance Minister at the time was Jack McConnell. He should have had something to say about the spiralling cost, but he kept as silent as Sturgeon. Silence defeats dialogue and hence the chance for reciprocity.

Michael Russell, who is rarely silent, said the project was "ill-starred from the beginning", adding that "perhaps the most sensible investment would be in a feng-shui consultant."

David McLetchie called the building "a national folly that brings politics into disrepute." He reminded members about the reality of "top-slicing", which means that "every pound that is poured down the Holyrood money pit is a pound less for public services in Scotland."

Fergus Ewing focussed on possible cost savings in a way which gave an insight into the extravagance of the designers:

> As the SNP's rural development spokesman, I met representatives of the Scottish Timber Trade Association, who told me that the wood that is being

---

[258] *Op. cit.*, cols. 595,6,7

used for the MSP block windows is oak, which will be laminated, or glued together. The oak is not grown in Scotland but in America. It will be shipped to Thailand, laminated and brought to Scotland.[259]

Donald Gorrie correctly observed that the parliament was effectively being asked for a blank cheque to finance the construction of a building whose aims were increasingly remote from the simple debating chamber with representatives' offices and necessary services, which is all a mere *democracy* requires. Why should the parliamentary budget be forced to cover a shop window too?

Gorrie continued:

> My quarrel is with *the shadowy coalition of people* who have been promoting this project from the start and who are described in David Black's excellent book. Those people have promoted the project relentlessly, *they have treated the Parliament with complete cynicism, contempt and dishonesty* and they have traded on the decent loyalty of many members to Donald Dewar. The previous two votes were presented as votes of confidence in Donald Dewar and not as votes on the new Parliament. On both occasions, we were given totally fictitious figures.[260] (emphasis added)

By then, as was noted late in the debate, 16,000 cubic metres of concrete had already been poured, so there was no going back. The parliament had been persuaded to vote for something which, had it known the true cost earlier, it would probably not have sanctioned. But the cost was quietly concealed until all the votes in parliament had been counted and the concrete had set. That was Brian Adam's "late amendment trick" in a different form. This is important to note because financial naivety and administrative incompetence are themes which run through Scottish devolutionary history from 1999 to the present, irrespective of the party in power. But not all the disasters have been caused by MSPs. Many can be laid at the door of the bureaugarchy which seems to have been working behind the scenes to turn Holyrood into a Potemkin parliament.

---

[259] 21 June 2001, col. 1883. According to David Black, the Thai oak laminators were paid 50 US cents/hour, which is one reason "Scots oak" was not used. The increased carbon footprint of material transported round the world to save on Scottish labour costs was not discussed.

[260] *Ibid.*, col. 1886-7

***

There was one further act in this "soft-soap opera", and that was the appointment in mid-2003 of Lord Fraser of Carmyllie to conduct a *post mortem*. But even that threw up difficult questions. Why waste more money on an inquiry into a project which would never be repeated? No lessons for the future could be learned as Scotland was unlikely ever to build another parliament. Hamish Gobson saw it as an attempt to "plough over the graves". When the new First Minister, Jack McConnell, announced the inquiry, he lent credence to this theory by saying he did not want "devolution to be symbolised by the Holyrood building site."[261]

That perhaps explains why McConnell did not speak in the long debate which was held after Lord Fraser presented his report. Neither did Nicola Sturgeon, even though by the time it was held, on 22 September 2004, she was Deputy Leader of the SNP. Perhaps she suspected something that Hamish Gobson claimed to see in all the bureaugarchic chicanery—namely that the parliament was not even *designed* to be a forum for real debate. A listen-to-me parliament can take any form it likes, so long as it does not develop a corporate character of its own and start acting independently of the real power in the land. Like trade unions in the USSR, Holyrood was there to be there, rather than to rock any boats, upturned or otherwise. A more serious parliament, Gobson argues, would pose a threat to bureaugarchic control. He suspects this one was intended to perpetuate "Scottish Office control" and the resulting democratic deficit by acting as an expensive form of *faux* political camouflage. This theme will be developed more fully in volumes 2 and 3.

As it operates today, Holyrood is closer to the old Scottish parliament, pre-1690 than to the Westminster ideal of a democratically-elected deliberative chamber that *takes ultimate responsibility*. From the fifteenth to the seventeenth century, the Edinburgh, parliament was little more than a form of consultative camouflage for the Crown—or what is now called the "Executive". Its agenda was set by a carefully selected committee, known as the Lords of the Articles, which occupied a place not dissimilar

---

[261] 19 June 2003, col. 948

to that of the modern, politicised bureaugarchy (see Appendix). If McConnell was "in on the secret" of control of the new legislature, then it is not impossible that he and those like him thought Fraser could bury the Holyrood controversy with a little judicial sleight of keyboard and a lot of emollient presentation. That was more or less what happened.[262]

***

Lord Fraser's Report was debated a year later, in September 2004, on a motion proposed by Robert Brown, a Liberal lawyer sitting for a bureaucratic seat in Glasgow. He suggested that Fraser was broadly right, even on the question of the shape of the chamber. That had been one of Dewar's touchstones as he wanted to avoid the atmospheric layout of the House of Commons in his "new kind of politics".

Initially, the design was to be horseshoe-shaped (like the Irish Dáil) in order to maintain eye contact between members, but that was replaced by the flat crescent we have today, where members face the blank wall behind the Presiding Officer's pulpit. They address the *building* rather than the meeting. Gobson thinks that this is the natural consequence of a grossly materialist conception of public duty. He once suggested that I call this book: *Talking to the Wall*. I said that would be misleading because, unlike the hard core of unteachables in Holyrood, walls at least have ears.

Lord Fraser discussed the layout of the chamber in his *Report*, highlighting the intention to devalue inter-personal debate at the expense of wall-friendly oratory:

> It was suggested in evidence... that this was simply the way in which the design had evolved and was a reflection of the "less adversarial" politics envisaged for the Parliament... [It had] been "approved through presentation and informal discussion with the Secretary of State". Dr Gibbons [a

---

[262] *The Holyrood Inquiry* (see above) is available online from the Scottish government, as is a report for the House of Commons "Building the Scottish parliament, *The Holyrood Project*". Fraser's study is clear and well-presented (270 pages plus innumerable documents in facsimile) but the criticism levelled by David McLetchie and quoted in the House of Commons study is fair: Fraser concentrated too much on the actions of individuals and too little on political failings. I take this to mean that the cogs in the machinery were examined but engineers who designed them were not. The bureaugarchs lived to fight another day.

civil servant] told the Inquiry that "under what he saw as *strong political direction*" the proposals agreed by Donald Dewar... had developed to be more akin to *lecture room seating*. This was in order to avoid the confrontational seating arrangements of the Westminster Parliament. Sra Tagliabue [Enric Miralles's widow] described the design of the Chamber thus: "I think it was also a way to make an elongated chamber, providing a totally different Parliament from the Westminster one. I think it was *very much appreciated*, because it was really *the opposite of the Westminster way of debating*."[263] (emphasis added)

"Lecture room seating" was precisely what Sturgeon needed, as it later transpired, since she seemed more at home informing passive listeners than debating with active equals. Bureaugarchs have a similar distaste for dialogue. Reciprocity is not the natural mood in lecture halls. The "democratic deficit" continues.

The shallowness and materialism of the bureaugarchic apologists was illustrated by the fact that all Robert Brown said on the "crescent" was that the "shape of the chamber did not have a major impact on either cost or programme [presumably: timetable?]".[264] He made no mention of the quality of debate in "lecture rooms", only of money. He ended with a boast followed by a meaningless cliché, while seeming to concede that the Fraser report really was intended to close down further debate:

> There is a growing view, which is shared by many visitors to Holyrood, that the Parliament is a landmark building and, indeed, one of the few iconic buildings of our era in Europe. It is a building that grows out of the land and the people of Scotland and it makes a statement about a new and confident Scotland that is intimate and conscious of its values and communities... *The Fraser report marks the end of an auld sang and allows us to draw a line in the sand.* Let us see ourselves as others see us. Let us go forward.[265] (emphasis added)

That was not everybody's view. Speaking for the Nationalists, Fergus Ewing did not mince his words:

> The people of Scotland have been perplexed, appalled, angry and frustrated by the Holyrood fiasco and the process that has led us to where we are now.

---

[263] Fraser Report, p. 132

[264] 22 September 2004, col. 10387

[265] *Ibid.,* col. 10391

> The fiasco has caused, in the public, a mood of disenchantment, disengage-
> ment, disdain and even, among some, detestation of us as elected represent-
> atives. I do not like saying that, but I believe that it is true.[266]

Ewing went on to make the most important point in the whole debate. It appeared that Dewar had manipulated the parliament by—let's
be upfront about this, as Gobson would say—*lying* to it in the crucial
first debate in June 1999 when there was a real danger that the parliament's opinion might differ from the bureaugarchs' one in circumstances which the bureaugarchs could not control. Dewar had rather
condescendingly mocked the SNP for having a whipped vote—i.e.
members were *ordered* by their party managers how they should vote. He
had made a point of saying that his own party was *not* whipped in that
debate. He must have known the difference between the fact and his
own words, but if so it did not deter him from misleading the chamber
on this vital point.

> I say to the nationalists that I am astonished… to discover that they are
> whipping on today's motion. I make it clear that, *on my side there will be a free
> vote.*[267] (emphasis added)

This was important because it was quite possible that that vote, which
went the government's way only by a tiny margin (64-61), could easily
have had a different outcome. A switch by just two MSPs would have
stopped the entire project in its tracks, pending reassessment *by the parliament*, at a time when the cost estimate was still £109 million, "including
fit-out". Others tried to organise a pause later, but the stumbling block
always was the first debate which had given the formal go-ahead before
the first sod had been turned.

Ewing referred to this when he said:

> We voted for a Holyrood halt, we voted to consider the facts and we voted
> for an appraisal of what those facts were, which would have involved con-
> sidering other site options. In neither case did the Parliament support the
> view that we took, because, *on a whipped vote—as we now learn, contrary to the
> lecture that we received from the late Donald Dewar on 17 June 1999*—every Labour

---

[266] *Ibid.*

[267] 17 June 1999, col. 520

MSP present voted in accordance with the party whip and the opportunities were lost.[268] (emphasis added)

Ewing had taken this information from Lord Fraser's Report. Under the heading "Parliamentary Debate on 17 June 1999", his Lordship had written:

> The minute of this Cabinet meeting, to which the Inquiry had the benefit of access, records that *Members of the Executive Parties would be expected to vote in favour* of the motion and the matter was actioned to Tom McCabe MSP, the Minister for Parliament.[269] (emphasis added)

Dewar's lie about whipping was the key act of anti-democratic malfeasance in this whole story. Did he think that the bureaugarchy might have risked defeat if had not misled the parliament ahead of this vote? If so, Gobson asks, was he in fact working for it rather than for the parliament, as the ordinary voter would naturally assume? Was he more pro-consul than First Minister of Scotland?

If so, there was precedent in the 1670s, for example, when the Duke of Lauderdale kept the Scottish parliament quiet on Charles II's behalf during the "Killing Time" when Scottish Covenanters were massacred and tortured wholesale by the likes of Sir George Mackenzie. Indeed, for most of the century after the Union of the Crowns, a royal "commissioner" managed the Edinburgh parliament on behalf of the Crown, which played the role that the bureaugarchy does today, though with more style and elegance. Perhaps Winnie Ewing had been right in an unintended sense when she implied at the opening—and Sturgeon agreed with her—that this parliament was a re-incarnation of the spirit of the old one. That spirit was uncompromisingly authoritarian.

Both Dewar's interference with the vote and his denial of that interference in the chamber were directly contrary to the ideals of openness and transparency which he had said he was in favour of when devising his new Constitution. No wonder he did not want eye contact between government and opposition in the chamber. It's easier to lie to a wall than to a person.

---

[268] 22 September 2004, col. 10393

[269] *Report., op. cit.,* p. 126, para. 9.35

Later in the debate, Margo MacDonald drew attention to the way the bureaugarchs in charge of the parliament's design and construction withheld information from their "underlings", the politicians. This was the same point in a different form. It took an Independent member, free of party shackles, to see the power relations in their true light—i.e. democrats *versus* bureaucrats.

The way in which Lord Fraser glided over what was surely the key to the problem he had been hired to investigate—how did the scheme end up costing so much?—suggests that he too might have been acting in the interests of the bureaugarchs. The alternative was that he was blind to such malfeasance. But that is unlikely as he had been an advocate since 1969 and a lecturer in constitutional law before he became a QC. He had been a (Tory) Lord Advocate, in which capacity he initiated the Lockerbie prosecution. Fraser was no greenhorn. He knew how to handle dodgy witnesses. He ought to have flagged this vote on a concealed whip as having been critical to the eventual expenditure of over £400 million. Yet he glided over it without comment. Why?

***

Once he got onto the details, Fergus Ewing provided the chamber with some light relief on the question of "risk allowances", which are contingency sums set aside for possible but unquantifiable costs.

> I will tell members my question to Mr McConnell. He is not here to answer it, but perhaps he phoned a friend and Mr Kerr will reveal all later. Mr McConnell knew that risk allowances existed. He was a maths teacher, I believe, and he performed various functions for the Labour Party, although perhaps like me he had no idea what risk allowances were before he came to the Parliament. Did he ask, — "What are risk allowances?" Did he ask, — "How much are risk allowances?" *Each of those questions has four words.*
>
> The cost of the Parliament has increased from an estimated £40 million to £430 million. I put it to the Parliament that Mr McConnell did not ask those questions… The consequence of not asking one of *those questions comprising four words* is that each word has cost the Scottish taxpayer a potential

£100 million.[270] (emphasis added)

It was a good peroration but, as Gobson pointed out, Ewing was a lawyer to trade not a maths teacher. Even so, he surely ought to have been able to count to five—"if only for billing purposes." Had he done so, the cost to the Scottish taxpayer of his second question would have been reduced from £100 million a word to £80 million—a saving which could have covered the cost of the Holyrood "site landscaping" (£18 million).

Ewing ended by talking angrily of "the mischief of a culture of secrecy, a lack of candour, arrogance and a lack of honesty." He said, "Truth was the first casualty of devolution."[271]

Not everyone was so acidic. When Liberals and Conservatives were debating, it could get quite matey:

> **Mr Stone (Lib):** Will the member take an intervention?
> **David McLetchie (Con):** No, thank you. I must move on.
> **Mr Stone:** It will be a nice intervention.
> **David McLetchie:** All right, Jamie. Carry on.
> **Mr Stone:** I thank the ever-courteous David McLetchie for giving way.[272]

Despite the mannerly tone, McLetchie went on to make what was probably, after Ewing's revelation that Dewar had hi-jacked the 1999 vote, the most important point to emerge from the whole debate. Do ministers in Scotland understand the working conventions of parliamentary government? McLetchie said of Donald Dewar:

> He knew that the *doctrine of ministerial responsibility* is far broader than simply acting in good faith, and that it covers decisions that are taken in good faith but which turn out to have disastrous consequences—just like this one...
> *Ministerial responsibility is an alien concept to the Scottish Executive.* This is a

---

[270] *Ibid.*, cols. 10394-5. In a posthumous tribute to Donald Dewar, McConnell gave this explanation for his appointment: "Donald was later to explain to the Queen that he appointed me a Finance Minister because I had been a maths teacher and he had assumed I could count." (*Dewar*, Alexander, *op. cit.*, p. 175) On the subject of education more generally, Wendy Alexander wrote in the same book: "I was so very proud of having a First Minister who had read so much that he could write his own speeches." (p. 31)

[271] *Ibid.*

[272] *Ibid.*, col. 10400

coalition that worships the principle of ministerial and collective *irresponsibility*, as shown by Sam Galbraith over the Scottish Qualifications Authority, Mike Watson over Glasgow hospital closures, Tavish Scott over the common fisheries policy, Cathy Jamieson over Reliance and Malcolm Chisholm over his disastrous health policy. We cannot go on like this. The principle of ministerial responsibility should have been triple underlined in the Fraser report.[273] (emphasis added)

It is almost impossible to overstate the importance of McLetchie's point. Without ministerial responsibility, parliamentary scrutiny of the executive is impossible. The problem he saw has, if anything, got worse since. In the first twenty years of the parliament's life, there was not a single resignation by a minister taking responsibility for a significant administrative mistake.

Ministers resigned due to sex scandals and allegations of financial irregularities, due to policy disagreements or because they wanted to spend more time in the real world. All those are personal rather than public reasons. Excluding ministerial reshuffles, there were 14 resignations between 1999 and 2019. Of these, 11 were for personal reasons. Of the three arguably political resignations, one was for an ill-advised remark by the minister concerned, and one was related to conduct in office (and hotly denied). *Only one was actually attributable to a Minister taking responsibility for a failure in a department he or she controlled.* However, that was over such a trivial matter—failure to forecast a snowstorm—that it is hard to believe that there were no other motives in play.[274]

This reveals an essentially elitist, "prerogative" attitude to power,

---

[273] *Ibid.*, col. 10401. The Ferguson ferry fiasco was later to provide an equivalent-scale example of "decisions that are taken in good faith but which turn out to have disastrous consequences." By then, as will be seen in volume 3, hardly anyone was taking personal responsibility for political disasters.

[274] The three exceptions were: Richard Simpson's in 2002 when, as Deputy Minister of Justice, he allegedly called firefighters "fascist bastards", as noted above; Lord Boyd's in 2006 when he was Lord Advocate over allegations of police misconduct in connection with the Shirley McKie (fingerprints) case; and Stewart Stevenson who resigned as Minister for Transport, Infrastructure and Climate Change in 2010 after admitting to having failed to anticipate the severity of a snowstorm that closed roads in the Central Belt. Five months after resigning, "Snowstorm" Stevenson was back in government as Minister for the Environment and Climate Change, so it looked like a pharisaic resignation only.

rather as the Crown and its officers had in the old parliament up to 1690. The office-holder gives orders to subordinates but is not personally affected by the way their orders are carried out. Ministerial office is really a "sinecure" which lasts only so long as the monarch—in this case the First Minister—continues to bestow favour. In Westminster, when a sense of personal responsibility is deficient, there is a well-established mechanism for enforcing it, through a motion of No Confidence. The Scottish parliament has similar procedures at its disposal, but it has largely failed to use them. In its first two decades, there were only three No Confidence motions introduced. Two of those were within the first two years. Only one was lodged *in the next seventeen years*—and that was for an allegation of misconduct by the minster concerned, so it did not amount to an attempt to enforce ministerial responsibility for the conduct of the civil service. [275]

The position of the First Minister under the Dewar Constitution has often been criticised for being "presidential", but a more accurate phrase

---

[275] In December 2000 Michael Russell introduced a motion criticising the Minister of Education for his indecision in connection with the Scottish Qualifications Authority. In February 2001, Bruce Crawford did the same with reference to the Minister of Transport's approach to trunk road maintenance. Then nothing happened for thirteen years, until, in May 2014, Neil Findlay introduced a motion criticising the Health Minister for "failure to disclose his involvement in the decision to reverse the planned closure of mental health services at Monklands Hospital." Since then: nothing. The reason is probably that Members saw them as hopeless, due to rigid party whipping. That was illustrated recently in connection with the Salmond Inquiry scandal. It will be described in volume 3, but here it is enough to say that Sturgeon, who had been accused of misleading parliament, said in the chamber: "If they think that they can bully me out of office, they are mistaken and they misjudge me. If they want to remove me as First Minister, they should do it in an election." (23 March 2021, col. 35—though the words Sturgeon says on film are more personal about Ruth Davidson than those in the *Official Report*, which members are allowed to alter after the fact) So, a motion in the parliament is "bullying" and the only people who can remove a First Minister suspected of dishonesty are the voters, *not the parliamentarians*. It is a radical devaluation of the institution to say that it can make no effective complaint against government ministers. Between elections, ministers are free to misgovern without any fear of parliamentary consequences. On this theory, *ministers are not responsible to parliament*, only to the electorate. The contrast with the House of Commons is stark. It is hard to conceive of a British Prime Minister standing at the despatch box and complaining that the Leader of the Opposition is "bullying" him or her because a general election is not in progress. This is *not* what Donald Dewar intended, but it is what Nicola Sturgeon has achieved due to the weakness of the Scottish parliamentarians who have tolerated it.

would be "electively autocratic". So long as one party or coalition can retain a majority, it is free to misgovern without any significant outside checks or constraints The lack of ministerial responsibility has been a consistent theme throughout the parliament's life, irrespective of the party in government. The fault, however, lies less in the constitution than in the deficient sense of personal responsibility of the individuals concerned. That is one problem that is *not* the result of the Dewar Constitution. As Hamish Gobson reminds us: "It's not the ships, it's the men that sail in 'em."

***

In the chamber, the Minister for Finance and Public Services, Andy Kerr, glided over the allegations about the bureaugarchy as smoothly as Fraser had Dewar's lie. Instead, he concentrated on gossip:

> Well, the Holyrood plot thickens: a Tory peer and former Tory minister and a Labour First Minister are in a big plot to keep secrets from Mr McLetchie and Fergus Ewing. What a lot of nonsense they talked in their speeches.[276]

Kerr did, however, concede that devolution had resulted in a rearrangement of Scotland's "administrative furniture":

> As I said at the outset, this Executive is a different organisation from the old Scottish Office. The Executive has its own aims, vision and values, and has developed a *distinctive Scottish approach to the governance of Scotland*. We have significantly different structures and accountabilities than existed before devolution.[277] (emphasis added)

The result of its being *Scottish* was that it was much better than the British version. Perhaps because he could not take such a conceit seriously, Kerr lapsed into clogged Aspiranto:

> The legacy of the Fraser inquiry for Scotland should be the best public sector procurement practice in the world and an innovative, creative and disciplined civil service that is outward looking, customer focused, effective and efficient. We believe that we have the best civil service in the world. Let us

---

[276] *Ibid.*, col. 10406
[277] *Ibid.*, col. 10412

prove the case.[278]

Robin Harper for the Greens criticised outcomes without attributing causes:

> Time after time, the [Fraser] report underlines instances of information that should have been passed on, information that was imprecise and muddled and *information that was deliberately withheld.* Time after time, we find poor and broken lines in the systems of communication at critical stages in the project's development. [279] (emphasis added)

So much for Andy Kerr's "best civil service in the world". Even his colleague, Wendy Alexander, would not join the boasting. She had helped Dewar plan the parliament and adopted a *faux* sentimental tone, expressed in native-user-standard Aspiranto. She admitted civil service failings but was worried about "Donald"—it's all first names at the top table.[280] "Donald would have been vexed into the wee small hours about how to rebuild the morale of the civil service". Then she presented an original view of why such an expensive building had been specified: it had a past to live up to.

> [Donald] wanted an iconic building because 1,000 years ago Scots made pilgrimages to abbeys, 500 years ago they petitioned clan chiefs in castles, 200 years ago they populated a stunning new town, and 100 years ago they protested against the powerful at our city chambers. Today they look to us.[281]

What I think Alexander meant by her invocation of Scotland's public architectural heritage was that "they", the people, "look to *our building*", rather than to "us" as people. Alexander had a reputation for cleverness. She was the daughter of a Glasgow manse, and has more degrees in her

---

[278] *Ibid.,* col. 10414

[279] *Ibid.,* col. 10416

[280] Lord Fraser himself commented on this in a different context in the House of Lords: "The Scottish Parliament thought that the House of Commons was so stuffy that it would refer to people instead only by their first names—so that world was whizzing round with Jacks, Jimmys and so on… The purpose of using "honourable Member" in Westminster is not only to calm people down but to identify who the person is for people outside, who have a right to know what we are doing and exactly who is doing it. If they are simply told that it is Jack or Jimmy, they will not know who it is." *Hansard* (HoL), 1 July 2011, vol. 728, col. 1980

[281] *Op. cit.,* col. 10418

CV than Hamish Gobson has shotguns hidden in his thatch. In terms of dialects of Aspiranto, she tended to speak more "manse" than "lecture room". "Let us disagree," she said to the wall, rather in the way her father might have addressed the ceiling with "Let us pray":

> Let us disagree without personal animus. Let us fight for what we believe in, as [Donald] did, with conviction untainted by malice. The eyes of the nation are upon us, and he set us a lesson to which we should live up.[282]

There was clearly something modish about that rather unScottish gush because when Alexander ended the chamber erupted into *applause*, for the only time in the debate. Members were happy to hero-worship a man they had just been told had lied to them while setting a national record for waste of citizens' money that stands to this day, despite the heroic efforts of the Ferguson's shipyard.

It was left to Dr Death to rise from the grave and get the debate back on track. For once, Swinney's "implacable dominie" act was entirely appropriate; applause in this context was disgusting. Gobson compared it to Victorian millionaires cheering at theft from the poor.

Swinney made a third, critically important, point about bureaugarchic malfeasance. Bovis, the lead contractors for the project, had been allowed by a civil servant to adjust their tender price when the other bidders were not. Naturally they won the tender and were able bill the Scottish taxpayer for pouring all those cubic meters of concrete.[283]

Based on this elite cronyism, Swinney issued a sensible warning which was related to McLetchie's point, but which has been ignored ever since:

> What we have here is a private culture where chats in the corridor and long-established connections are used as substitutes for frank and open government. We must seek an assurance that that culture has ended and that we

---

[282] *Ibid.,* col. 10418

[283] This is discussed in the House of Commons report, which notes without comment that "Bovis was the highest tenderer." (p. 10) Fraser commented on this in his report: "It does appear to me, on elementary considerations of fairness as between competing tenderers, that if one tenderer was effectively permitted to change a very material aspect of the financial basis upon which its tender was submitted that is an opportunity which should have been afforded to the others." (p. 93) This was bureaugarchic malfeasance of an unusually naked sort. No action was ever taken.

are now operating in a frank, open and transparent climate. If ministers did not know in 1998 and 1999 what was going on with the Holyrood project, how can we have confidence that ministers know that public money is being spent wisely today?[284]

Swinney ended by returning to Dewar's lie:

If the report contains lessons for the Executive to learn, it also contains lessons for the Parliament to learn about how we discharge our duties. In June 1999 and again in April 2000, the Scottish Parliament had credible opportunities to influence this project for the better. On both occasions I, and colleagues across the political spectrum, voted to pause and redirect the project. If that course had been followed, the project would have better commanded the confidence of the people of Scotland. The fact that the Parliament chose not to take those opportunities in *a climate of misinformation, deceit and blind party loyalty* tells us that, if we are to serve the people of Scotland effectively, we must have political debate that is open, honest and transparent.[285] (emphasis added)

The SNP criticising Labour for "blind party loyalty" was cheap, given the obsession with loyalty within the Nationalist movement. Nonetheless, the contrast with Wendy Alexander's off-topic sentimentalising was clear, and it is from this point, and due to this sort of thing, that some commentators began to sense that the Scottish Labour party was starting to lose whatever hard edge it may once have had.

John Home Robertson followed Swinney and, instead of taking up his points, lapsed into querulous whataboutism and an unappealing mix of self-pity and self-congratulation:

I agree with everything that Wendy Alexander said about Donald. I am sick of hearing people deriding Holyrood as a "fiasco". Yes, it is far too expensive, just as the Palace of Westminster was far too expensive in 1849 and just as the Sydney Opera House was in 1973. It is right that we should learn the lessons to be drawn from the Fraser report. I hope that it is not too much to ask Scotland to move on from our national traditions of self-doubt and mutual recrimination. We have a hard-won new constitutional settlement. We have a new Parliament, which can and will achieve great things

---

[284] *Op. cit.,* col. 10420

[285] *Ibid.,* col. 10421

for our people. Now, we have an *inspirational new home for our new democracy*.[286] (emphasis added)

Apart from Ewing, McLetchie and Swinney, the only other member to see the root of the problem was the Scottish Socialist, Frances Curran, a Glasgow "list" MSP who sounded as if she had "read her Gobson". She started with the bureaugarchs:

I am afraid that I hear the sound of the establishment closing ranks when I read the Fraser report. The biggest scandal about the whole sorry business and about the building that we are sitting in is that every key decision about it—its financing, architecture, design, the construction contracts and the site—was taken in London...

It is utterly inconceivable that Donald Dewar, who was a member of the British Cabinet and answerable to Tony Blair, could have taken those decisions alone. Wendy Alexander said that Donald Dewar understood symbolism. Other people also understand symbolism. There is still no answer to the question of why Calton Hill was rejected...

Lord Fraser may not be close to the Labour Cabinet, but he is a lifelong Tory and a lifelong unionist. It is unbelievable that in the report he refuses to attribute to Westminster any blame for the decisions that were taken...

Much of this discussion is obscure to most people who are watching the Parliament. They know that someone made a fortune out of this building and they want to know who. Was it the consultants? Was it the architects? We still do not know how Bovis got the contract—that is a complete secret. Who made the money and who let them get away with it? We will search in vain in the Fraser report for an answer to that question.

The Fraser report has come and gone and the same people are paying for the Parliament building. Is it people at Westminster? Are Cabinet ministers paying for it with their jobs? Are the MSPs on the corporate body paying for it out of their very high salaries? Are senior civil servants paying for it? None of those people appears to be paying for the cost of the Parliament or the mistakes that were made. The people who are paying for the Parliament now are the same people who were paying for it before—ordinary people in Scotland. That is where the problem lies.[287]

After that, the discussion sank into flabby-minded trivia. I'll give a

---

[286] *Ibid.,* col. 10423
[287] *Ibid.,* cols. 10431-2

few examples for the record.

"Snowstorm" Stevenson, who appeared to *think* in Aspiranto, said: "If the past five years have told us anything about what needs to be changed in Scottish public life, it is about the way in which we make our decisions and implement them." Since public life consists of nothing other than making decisions and implementing them, this was hardly illuminating. But it sounded profound, as did this: "If we learn anything from the experience, it should be that what starts as a shambles ends as a shambles." He ended with an observation that he derived from having read a book by the founder of the Intel Corporation, an American electronics company: "The title of his book, *Only the Paranoid Survive,* is a perfect lesson for us. This project was characterised by optimism when pessimism was required. Paranoia is what we need on these kinds of projects. We need to think the worst and prepare for the best."[288]

Helen Eadie had an attack of guilt and decided the whole project was really her own responsibility. "I join Robin Harper in saying how humbly sorry I am for the exorbitant cost of the building."[289]

Andrew Welsh for the SNP started sensibly by saying Scotland was being run as a "quango state", but then he veered off course and ended up in pure, Mumbo-Aspiranto: "The future will be what we make it."[290]

Sarah Boyack for Labour noted how few people liked the look of the building, and then said,

> The tragedy is that the process has alienated people in Scotland from the democracy that this place was meant to make theirs. We must turn that around. That will not be easy, but we need to think back to the aspirations that people voted for in 1999: openness, transparency, the sharing of power, and equality. That is why we established the Parliament.[291]

Dr Jean Turner, an Independent, agreed with Boyack about the appearance of the building, but in terms which could also be taken as a description of privilege in any elite: "I have not come to like the outside

---

[288] *Ibid.,* cols. 10433-5

[289] *Ibid.,* col. 10437

[290] *Ibid.,* col. 10441

[291] *Ibid.,* col. 10443

yet, but I adore the inside."[292]

Loyally for Labour, Rhona Brankin said: "Scotland now has a world-class Parliament building," and this will result in "a modern, representative and participative democracy for Scotland."[293]

It was unusually late for "family-friendly" Holyrood—after 6 o'clock—when Alex Neil stood up to close for the SNP. "This has been a very good debate, partly because we have had enough time for debate. Members from all parties have been able to speak and have been given enough time." He even managed a rare shaft of wit: "If Helen Eadie had spoken for eight minutes rather than six she would have managed to prove that the Tories were responsible for the disappearance of Shergar as well as everything else."[294]

Mike Watson spoke for Labour in one of his last appearances in parliament before being sent to jail for setting fire to hotel curtains when drunk. He illustrated the fundamental problem with any parliamentary clan which treats power as a benefit not a responsibility and enjoys expressing contempt for "bottom tablers". In summing up Frances Curran's contribution he completely distorted the thrust of her point about the contract shenanigans. Watson said:

> I was interested in the SSP position, which was clarified to some extent today by Frances Curran, who revealed some of her prejudices when she said that the fundamental reason why she did not want the building was that people made a profit out of it.[295]

Compare that with what Curran actually said (see above), and ask yourself: was "curtains" Watson really up to the job of representing constituents in a serious parliament? Decisions are taken after debate and debate depends on mutual respect. For reason to prevail over abuse, that must include not misrepresenting previous speakers' contributions. Watson seemed to Gobson to have something in common with Jeffrey Archer, the popular novelist and disgraced MP, of whom his wife, Mary,

---

[292] *Ibid.*, col. 10451
[293] *Ibid.*, cols. 10454,10455
[294] *Ibid.*, col. 10457
[295] *Ibid.*, col. 10466

once said, "He has a gift for inaccurate precis."

That day's debate lasted from 2.30 p.m. to 7 p.m. At £200,000 per hour, that amounted to about £900,000 in taxpayers' funds (18 POYs). Yet nothing came out of it. The discussion was as wasteful as the building in which it was held.

***

A fortnight later, on 9 October 2004, the new building was formally opened by the Queen. This was another event which Sturgeon did not attend. According to her biographer, David Torrance, she "boycotted" the ceremony.[296]

Dressed in the kilt, George Reid, as Presiding Officer, made a speech which echoed many of the sentiments expressed in *haute civique* circles in Scotland, or at least Edinburgh, about the purpose and point of the parliament. It is worth quoting as a clear example of bureaugarchic camouflage technique.

After a Gaelic psalm had been sung, Reid got straight down to sentimental Aspiranto. He described the parliament as "a place where the ears of politicians are open to the voices of the people" and therefore part of the "community of the realm", as it brought together "People, Parliament and Palace" (capitalisation in the Scottish Executive transcript). He said the "the Parliament belongs to its people. It has been built to invite them in." Apparently, the police with machine guns at the entrance are merely decorative, as the parliament is a place of "shared conversation, not sterile confrontation." It was also "a place where we know our enemy. And have the wisdom to understand that it is often us."

Then Reid burst into tears, metaphorically speaking, and talked of "A Scotland where we face our fear of failure. Where we confront that Caledonian cringe which merely reinforces doubt." I have no idea what he was thinking about, perhaps some long-buried personal trauma? But Gobson merely scoffed: "What on earth do they teach them at Dollar Academy?"

As anyone familiar with Communist propaganda knows, personal

---

[296] *Nicola Sturgeon, op. cit.*, p. 123

self-abasement is often accompanied by a spasm of national boasting. After claiming that the building was "designed like the leaves of a plant whose green stems stretch out to the hills"—whatever that meant—Reid said, "Our architecture is domestic, not patrician. Our people live right beside us." Scots, he implied, are superior to those blighted peoples whose national capital is separated from their largest population centres. There is virtue in political propinquity, apparently. Brazil (Brasilia rather than Sao Paulo) springs to mind as a victim of that blight, as does Australia (Canberra rather than Sydney) and the United States (Washington rather than New York). But Gobson points out, *pace* Reid, that the same applies to Scotland (Edinburgh rather than Glasgow). "We are so virtuous," he says, "that we are superior even to ourselves.

To describe the Holyrood building as "domestic" architecture was pure bunk. Was Reid suggesting that we all live in glass and concrete structures, picked out with Kemnay granite and Thai-laminated American oak, which have been made to look like upturned boats, or parts of a forest, and which have their windows covered with irregularly bent sticks?

Gobson suggested Reid might have been "channelling" the bizarre poem written for the occasion by Edwin Morgan, the elderly Scots "Makar", or Poet Bureaugarcheate. Morgan commented on the building's design in verse by saying it was: "No icon, no IKEA, no iceberg," adding for clarity that it featured "curves and caverns, nooks and niches, huddles and heavens syncopations and surprises." He summarised the architectural part of his poem by saying: "Leave symmetry to the cemetery."[297]

Reid moved on to Hugh McDiarmid, the short, sour, English-hating poet who was by then already laid out with symmetry in a cemetery. He is famous for having objected to national critiques based on size. "Our – Scotland small? Our multiform, our infinite Scotland small?" From McDiarmid we moved on to "the Proclaimers". This is a band which was popular in Scotland at the time. They may have been good, for all I know, but Reid surely took leave of his senses when he compared them with Robert Burns. Apparently, they sang: "We're all Scotland's story

---

[297] Full text available on the Scottish Parliament website

and *we're all worth the same.*" (emphasis added) Not even Burns thought that, as we know from his willingness to go slaving in Jamaica. And even if he had believed in universal equality, Burns would surely have expressed himself less prosaically. Gobson suggests that Reid's typist got her fingers in a twist and mixed up national "band" with national "bard".

Those with sensitive political antennae would have detected the muffled sound of bureaugarchic drums beating when Reid told us that the founding principles of the parliament were: "Accessibility, Accountability, Equality of Opportunities, and the sharing of power between our government, parliament and people." (capitalisation in original)

Finally, we were encouraged to "listen to the building", an idea which was not explained before Reid returned to the theme of superiority to England. "This is not a place where, like Westminster, we sit at two swords' lengths apart. It is a campus… It is a village… It says to all… 'Come on in.' This is a place where Scotland's horizons should be stretched, not squeezed."

Hamish Gobson, who tends to see the iron hand in the velvet glove, wrote about the day: "George Reid's half-comic, half-sentimental speech blessing the £400 million building was a mixture of inferiority complex (fear of failure) and superiority complex (Scotland's big, really). The 'Caledonian cringe' he seemed to be promoting from behind his enormous sporran looked out of place in such a lavish building, with members paid equally lavishly to debate any subject they wanted, irrespective of its usefulness to the Scottish public." Where is the "Accountability" in that, he asked?[298]

---

[298] MSPs are paid on a formula (agreed in 2002) which gives them 87.5% on MPs' salaries in Westminster. From April 2020 MSPs were paid £64,470, with various increments up to the rank of First Minister, who is paid £157,861 (plus six categories of expenses, a pension and a "failure bonus" if not re-elected). For comparison, the Prime Minister of the UK earns £164,080. The Clerk/Chief Executive of the SPCB was paid a total in 2020-21, including both salary and pension accrued during the year, of £370,000. (Report and Accounts, *op. cit.*, p. 38)

Chapter 7

Deputy Leader

The first words Sturgeon spoke in the first debate in the new Holyrood chamber were pure Aspiranto. Referring to the siege of Beslan in north Ossetia by Chechen terrorists a week earlier she used an off-the-peg cliché, "our thoughts and prayers". There is no sign that Sturgeon has ever been religious or, if she is, to which higher authority she prays. Most likely, the words were deployed carelessly as conventional, non-lethal deception aimed at any religious Nationalists who might have found themselves watching Parliament TV at the time. It was a regrettably cheap start to her career in a regrettably expensive building.

She moved quickly on to the subject of herself, and her new position as "deputy leader of the Scottish National Party and, indeed, leader of the nationalist group in the Scottish Parliament." Graciously, she tried a little wit, perhaps to show that she wore the cares of high office lightly.

> If press reports are to be believed—and, on occasion, that is a big if—some Labour back benchers have spent hours in recent days dreaming up *playground taunts and infantile insults* to hurl at me across the chamber. I am just glad that, after five years, we have at last found something for them to do.[299] (emphasis added)

As soon as she got onto the subject of the Holyrood building, the wit died. "It stands as our best hope of restoring confidence in Scottish self-government", she said. But that would happen "only if all of us live up to the grandeur of our new surroundings". As she spoke, Hamish Gobson's thoughts and prayers were for the English language. To associate the concrete éclair at Holyrood with the word "grandeur" was, he said, "[expletives deleted]".

Sturgeon continued by explaining what she meant by "live up to".

---

[299] 7 September 2004, col. 9879

The answer was "delivering real change to the people of Scotland".[300]
"Delivering change" is Aspiranto for "forcing everybody to do what the
speaker wants." The Chechen terrorists in Beslan were attempting to
"deliver change" in their own way. The atomic bomb had "delivered
change" to Hiroshima in 1945. But Sturgeon herself never changed:

> Will the First Minister consider that perhaps the best way of marking the
> opening of this fabulous new Parliament building and ensuring that it rep-
> resents the fresh start that each and every one of us wants is to demand for
> it the *powers that will match its price tag*?[301] (emphasis added)

David McLetchie followed her, also on the subject of the new building:

> As a patriotic Scot, it upsets me that our Parliament has become a source of
> shame when it should be a source of pride. Does the First Minister agree
> that we have spent the past five years building offices for the Parliament and
> that we must spend the next five years building respect for the Scottish Par-
> liament?[302]

Jack McConnell responded as First Minister by suggesting that he
had more in common with the Nationalists than with the Tories:

> I welcome Mr McLetchie back to our jousts. I suspect that he and I may
> find it harder to agree than Ms Sturgeon and I will do in the months and
> years ahead. I welcome that prospect.[303]

After a short "comfort break", the debate moved to the government's programme for the next session. The opening speech was made
by Jim Wallace, the Liberal leader, who was Deputy First Minister as well
as being education minister. Sturgeon replied by noting "the disappointment that many people feel about the early days of devolution". Then
she reached again for the keywords "grandeur" and "price tag":

> The new parliament is now a reality. It is granite, bricks and mortar; it is
> living and breathing. The challenge now for all of us is to live up to it, and

---

[300] *Ibid.*

[301] *Ibid.*, col. 9884

[302] *Ibid.*, col. 9885

[303] *Ibid.*

to ensure that what is delivered within this fabulous chamber matches the grandeur of the surroundings… How much better it can be and how much more we can achieve as a country if we equip our Parliament with the *powers to match its price tag*.[304] (emphasis added)

The debate achieved little more than many held in rooms without the grandeur. At least one academic suggested there might be a connection between the opulence and the impotence:

Even the architecture of a parliament can affect the way it operates. As a general rule, *the more imposing the chamber, the less efficient the legislature*.[305] (emphasis added)

In Holyrood, the blame for the parliament's performance cannot be laid entirely at the door of Catalan architects and Kemnay grandeur. There was also obstructionism. Sturgeon demonstrated her own technique in this debate:

George Lyon (Argyll and Bute) (LD): In the spirit of building confidence in this Parliament, does the member agree that we need to take tougher action against absentee lairds who might wish to interfere and meddle in matters that should rightly be decided here in Scotland?

Nicola Sturgeon: I was listening to the First Minister on the radio, I think on Sunday morning, and he said that the people of Scotland were heartily sick of yah-boo politics and that they expected something more. I guess that George Lyon was still in his bed at the time.

Scotland is a country with enormous potential…[306]

She gave the First Minister similarly dismissive treatment while taking about his "Blair-lite" plans for schools:

In the past few days he has stumbled on each occasion on which he had

---

[304] *Ibid.*, cols. 9899-9900

[305] "Sovereignty and Independence in the Dominions", Ged Martin, in *The Challenge to Westminster, op. cit.,* p. 99. Professor Martin gives an example: "Australia managed for sixty years with much-loved and very cramped temporary premises until a permanent Parliament House was completed in 1988 at a *cost of £500 million.* It was the largest construction project in the Southern Hemisphere… While working conditions have improved, there is a general impression that the *executive has become more remote from the backbenchers.* One politician complained in the new House of Representatives that… 'I have been at crematoria that have been more fun.'" (p. 100, emphasis added)

[306] *Op. cit.,* col. 9900

tried to articulate new ideas about the future direction of the country… It is as if Mr McConnell knows that he has to say something that sounds big, bold and different, but he does not really have any ideas of his own, so he borrows some from Blair. The only problem is that he does not really believe them, so he backtracks before the ink is dry on the press releases. That is government by headline, not substance.[307]

The tactic of answering questions by giving a Jeffrey Archer-like precis of the questioner's presumed position, then answering a question that was not asked, is considered clever by a certain type of provincial politician. It is another way of avoiding "openness and transparency". Sturgeon had done this regularly with Tories, now the First Minister was getting the cold kiss from "authentic Scotland". The result was that she made no impact when she talked in plain English about real problems, such as

> …low economic growth, inequality, failing public services and the gaping chasm that exists between the public and decision makers… It takes longer to travel between Glasgow and Edinburgh by rail today than it took 30 years ago. That beggars belief, but it is true.[308]

Both leaders seemed intoxicated with their ability to deceive by talking in Aspiranto when others imagined they were speaking English. The only question was who was better at it. After McConnell said: "We must raise our game." Sturgeon used the phrase six times before she sat down. First, she quoted McConnell, then said, "Let us *raise our game* by bringing our infrastructure up to scratch." A paragraph later, it was: "Let us *raise our game* by doing more to tackle population decline." She made the same point twice, then said, "We should also *raise our game* by tackling pensioner poverty." Then: "Finally, we must *raise our game* in relation to the delivery of public services."[309]

Tommy Sheridan joined in the joke, saying, "The First Minister can hardly raise his game, raise his vision, or be more daring while willingly submitting to the British straitjacket of free-market profit worship." But

---

[307] *Ibid.*, col. 9902

[308] *Ibid.*

[309] *Ibid.*, cols. 9903-4

he was not joking when he said he preferred the example of Venezuela as a model for the new Scotland:

> **Tommy Sheridan:** Last year I had the pleasure of visiting the Bolivarian Republic of Venezuela, and of meeting President Hugo Chávez and Vice-President José Vicente Rangel.
> **Stewart Stevenson:** This is just a rant.
> **Tommy Sheridan:** Presiding Officer, I thought that this was a new Parliament and that the child Stewart Stevenson would have learned to behave appropriately for an adult Parliament, but he has still got his short troosers [*sic*] on. We discussed how the Bolivarian Republic of Venezuela intends to harness its vast oil reserves to raise living standards and improve the quality of life of all its citizens.[310]

To be fair to Sheridan, that was said when Chávez was still President and, though the Bolivarian Republic was enduring strikes and popular revolts, it had not yet suffered a coup d'état, followed by a catastrophic deterioration in "the quality of life of all its citizens".

It is easy to laugh at such ideas, but it is worth remarking that his was about the only alternative approach to national development that was advanced in opposition to the First Minister's empty keywords and re-heated talking points. It is also relevant to this story because Sheridan presaged the logic of the SNP case at the independence referendum a decade later.

> **Tommy Sheridan:** Instead of the £10 billion of revenue that was raised from [Scottish] oil reserves last year going into the pockets of private multinationals, it should be deployed to improve the living standards and quality of life of all our citizens. If that can work for countries such as Venezuela and Norway, it can work for countries such as Scotland.
> **Stewart Stevenson** *rose—*
> **Tommy Sheridan:** In Scotland and in this Parliament we have people like Stewart Stevenson who are obsessed with the Barnett formula but not with the type of revolution that we require to harness the wealth and resources of our country. Leave the Barnett formula to the anoraks such as Stewart and the other faint hearts. We need to raise our vision in this Parliament. *This Parliament is far too grand to retain the powers of a mere parish council.* Yes, let

---

[310] *Ibid.*, col. 9916

us use the limited powers that we have. Let us abolish council tax and water rates and replace them with a progressive income-based alternative. Let us introduce free school meals for every child and raise dietary and nutritional standards for our children. Let us abolish the pill tax that is a tax on the ill in this country. Let us ensure that all public contracts in this Parliament go to companies with recognised trade unions, to improve employment standards and conditions. But let us not forget that if we really want to raise our vision, if we really want to be more daring and if we really want to raise our game, we will have to win and secure the confidence of the Scottish people in a genuinely independent nation and a democratic republic that owns and controls the natural wealth and resources of our country. Only then can we harness them to eradicate poverty, promote peace and tolerance throughout our world and expel barbaric nuclear weapons from our shores.[311] (emphasis added)

Sheridan might have been on the electioneering stump. It is impossible to *debate* with people who are really speaking to distant, imaginary rallies, rather than to the wall in front of them. Nonetheless, Sturgeon took up one of Sheridan's themes and pointed to how successful an independent Scotland could be if it kept its resources to itself and did not allow English or foreign access:

We have won the lottery in terms of our natural resources. North sea oil and gas—half of which is still to be exploited—is currently earning the United Kingdom Treasury £8 billion a year, which, according to one of Labour's former economic researchers, debunks the myth that an independent Scotland could not stand on its own two feet and prosper.[312]

The theme of success was mentioned by many speakers, though usually in a vague, generalised way, with no concrete recommendations on how to generate wealth at national level other than by hoarding the country's hydro-carbon winnings. That was empty rather than ominous. Then a bank of soul-freezing Aspiranto rolled in, like haar from the North Sea. Alex Neil referred to a government report entitled *A Smart, Successful Scotland* as if it was a serious document. Robin Harper talked of "a smart,

[311] *Ibid.,* cols. 9916-7
[312] *Ibid.,* col. 9900

successful, sustainable Scotland."[313] Richard Baker, a Labour "list" member, said he wanted Scots to be "more confident about their talents, because we want to have a more confident nation."[314]

Jim Wallace, as Deputy First Minister, presumably spoke for the Cabinet when he said he wanted "to equip our young people with the skills and confidence that they need to lead successful, enterprising and ambitious lives, to support confident communities."[315] Sturgeon herself said: "Our job is to build a Scotland that is confident about itself and its place in the world."[316]

Meanwhile, the otherwise respected Fraser of Allander Institute, which monitors the Scottish economy from a bureaugarchic perspective at Strathclyde University, raised its game and published an expensively confident 66-page, government-backed report entitled: *Measuring Scotland's progress towards a smart, successful Scotland*. The idea was clearly catching: Madison Avenue meets the M8. The only group which refused to debate in the language of J. Walter Tamson was the Scottish Socialists:

> **Frances Curran:** I was unsure about it at first but, after my first week here, I think that this is a wonderful building… The question about this Parliament—the lawmaker, not the building—is whether it can talk to the almost half of the population who never put a cross on a paper to send any of us here and who do not participate in voting, such as young people and the less well-off. At the moment, they obviously do not think that this Parliament has much to offer them. After the First Minister's speech this morning, I can see their point. There is a view… that this place is occupied by an elite who represent the privileged. The key question for the Parliament is: who is the Parliament going to represent?
> **Members:** The people.
> **Frances Curran:** Which people?
> **Members:** All the people.[317]

The revivalist tone echoed the biblical language which the Minister

---

[313] *Ibid.*, col. 9913
[314] *Ibid.,* col. 9938
[315] *Ibid.,* col. 9892
[316] *Ibid.*, col. 9901
[317] *Ibid.* col. 9940

of the Canongate Kirk, Rev. Charles Robertson, had used in the Time
for Reflection earlier. He skilfully captured the tone of empty verbalising,
saying, in pulpit Aspiranto, that the parliament was

> a complex of buildings that will neither pall nor bore, in a setting that joins
> the tangible with the intangible. The kaleidoscope of reflections that pass
> across the glass panels lining the walls of the chamber, the complexity and
> sophistication of the engineering marvel of the roof, the majestic sweep of
> the magnificent staircase that brings you here, or any one of the other many-
> splendoured things that makes this place the unique and precious thing that
> it is—the beauty of each and all of those will inspire and uplift you as, from
> this day forward, you go about your business in this place.[318]

Since Patrick Harvie was eventually "uplifted" enough that he as-
cended into government, and now sitteth on the right hand of Sturgeon
the First Minister as co-leader of the ruling coalition, it might be appropriate to end with his eulogy for the building:

> Members from all parties have talked of their feelings when speaking for the
> first time in this beautiful chamber. It is beautiful and I like it a lot, but I feel
> a sense of responsibility. This room will ring with the voice of Scottish gov-
> ernment for many generations to come; generations of Scottish politicians
> yet unborn will be here. The chamber should be a reminder to us all to hand
> on a better Scotland to them.[319]

Let us not leave this ocean of verbal grandeur without mentioning
two concrete facts. First, the debate lasted all day, so, on a *per diem* basis
it cost £1 million. That was a large sum of other people's money to de-
vote to self-congratulation at what amounted to a house-warming party.
But, as both Sturgeon and Sheridan pointed out, Scotland had so much
oil that it could afford to indulge itself.

Secondly, the average price of oil in late 2004 was $40 a barrel. The
debate could be said to have cost, at the exchange rate then prevailing,
about 35,000 barrels of Brent Crude, or 1,000 for each of the 35 MSPs
who spoke in it (equivalent to 160,000 litres of petrol). Perhaps that is
why Sturgeon talked, in her own thousand barrels' worth, of "a Scotland

---

[318] *Ibid.*, col. 9868
[319] *Ibid.*, col. 9967

that is clean, green and sustainable"?[320]

***

Sturgeon made another contribution of general significance a month later when, on 7 October, she spoke to a motion, introduced by Jack McConnell, about "Scotland's International Image". Specifically, McConnell had moved:

> That the Parliament shares the Scottish Executive's ambitions to build rela-
> tionships across national and regional boundaries to deliver social, political,
> cultural and economic gain; welcomes efforts to promote Scotland's inter-
> national image and to attract people to visit, live, work, study and do busi-
> ness in Scotland; acknowledges the importance of promoting Scotland's in-
> terests overseas; agrees that Scotland has a role in meeting the shared re-
> sponsibilities of the international community, and welcomes the publication
> of the Executive's first international strategy.[321]

All this "sharing", "welcoming", "acknowledging", "agreeing" and more "welcoming" reads like the preamble to a European Commission Directive. That would be nebulous enough, but at least EU Directives are "directing" something. This motion, like so many others in Holyrood, had nothing beyond the sharing, welcoming, acknowledging, agreeing, etc. The entire debate was a pure expression of attitude. It could have been held in a pub. Because it was not, this effusion of atti-tudinising cost the equivalent of 2,800,000 litres of petrol.

McConnell started by saying how "European" the new parliament building was:

> Scotland has always looked to Europe for inspiration. Our auld alliances run
> deep. We are now forging new friendships in an enlarged European Union.
> This building is itself a reflection of our long-standing connections with Eu-
> rope, and this chamber is set up in a distinctive European style.[322]

---

[320] *Ibid.,* col. 9901. Scotland's average daily consumption of oil for all purposes is about 150,000 barrels. 35,000 is nearly a quarter of that.

[321] 7 October 2004, col. 11073, motion S2M-1831

[322] *Ibid.,* col. 11065

The "distinctive European style" of the chamber meant ditching Scotland's past.

> Since 1 July this year, this Government has undertaken an extensive pro-
> gramme to promote contemporary 21st century Scotland to people from
> around the world. We have introduced the strategy because the image of
> Scotland as a place of great myths, castles and misty mountains alone simply
> does not reflect the reality of modern Scotland. In the five years of devolu-
> tion, Scotland has changed for the better. It is a country in which we are
> doing and saying different things and in which there are signs all around us
> of economic, social and cultural renewal. However, the world's perception
> of us is based firmly on an image of the past—an image that certainly puts
> us on the map but does not demonstrate either progress or aspiration.[323]

The First Minister's idea for promoting smart, successful Scotland was to call it "the best small country in the world". That acknowledges, shares, welcomes and agrees with the psychological complexes which George "the sporran" Reid confessed to at the parliament's opening cer-emony. According to McConnell, the result was that:

> We need to work as hard as we can to demonstrate that Scotland is hungrier
> for success than anyone else.[324]

"Hungry for success" – heard that phrase anywhere before? Was it beyond the ex-schoolmaster to think of something original to say on such an important subject? Or did he not have the confidence to speak in plain English?

McConnell went on with an embarrassing list of spring-heeled initi-atives which seemed to be predicated on the Reidish worry that Scotland was not good enough to earn the approval of the world beyond the local grandeur. He talked of Chinese broadcasters who had come to Scotland and were "producing documentaries". He said that his government had "produced new promotional materials on fresh talent". And he noted that a website called "scotlandistheplace" had had "150,000 hits or page impressions from all corners of the globe since its launch in May." For those of little faith, he added with a hint of swagger: "However, that is

---

[323] *Ibid.,* col. 11067
[324] *Ibid.,* col. 11068

just the start."[325]

McConnell clearly had a streak of the class warrior in him as he was willing to characterise the opposition in cartoonish terms:

> Unlike those on the Opposition benches, who think that Scotland is a terrible country that nobody would ever want to come to, we believe that Scotland is a great country that people would want to come to.[326]

False dichotomies undermine reasoned debate as effectively as inaccurate precis does. *Measured* disagreement, which is the basis of all civilised interchange, seemed beyond the First Minister. At least, he gave no sign of it in this debate. Gobson described him as being "all black and white with no grey matter in between."

Aspiranto snobbery comes at a cost in terms of the clarity of public thought. It extends well beyond the parliament into, for example, education. Eighteen months after this debate, while "Hungry Jack" was still First Minister, the Scottish official education standards body, HM Inspectorate of Education, published a booklet entitled *Hungry for Success: Benchmarks for Self-Evaluation*. The "Aim of This Publication" section included this cotton-wool sentence: "In evaluating the effectiveness of the implementation of *Hungry for Success*, it is important to consider, in particular, the outcomes and impact of action taken to improve school meals and other aspects of food in schools." (p. 1) Essentially this says: evaluation must take account of results. Do the teachers of Scotland not know this? Is it not obvious?

McConnell appeared to need high-octane Aspiranto to sell his plan for a programme of national boasting:

> We are harnessing the energy, expertise and enthusiasm of all those with a passion for Scotland. Everyone who is in a position to promote Scotland, including public agencies, Scots abroad and our top companies, should speak to the world together—many voices, delivering a consistent and clear

---

[325] *Ibid.* This was not an aberration. In 2022, the home page of the replacement for scotlandistheplace, www.scotland.org, makes these fatuous claims: "Scotland is kindness, respect and generosity. Scotland is determination, creativity and curiosity. We are castles, lochs and mountains. We are students, explorers, innovators. We are Scotland and good things live here. We've come a long way and you could too." Amusingly, the page ends with a link headed: "Where is Scotland?"

[326] *Ibid.*

message about modern Scotland.[327]

As if that was not impressive enough, McConnell then launched into a description of how "small" Scotland was going to help transform China:

> We can work with China to help deliver economic reform, eradicate poverty and promote a positive change in human rights. We already have the advantage of many established links. Scottish Development International has new offices in Beijing and Shanghai, but to support them and strengthen Government ties, I have decided to locate a Scottish Government official in Beijing on a full-time basis.[328]

The claim that a single Scot in a country of 1.3 billion people could help "deliver economic reform [and] eradicate poverty", while simultaneously Scottifying the Chinese Communist Party's approach to human rights, was "confident" to the point of imbecility.

This atmosphere of adolescent self-assertion and consensual reputation massage was broken by the new Leader of the Opposition. Quite reasonably, Sturgeon ignored McConnell's ludicrous claims and hit him instead with reality. That was well stated in plain English until she, too, veered off into personal fantasy, this time of an exaggeratedly negative sort, as opposed to the First Minister's exaggerated boosterism. That allowed her to bend her point round to a predictable complaint about the constitution. As Gobson commented: "All roads lead to Home Rule." After that, all attempts at dialogue were futile:

> **Nicola Sturgeon:** Yesterday, the Scottish Executive announced the establishment of a permanent representation in Beijing. I welcome that, but I remind the First Minister that, when he visits China next week, he should raise loudly and clearly the Scottish people's concerns about human rights issues in that country. Let us compare ourselves not even with any other independent nation—which is what Scotland should be—but with other autonomous regions. The Flemish region, which has a similar population to that of Scotland, has 77 offices in 54 countries. Scotland has only one such office, which is Scotland House in Brussels. We need Scotland Houses in a

---

[327] *Ibid.,* col. 11069
[328] *Ibid.,* col. 11071

range of countries that are politically, culturally and economically important to us. We cannot rely on the Foreign Office to represent Scotland properly.

Mr Keith Raffan (Mid Scotland and Fife) (LD): Will the member give way?

Nicola Sturgeon: Sorry; I must make progress. Scotland is not a priority for the Foreign Office. Without putting too fine a point on it, I might add that many of the people who work in that organisation know little about Scotland and care even less.

The First Minister: That is rubbish.

Nicola Sturgeon: Perhaps the First Minister should listen. The fourth and final thing that we should do to enhance our international profile is the most obvious and important of all: we need to be independent. We need the same powers and the same international status as our neighbours and competitors. It is as simple as that.

The First Minister: Will the member give way?

Nicola Sturgeon: Not just now. We need to be independent for practical reasons. As the First Minister said, most of our work in the Scottish Parliament is influenced by the European Union. It is absurd that our voice is not heard directly in Europe where the big decisions are taken.

The First Minister: Will the member give way?

Nicola Sturgeon: Not just now. Listen to this. We also need to be independent for symbolic reasons.

The First Minister: Will the member give way?

Nicola Sturgeon: No. When we have Governments in London and in Edinburgh telling the entire world that Scotland is too poor and too weak to stand on its own two feet as an independent nation, how can we expect to be taken as seriously as independent Ireland? We need to be independent to have our own voice in the world.

The First Minister: Will the member take an intervention?

Nicola Sturgeon: No. The last time that I took an intervention from the First Minister he made another four-minute speech.

Ms Wendy Alexander (Paisley North) (Lab): Will the member take an intervention?

Nicola Sturgeon: The First Minister will not give Wendy Alexander the chance to speak very often, so I do not see why I should...[329]

David McLetchie tried to restore the courtesy of debate. He

---

[329] *Ibid.*, cols. 11076-7

answered Sturgeon's point about Scotland being considered "too poor and too weak" by mentioning all the Scottish Enlightenment heroes and showing how many Scots had influence in London in 2004. Then he came to an important point about McConnell's speech:

> It is somewhat typical of the Executive that it thinks that our international reputation can be improved by the launch of a strategy… Ultimately, Scotland's international image cannot be transformed by clever public relations. *Image is based on substance, so we need real improvements, not cosmetic makeovers.* I believe that the current weaknesses in Scotland are the result of the wrong political approach. Our international image will improve only if we are prepared to reform our public services and strengthen our economy.[330] (emphasis added)

For the SNP, Kenny MacAskill seemed to think his own country little more than a commercial "brand":

> Talking the talk is not walking the walk. We need to do more, to go further and to push harder and the best way of doing that is for Scotland to become an independent nation state… On trade… it is clear that Ireland is the model—Ireland is the Celtic tiger that leaves everyone else in its wake… On tourism… VisitBritain means us no harm, but it is not possible to sell Scotland fully under a British identity: Scotland needs to be sold as the unique *brand* that is Scotland.[331] (emphasis added)

Hamish Gobson asks if Nationalists can really be serious about a country they consider "a brand". Do you love your brand? Would you die to defend your brand? Can a brand declare independence from other brands? Most of all, does a mere brand need £414 million spent on a building in which brand managers debate broad-brush strategies in cartoonish clichés, using a coded language in order to deceive the population of the brand? Should it be called a parliament at all? Maybe, Gobson suggests, it is just a staggeringly expensive boardroom with armed police outside to make sure the visitor understands that the word "Welcome" in this context is really Aspiranto for "Fuck off, bottom tablers! Le brand c'est nous!"

---

330 *Ibid.,* col. 11081
331 *Ibid.,* cols. 11087-8

Mark Ruskell tried to rescue the debate for the Greens by cutting out the hot air and going specific. He criticised the government's road improvements, like the M74 and the Aberdeen by-pass, and for "entertaining the fallacy [*sic*] of having a second Forth road bridge."[332]

This made no impact, despite the fact that Ruskell did have an unusual point to make about what might be called "post-holiday tourism":

> People are coming to Scotland to look for answers on how we can tackle the root causes of climate change. They are not going to find the answers in the tartan tourist brochures that will be handed out at airports when they arrive or in tours around flood defences, which only deal with the symptoms of climate change, not the root causes.[333]

Still on "tourism", Robert Brown said for the Liberals: "People now come to Scotland to see how home rule is working out."

> This Parliament must become not just an iconic building, but an iconic democracy—by our style, by the way in which we approach things and by developing our own ways of doing things in the light of best international practice.[334]

Jamie McGrigor for the Tories drew attention to sewage, which a Liberal member objected to as not being relevant to Scotland's international image.

> **Mr McGrigor:** I am led to believe that Scottish Water has said that it will accept no further connections in Campbeltown, which puts an unbelievable burden on the local council and anyone planning to expand. What does that do for Scotland's international image? A country is judged by elements of its infrastructure, and water and sewerage are pretty basic elements.
>
> **Mr Raffan:** On a point of order, Presiding Officer. I fail to see what water connections and sewage disposal have to do with Scotland internationally.
>
> **The Deputy Presiding Officer (Trish Godman):** I am sure that Mr McGrigor will get to the point.
>
> **Mr McGrigor:** Mr Raffan ought to admit that a smell of sewage certainly has something to do with image. In Scotland a visitor who is unlucky enough

[332] *Ibid.,* col. 11091

[333] *Ibid.,* col. 11090

[334] *Ibid.,* col. 11095

to be in the wrong place at the wrong time and smells sewage is going to think that Scotland is moving backwards.[335]

Sylvia Jackson for Labour moved forward, putting sewage behind her as she returned to "Scotland the brand":

> Building the brand is important. The Scottish Executive's research discovered that people abroad know about the older images of Scotland, but we must build on the new aspects such as the Parliament—the building, the values and how we work—and somehow get those aspects into the branding.[336]

It took Colin Fox for the Scottish Socialists to take the true measure of this debate and introduce an element of humour. Referring to the visit that the smart, successful First Minister and his wife were soon to pay to Beijing, he said:

> The First Minister should know that a worldwide poll that was conducted recently on the internet found that the most famous Scotsman in the world is not Sean Connery, Ewan McGregor or Billy Connolly but groundskeeper Willie from "The Simpsons". Perhaps when Janet or Jack goes to Beijing, he will bear that in mind.[337]

Dr Death could not see the joke, so he heaved the discussion back to brand management, which he did in a curious mix of broken English and half-assimilated Aspiranto:

> In the good old days when I worked for a living in the real world, I used to design strategies for private companies. A strategy is not just a collection of actions that are designed to make one feel busy. They must give a cohesive and purposeful direction to an organisation or country as to what it wants to achieve. The international strategy that the First Minister published this morning is certainly a busy agenda and a complex set of actions. However, I question the extent to which those actions are grouped together into a cohesive international strategy. In that strategy, I do not see what we are trying to promote as being the key credentials and identification of

---

[335] *Ibid.*, col. 11097

[336] *Ibid.*, col. 11099

[337] *Ibid.*, col. 11100

Scotland.[338]

What did Swinney mean by the words "key credentials and identification of Scotland" when arranged in that order? I have no idea. Gobson said in his blog that he considered it demeaning to be talked of not as a citizen but as part of a marketing strategy.

However, Swinney's point was popular with the chamber. Most of the members present seemed to share his materialistic view of Scotland. Labour was "singing from the same hymn-sheet". Helen Eadie told the chamber that all Scots should think the same about national branding:

> We appear to lack a single focused body that can co-ordinate all the organisations and identities that Scotland offers. Those different identities do not need to be diluted, but harnessed into a united front that says "Scotland" to a world audience. We are all guilty... We must sell under one banner the diversity of Scotland and what that represents in total.[339]

The debate wound down without any overall conclusion, and with only one more outburst from a frustrated Nationalist, Michael Matheson, who called Jim Wallace "a hypocrite."[340] Soon it was time for lunch. Other tables, other brands—the world moves on...

What was achieved for the taxpayers' £½ million is hard to say, but the debate did reveal the type of person Sturgeon needed to dominate if she were ever to leverage herself into the nation-breaking position. In her disdain for almost all the non-Nationalist members, she appears to have taken the correct measure of the chamber. However revolutions are not made by disdain, they also need dynamite. What Sturgeon wanted was a signature issue which the SNP promotional machine could use to blast its opponents from their mental dug-outs over the long haul. In the Swinneyish language of business management, she needed a "cash cow". That is a revenue stream from an established source that can be "milked" indefinitely. The political variant is an *issue* which can be milked indefinitely—a "vote cow".

To work for the SNP, the issue had to be important, popular and

---

[338] *Ibid.*, col. 11103

[339] *Ibid.*, col. 11104

[340] *Ibid.*, col. 11117

deeply damaging to Britain. Apart from the constitution—a subject on which the Nationalists were in danger of becoming a bore—there were few issues which came before the parliament that met all three criteria. Nothing less would be required if the Nationalists were to light the fiery cross and reverse their decline in electoral popularity.

Six months after this debate, a question arose concerning an issue which is still, nearly twenty years later, one of the most important and controversial in Scottish politics: nuclear weapons. There were to be four substantial debates before the next Scottish election. The specific question was whether or not the British government should order replacements for the Trident-armed nuclear submarines which are based at Faslane on the Clyde. This was, of course, a matter reserved to Westminster, but the SNP was determined to make its voice heard by demanding a veto on British defence policy. At last, a high-profile, indefinitely sustainable, multi-megaton vote cow!

***

The biographical interest in the first Trident debate was that the proposer of the motion was Roseanna Cunningham, Sturgeon's defeated rival for the leadership of the Party after Swinney resigned. Many observers thought that the blonde radical had been in a sort of muffled sulk since her defeat in the race for Party leadership the previous August. But she spoke confidently on 24 March 2005.

Since the arguments about weapons of mass destruction in the nuclear age are likely to be as eternal as the urge to make war, I propose to examine them in the light of recent developments, especially in Ukraine, which have reminded the world of some eternal truths which a long peace had caused many to forget. This is not hindsight. Given the lead times necessary for the development of nuclear weapons systems, the discussion in 2005 was as relevant for the situation today, in 2022, as it will be in 2055 by which time the *Dreadnought* class of Trident missile-armed submarines will have replaced today's *Vanguard* class. The first is expected to come into service soon after 2030, after which it will have a service life of over 40 years. Nuclear defence policy is one of the few issues which hardly changes from decade to decade.

The Motion Cunningham moved said:

> That the Parliament is opposed to the existence of weapons of mass de-
> struction in Scotland; believes that the existing Trident nuclear system which
> costs almost £1 billion annually to keep in operation should be scrapped;
> recognises that a decision on the replacement of Trident will require to be
> taken within the next UK Parliament; further recognises that the cost of
> replacing Trident would be over £20 billion, and wishes to register strong
> opposition to any proposal by Her Majesty's Government to procure a re-
> placement for the Trident nuclear system.[341]

At first sight, this does not make it clear whether the Trident system
alone should not be renewed, or whether all nuclear weapons should be
abandoned by Britain. In other words, was this a practical issue—there
are better ways to deter enemies than by having nuclear-armed submarines—or was it a moral one: all nuclear weapons should be discarded
by Britain as an act of ethical self-advertisement?

Cunningham soon cleared that up when she said: "The moral argument against nuclear weapons remains as strong as ever"; and "I believe
that no country should have nuclear weapons."[342] That was clear in theory, but what did it mean in practice, given that, even if Britain abandoned hers, seven other countries would still have their nuclear weapons?

Instead of addressing that obvious problem, Cunningham turned to
the more saleable issue of cost:

> If we do not ditch it now, Scotland's share of the money blown on a re-
> placement for it would be in the region of £3 billion over 10 years, at an
> annual cost of £300 million. I do not believe that Scotland can afford to
> spend its money on that.[343]

It should be borne in mind that, as will be seen in volume 3, £300
million was the price of two Hebridean ferries from Ferguson's yard in
Port Glasgow. It was far less than the cost of the building Cunningham
was speaking in. Scotland clearly *could* afford such sums. The real

---

[341] 24 March 2005, col. 15692, motion S2M-2640
[342] *Ibid.*, cols. 15689, 15690
[343] *Ibid.*

argument was about whether it *wanted to* or not. Curiously, Cunningham did not make a strong argument on this point. Her speech was unusually short for the proposer of such a motion. She devoted much of the second half of it to excusing her choice of subject.

> I make no apology for debating nuclear weapons in the Scottish Parliament. I do not deny that the subject matter is outwith the Parliament's current competence, but we have debated such issues before and we will do so again. It is an issue of huge importance to Scotland and *we are Scotland's voice*. We must be heard.[344] (emphasis added)

Here Cunningham raised the issue of the purpose of the parliament. Was it to choose a government and then oversee its actions, or was it to be a forum for self-expression by MSPs who wanted to sell their personal "brand" to party managers?

Cunningham briefly mentioned the three amendments to her motion which had been lodged by other parties. She could accept the Green Party one, she said, but that the Liberal one was "weaselspeak", and the one lodged by a Labour member was "profoundly confused". She added mysteriously about the proposer, Scott Barrie: "He was obviously never on any of the anti-nuclear marches that I was on."[345]

Cunningham ended with another reference to the anti-nuclear marches which had once attracted Sturgeon:

> I want Labour and Liberal Democrat members individually to look to their consciences as they consider how to vote this afternoon… I know that many members have a long-standing commitment to the cause of nuclear disarmament, and some of us have been on the same demonstrations together down the years. Today, the Parliament has the opportunity to keep faith with those principles by supporting the motion in my name.[346]

Scott Barrie defended his motion which, to this reader at any rate, was perfectly clear.[347] It is hard to see Cunningham's confusion. Barrie

---

[344] *Ibid.*, col. 15691

[345] *Ibid.*

[346] *Ibid.*

[347] Barrie's was motion S2M-2640.4: "That the Parliament acknowledges that defence and national security are matters reserved to the UK Parliament and acknowledges, in the words of the Government's Strategic Defence Review, 'the goal of the global

was a former social worker who was now Labour chief whip. He is one of the few ministers in the Holyrood parliament ever to resign from office on a point of personal *principle* in opposition to party policy (against bridge tolls, in 2007; the next such resignation did not take place until 2022). *Barrie* thought it was *Cunningham* who was unclear:

> Ms Cunningham's motion, on behalf of the SNP... opposes weapons of mass destruction in Scotland but says nothing about such weapons elsewhere. It gives the impression that we do not want them here but we do not care about anyone else. The motion criticises Trident but says nothing about whether the money that would be saved should be spent on alternative defence projects or—as is more likely—no defence projects at all...
>
> Often, in parliamentary debates, SNP members claim to be internationalist yet, when it comes to defence, they display the worst aspects of any little Englander approach. They want us out of NATO; they want to deny our international defence commitments; and they would hide behind the skirts of the rest of the western world but promise nothing in return.[348]

Barrie was followed by a Liberal, Robert Brown, an English-born lawyer who grew up in Aberdeenshire. He defended his Party's motion which seems to me, *pace* Cunningham, perfectly reasonable, if a little unfocused. It essentially sought to promote nuclear disarmament, but only when all countries act together. Cunningham's description of it as "weaselspeak" sounds lazy. Perhaps she did not want to be bothered to refute the Liberal argument in detail?[349]

---

elimination of nuclear weapons'; welcomes the many moves taken to reduce the number of weapons in the world including UK support for the convention to ban anti-personnel landmines, end-user certificates and other restrictions on the arms trade and the significant reductions in the UK's nuclear weapons stockpile; notes the position of the Scottish National Party, in favour of withdrawal from the United Kingdom and NATO; recognises that withdrawal from the United Kingdom and from NATO would put at risk 25,000 direct MoD jobs in Scotland, 6,000 more dependent on MoD contracts and 12,000 more jobs supported by the military presence, and notes that between 2000 and 2004 the MoD placed 2,500 contracts in Scotland worth around £2 billion, all of which would be at risk under the SNP." (col. 15694)

[348] *Ibid.*, cols. 15692, 15694

[349] Brown's was motion S2M-2640.2: "That the Parliament believes that the Nuclear Non-Proliferation Treaty is central to nuclear weapons control; supports the universal ratification of, and adherence to, the Comprehensive Test Ban Treaty; regrets that technology in the production of weapons of mass destruction, including nuclear weapons, continues to advance and to proliferate around the globe; supports the retention,

Brown offered an explanation for Cunningham's approach:

The reason why the SNP is raising the issue today has nothing to do with
Trident but has to do with two things, both *arising from the forthcoming general
election*. The first is the need to secure the party's left flank against the Scottish Socialist Party and the black-and-white mirror world that the socialists
inhabit. The other is the need to secure the party's right flank against the
problem that its manifesto costings do not add up.[350] (emphasis added)

The Greens' motion was proposed by Chris Ballance, an English
Quaker and playwright who once owned a second-hand bookshop in
Wigtown. His argument was flawed in the same way as Cunningham's
motion because he took a local rather than a global view, even though
nuclear weapons on ballistic missiles are by definition a "cross border"
problem. No country nukes itself. Ballance started by saying:

There are two groups in this Parliament. There is the Lib-Lab-Con party,
which is in favour of Trident, and there is everyone else, who represent the
85 per cent of Scots who say that they oppose nuclear weapons *on our soil*.[351]
(emphasis added)

This was a common position, which many have taken, but which
President Putin showed in 2022 was dangerous. Ukraine gave up its

---

against this background, of Britain's nuclear deterrent until real progress can be made
on the multilateral elimination of nuclear weapons; believes that for nuclear non-proliferation and weapons reduction to be achieved, nuclear-armed countries such as Britain must be willing to participate in any disarmament process; believes that a decision
to commit any research or other funding for the preparation of any successor to Trident must be first approved by the Westminster Parliament and that no effective case
for a successor to Trident has yet been made, and calls on the UK Government to
press for a nuclear weapons convention to formalise the commitment of all nuclear
weapon states to nuclear disarmament." (col. 15697)

[350] *Ibid.*, col. 15695

[351] *Ibid.*, col. 15697. The Green motion was S2M-2640.3: "That the Parliament is opposed
to the existence of weapons of mass destruction in Scotland; believes that the existing
Trident nuclear system which costs almost £1 billion annually to keep in operation
should be scrapped; recognises that a decision on the replacement of Trident will require to be taken within the next UK Parliament; further recognises that the cost of
replacing Trident would be over £20 billion, notes that communities and the environment across Scotland are endangered by nuclear convoys, by the dismantling of nuclear submarines at Rosyth and the testing of depleted uranium shells at Dundrennan;
furthermore calls on Her Majesty's Government to honour its international obligations under the Nuclear Non-Proliferation Treaty." (col. 15699)

nuclear weapons following the agreement with Russia recorded in the Budapest Memorandum (1994). They were handed to Russia in return for a Russian guarantee of Ukraine's territorial integrity. Twenty years later, Russia invaded and annexed Crimea and fomented war in the Donbas. Eight years after that, Putin ordered the invasion of the whole country. At the same time, he threatened the rest of the world by saying on Moscow television on the day of the invasion (24 February): "To anyone who would consider interfering from the outside – if you do, you will face consequences greater than any you have faced in history." Prudent political leaders took this as a threat of the use of nuclear weapons, which Russia possessed and which Ukraine no longer did.

That may seem like an unfair point to make in connection with a debate seventeen years ago, but defence is a question of countering threats that *might* arise sometime in the future. Russia was nuclear-armed in 2005 and Putin was unpredictable, even then. One wonders how many participants in this debate were aware of Russia's long history and current realities. If not, what were they doing speaking for Scotland on the subject, as Cunningham claimed they were? And being paid to do so, Gobson adds.

Disappointingly, the ensuing debate did not elucidate the position of the large proportion of Scots who were said to have wanted to put their own country at risk in the name of Ballance's private morality. Did they want England to bear the nuclear risk for them, or the United States? Or did they simply want their country to be open to the kind of attack which Russia visited upon Ukraine? Better dead than unGreen? All Ballance said in this regard was "We need urgently to give the world a lead."[352]

This claim for Scottish moral authority was empty utopianism. Many other speakers took a similar line, even though it was open to question whether President Putin would have submitted to the dictates of Ballance's conscience.

And what about China? It did not come up in this debate. Indeed, "Russia" was mentioned by only one speaker, Tommy Sheridan, and that was only because he tried to ridicule Jamie "Sewage" McGrigor, the lairdish Tory who he presumably saw as a class enemy:

---

[352] *Ibid.*, col. 15698

When I listened to the Tories' arguments, it felt like groundhog day. They never change. Jamie McGrigor did not take an intervention as he told us that getting rid of nuclear weapons would leave us defenceless. He wanted to know who would guard our borders. The question that I wanted to ask him was: from whom are we going to be defenceless? After 1945, people like Jamie McGrigor tried to tell us that we needed nuclear weapons because the Russians were just over the hill and would invade us if we did not have them. I do not know what they were going to invade us for; after all, they have enough rain in their own country. Moreover, throughout the 1980s, they certainly had nothing like the level of unemployment that we had under the Tories.[353]

McGrigor had said: "If the SNP got its way, there would be no British Army, no Royal Navy and no Royal Air Force. The withdrawal of Trident is part of a greater SNP policy that would leave Scotland defenceless."[354] Sheridan carried on with swaggering sarcasm:

I have seen no reports that say that the good people of Ireland, Sweden, Finland, Norway and Iceland cannot get a good sleep at night, and yet they do not have any nuclear weapons. They are—to come back to Jamie McGrigor's point—defenceless.

The SNP argument in this context was put with patronising certainty by Richard Lochhead, a "list" member who had been an environmental development officer in Dundee before entering parliament.

When I last considered the geopolitical situation, other countries round the world were not queuing up to attack Scotland… Nuclear weapons are a legacy of the cold war, which finished a long time ago. Children who will leave school after the summer were not even born when there was a cold war— that is how long ago it was. *Nuclear weapons are no longer relevant in our national security strategies… They do not have a role to play in the 21st century.* Scotland has an opportunity to become a nuclear weapon-free country and to play a role in making the whole world nuclear weapon free. In 1998, the new agenda coalition, which was led by the Irish and launched in Dublin, began a campaign to achieve nuclear disarmament. Small countries can play a role in

---

[353] *Ibid.,* col. 15705

[354] *Ibid.,* col. 15700

making the whole world nuclear weapon free.[355] (emphasis added)

The fate of the Irish initiative is unknown, but it has demonstrably failed. The world is still awash with nuclear weapons. Small countries' influence has not worked to restrain Russia, China or North Korea. Yet less than two decades after Lochhead asserted that nuclear weapons "do not have a role to play in the 21st century", we are in the middle of a war in Europe in which one side is threatening to use them, and is pulverising the other due its nuclear impotence.

Perhaps the most baffling example of strategic unreality came from the Green, Mark Ruskell, a "list" member who had studied environmental science and sustainable agriculture. He was especially critical of Robert Brown, who had put the Liberal motion:

Mr Ruskell: Robert Brown fails to understand that the West's nuclear arsenal is built on a house of cards… If we moved to reduce the nuclear arsenal in the UK, the whole edifice would come down and countries such as North Korea would be brought into a position in which they could [*sic*] disarm.
Robert Brown: Given the state of North Korea, how on earth would getting rid of the nuclear deterrent in Scotland or the UK encourage the North Koreans to do likewise?
Mr Ruskell: Countries have lost faith in the non-proliferation treaty, and we must move and show leadership. Countries must be brought back into the moral consensus.[356]

Unless I have read Ruskell's contribution wrongly, it seems to me to imply that the moral consensus of the West must be asserted by "showing leadership" to Russia, China and North Korea. Who exactly did Ruskell think would be able to "show leadership" to Presidents Putin and Xi and Supreme Leader Kim Jong-un? He did not say.

The final point about this debate is that *Sturgeon made no speech in it.* Was that because her rival and sometime friend, Roseanna Cunningham was showing out as "sales lead" for their brand's vote cow? In any event, right at the end of the hour and a quarter, the new SNP leader did come

[355] *Ibid.*, col. 15702
[356] *Ibid.*, col. 15709

into the chamber. This provoked a withering response from Karen Gillon, the democratic Labour member for Clydesdale. Gillon is a religious woman who used to work in community education. She said she was annoyed at Sturgeon's treating the parliament with disrespect by dropping in and expecting to be able to speak without having listened to much of the debate.

> **Karen Gillon:** On the occasion of its first opportunity to choose a debate after Nicola Sturgeon's most recent performance at First Minister's questions, the SNP has chosen to have a debate not on the health service—the issue that matters most to the people of Scotland, according to Nicola Sturgeon—but on nuclear weapons, a matter for which we have no responsibility and on which we have no choice and no veto. But there goes the SNP, once again.
>
> **Nicola Sturgeon:** Will the member give way?
>
> **Karen Gillon:** Nicola Sturgeon could not be bothered to turn up for the debate. She cannot come into the chamber now and think that she can nip into the debate in the middle of my speech. If the subject was important to her, she would have been sitting in the chamber for the whole debate, just like everybody else did. We will see what subject she raises at First Minister's Question Time [FMQT] today.[357]
>
> **Stewart Stevenson:** Will the member give way?
>
> **Karen Gillon:** No, I think I will just carry on.
>
> > [*Interruption.*]
>
> **The Deputy Presiding Officer:** Order.
>
> **Karen Gillon:** Oh well, on you go, Stewart.
>
> **Stewart Stevenson:** I thank the member for giving way. Will she acknowledge that the SNP's last debating day, which was only two weeks ago, was spent on health, which is a matter of importance to the people of Scotland?
>
> **Karen Gillon:** Absolutely, but how many minutes did that debate take up? It was not as many minutes as Nicola Sturgeon has taken up at FMQT on

---

[357] Gillon was acting in accordance with House of Commons practice which is that members should not expect to make an intervention without having been present in the chamber for a reasonable period during the debate. It is also considered a discourtesy to leave the chamber shortly after making an intervention, which appears to have happened on this occasion. It is disrespectful to any meeting simply to pop in, interrupt, then pop out again, as if you are some sort of "supervisor" come to check up on your junior staff whose detailed deliberations are beneath you.

the subject. Since that debate, another two weeks of Nicola Sturgeon telling us about the crisis in the health service have elapsed and yet, once again, we come to the chamber for an SNP debate and there is no debate on the issue. The truth is that, when the issues are difficult and the chips are down, it is not Nicola Sturgeon who runs the SNP but the Notting Hill Nats and Alex Salmond—Nicola dances to Alex Salmond's tune. Issues on which the Scottish Parliament has responsibility and on which we can change things are side-lined. Once again, the SNP ducks the real challenge, which is to grasp their role as MSPs. It seems that they would rather act as a support band to their London bosses.

[*Interruption.*]

The Deputy Presiding Officer: Order.

Karen Gillon: The SNP sees a note of truth in what I have said. All of us are committed to achieving world peace and nuclear disarmament. We may differ on how best to do that, but all of us are committed to doing so. My colleagues Scott Barrie, Jackie Baillie and Michael McMahon exposed the difficulties of a party having a policy that is built on a slogan. I expected that from Tommy Sheridan—the Trots have been doing that for 30 years, and never have they had the aspiration of Government. However, the SNP tells everyone that it is a serious party of Government. Therefore, we could be forgiven for expecting from it today a slightly more thought through policy.[358]

Rob Gibson, the Gaelic oath-taker, wound up for the SNP in terms which reflected Cunningham's imprecisely worded motion. He seemed to assume that the *British* government was the only one capable of introducing nuclear weapons to Scotland, quite forgetting Vladimir Putin. Russia has approximately 534 missile launchers already deployed (land, air and submarine-based) which are capable of delivering 2,565 nuclear warheads into any part of Scotland Putin chooses.[359] No permission from Holyrood would be necessary. Gibson's peroration was therefore either ignorant or absurd:

At the SNP conference, the loudest cheer is always for the speech on the

---

[358] *Ibid.,* cols. 15713-4

[359] See: "Russian nuclear weapons, 2022", Hans M. Kristensen & Matt Korda, *Bulletin of the Atomic Scientists* (2022), 78:2, pp. 98-121. Beyond the figures mentioned, Russia has approximately the same number in reserve.

motion that says that we will get rid of nuclear weapons *from our soil*.[360] (emphasis added)

***

The first test of the new Salmond-Sturgeon dyarchy was the UK general election held on 5 May 2005, as mentioned by Robert Brown in the nuclear debate. The results were not encouraging. The SNP polled a mere 17.7% in Scotland (and 1.5% in the UK, less than UKIP's 2.2%). The Party fielded candidates in all 59 Scottish seats but won only 6. That was one more than in 2001, but it did not represent fundamental progress as its share of the popular vote was actually *down* by 2.4%. Less than one in five Scots supported the Nationalists. Crucially, the Liberals achieved a higher share of the vote than the SNP, who slipped to third place. The SNP's 17.7% was the smallest since 1987, when Mrs Thatcher was in her pomp. Swinney had persuaded 460,000 people to vote for the Party in 2001, but Salmond and Sturgeon managed only 410,000 in 2005. Labour won 41 seats in Scotland, which was nearly *seven times* the SNP total. Things did not look good for a Nationalist upsurge in the two years left before the next Holyrood election, in May 2007.

Strictly speaking a "dyarchy" implies two *independent* powers in charge, whereas Salmond and Sturgeon were far from independent of each other. But with one operating in Westminster and the other in Holyrood, the Party leadership was not quite so close-knit as might have been wished. Furthermore, the Party's representatives in both places were difficult to control. Salmond had once said that managing them was "like herding cats". Perennial indiscipline was one of the reasons why he gave up the leadership in 2001. It should not be surprising that a pro-independence party produced politicians who were – well – *independent!* But in smart, successful Scotland, image and appearance are the basis of brand equity. Everyone must look, sound and act the same. The cats had to be converted into sheep.

Ostentatious disdain for trivial external discipline has a long and honourable history in Scotland. In 1892, Keir Hardie, who came from

---

[360] *Op. cit.*, col. 15717

Lanarkshire, went to Westminster to take his seat (for West Ham) dressed in a tweed suit and a deer stalker hat when most of the other honourable Members were wearing frock coats and top hats. In Holyrood today, some members seem to want to demonstrate their lack of respect for "bourgeois convention" as far as dress is concerned. Like the Bolsheviks, they flaunt their bohemianism. Despite that, the only half-Bolshevik elected to Holyrood in 1999, Tommy Sheridan, appeared for the first swearing-in ceremony dressed smartly in a suit and tie (which made his clenched fist gesture, while making his affirmation of allegiance to the Queen, look slightly comic).

Outwardly, Sturgeon began her political life closer to tweedy Hardie than to snappy Sheridan. As Iain Macwhirter noted, she appeared to have an almost mannish disdain for "feminine vanity", from hair and make-up to the occasional "wardrobe malfunction". However, once she became leader in Holyrood, that began to change. Pressure was brought to bear on her to smarten up her image. Both her hair and lip colours changed, and she started dressing in a more "executive" style, though with an uninspired, off-the-peg look. Perhaps that was part of her disguise. A few years later, the style pressure mutated into "Project Nicola" which has made her look today as if she dresses at someone else's expense.

Between her appointment as Deputy Leader and the independence referendum in 2014, the visual sea-change which came over Sturgeon was accompanied by a radical tightening up of discipline within the Party, focussing on the "awkward squad". They had been the soul of SNP from the days when Party officers were free to dress as they liked and express their own opinions. Douglas Young, the leader of the party during World War II, was perhaps the most awkward of them all. He went to jail for insisting that the Treaty of Union prohibited Scots from being conscripted for "English" wars. He had a curious mix of warped pragmatism and equally distorted idealism. In early August 1940, in the middle of the as yet undecided Battle of Britain, he wrote to a friend: "The SNP must not be thirled to democracy in case democracy should be the wrong camp."[361]

---

[361] Quoted in *SNP Leaders, op. cit.*, p. 150

Young came close to De Valera-ism when he argued that resistance to Hitler amounted to supporting "British imperialism". He made an extremely sophisticated constitutional argument to the court that jailed him, but to no effect. Though a cosmopolitan polyglot and academically brilliant—he ended his life in the 1950s teaching classics in an American university—Young talked at times as if the fates of the Russian and Jewish people were of no concern to a Scottish Nationalist.

It is doubtful if such a colourful, intelligent and unbiddable man would have submitted to the discipline which Salmond-Sturgeon imposed on the Party. His generation believed that political independence should be reflected in personal independence. Today's natty-suited Nats do not. They are not *living* a cause; they are working for it, like any other person whose job requires a suit, a salary and an easy way with ring-binders.

Sturgeon's new image had a social aspect, though of course for a political purpose. No more scuttling quietly under the dining-room table to read Enid Blyton at birthday parties. Now she was to be an extrovert in office suits and very high heels, who had to scuttle across the floors of noisy meeting rooms with the self-confidence of an Alaskan king crab. But the introversion never really went away; it was just subsumed by the requirements of towering ambition. Sturgeon understood, like Hillary Clinton, that if success were to be achieved, she had to shed the cold, stiff-necked manner for which she had become known. The change was an act of political *will*.

***

The only important debate in which Sturgeon engaged between the first and the second Trident colloquia was the one traditionally held to discuss the First Minister's programme for the next year. By custom, it took place shortly after MSPs returned from their summer break, in early September.

The debate was a dull, lack-lustre affair which showed, depending on your view, either that the Labour government in Edinburgh had run out of inspiration or that, in Jim Sillars's "provincialized" Scotland, power was simply not so sexy as it is in London or Washington. Devolved politics are mainly administrative and lack the glamour of important and potentially dangerous choices. In any event, the cut-and-thrust of real political argument is impossible to achieve in a "lecture hall" setting. Consensus politics takes the blood out of debate and, in Jack McConnell's opening speech, that showed. It was almost as if he had set out to bore the chamber into submission. He ended by saying the policies he had outlined amounted to "a programme for a strong and ambitions Scotland—*the best small country in the world.*"[362] (emphasis added)

Sturgeon, as Leader of the Opposition to the Liberal-Labour government, followed him. She started with what was probably meant as a joke. While talking about his "hungry for success" programme, McConnell had said: "I know from my visits to schools that big changes are going on in the school canteen—I even came across broccoli curry recently in one canteen. I am not saying that I ate it, but the kids loved it and that is important."[363] This was the possible joke:

> I do not know about broccoli curry, but the First Minister certainly likes his mince.[364]

However, Sturgeon's first substantive point was one that readers *today* would probably take as the real joke since this was already the *sixth* year of the SNP using the phrase, "the unfair Tory council tax", or variants of it. As of this writing, the "fair" SNP has been in power for fifteen years without abolishing the "unfair" council tax. This was her comment in context:

> Is it not true that 20 bills thrown together adds up neither to a vision for Scotland nor to a coherent set of responses to the big issues of the day? For example, where is the bill to get rid of the unfair, ever-rising council tax and to replace it with a fair system that is based on ability to pay? The [coalition] Liberals would surely have insisted on such a bill if they had any gumption at all.[365]

---

[362] 6 September 2005, col. 18773

[363] *Ibid.,* col. 18769

[364] *Ibid.,* col. 18774. "Mince" can be used in Scotland to denote confusion – as in "his heid is full o' mince" – i.e. he cannot think straight.

[365] *Ibid.*

The rest of the speech was saloon bar stuff. Too much crime unpunished; too many criminals showing disrespect to the courts; the police ignoring this. And, er – that was all.

Dull, dull, dull – then Tommy Sheridan stood up and made a practical point:

> I will be uncharacteristically helpful to the First Minister and ask him to remind the principal [*sic*] Opposition [SNP] and his own partners in the Executive [Liberals] that, if they wish to abolish the council tax, they will be able to vote for that very soon, as the passage of the member's bill to abolish it begins on Thursday.[366]

Late in the debate, Sturgeon emphasised the importance she attached to such a measure in the years before she herself had a "gumption malfunction" and quailed at the thought of abolishing a tax she thought "unfair". Curiously, it was now "Labour's" council tax!

> The First Minister… failed to mention pensioner poverty. That is not surprising, however, given that it is *Labour's council tax* that contributes most to pensioner poverty in Scotland… A Government that was interested at all in fairness in the taxation system or in lifting pensioners out of poverty would have included in its programme a bill to abolish the council tax. It would have replaced the council tax with a fair system that is based on the ability to pay. I am sure that the Liberals would support such a move, even if they could not muster the backbone to demand that it was put into the programme.[367] (emphasis added)

Volumes 2 and 3 will show the SNP failing to "muster the backbone" to abolish the council tax, or to show "gumption" on local government finance generally. In a world in which presentation trumps principle that would be unremarkable, except that Sturgeon talked for years with contempt for all who did not do as she recommended *but never herself did*. Does this amount to inconsistency, weakness or simple egocentricity (the inability to see the world from any point of view other than your own *at the moment*)? Or is the mark of a true leader the ability to wear the mask of command in order to keep the real face well concealed? Is

---

[366] *Ibid.,* col. 18785. Sheridan's proposal failed.

[367] *Ibid.,* col. 18797

consistency, like "openness and transparency", just for what Leona Helmsley called "little people"?

The Minister of Justice, Cathy Jamieson, responded to allegations about criminals and the police ignoring the law by saying she was going to introduce more laws. Her end of the bar was exercised by "kerb crawling", "extreme pornography", "hate crime" and "knife crime".[368]

David McLetchie made an important point about this desire to make Scotland perfect by passing more laws, when the courts, the police and criminals ignore so many of the laws already passed:

> In six years, the Scottish Parliament has passed 89 acts and 3,645 statutory instruments, with more on the way. I doubt that there are many people who think that all that frenetic legislative activity has solved any of the fundamental problems facing Scotland.[369]

A count of Statutory Instruments (SIs) reveals that 2,502 SIs were passed from 1999 to the end of 2005.[370] McLetchie's figures were high, though that did not diminish the force of his point. What obliquely reinforces it is that *nobody objected* to his exaggeration. Probably nobody noticed. If so, that would imply that MSPs had little idea of the amount of legislation the bureaugarchic machine was churning out in all those SIs. They were *passed into law at the rate of more than 3 per sitting day of the*

---

[368] *Ibid.,* col. 18795

[369] *Ibid.,* col. 18800

[370] www.legislation.gov.uk gives these totals of Scottish Statutory Instruments: 1999 – 124; 2000 – 281; 2001 – 398; 2002 – 395; 2003 – 407; 2006 – 420; 2005 – 477. Since then, they have averaged just over 400 per year, with no significant trend either up or down after the SNP took over from Labour. Most concern trivial issues, but a few have important general effects. The default practice is to debate them, if at all, in Committees. While this might be appropriate for "bread and butter" measures, it is not so for controversial ones. SIs amount in some circumstances to "proclamations" like those made under the Royal Prerogative. It was partly to control prerogative government that the 1688 Revolution was undertaken. Today, the use of delegated legislation (i.e. SIs etc.) is commonplace in both England and Scotland. As such it will be discussed when Sturgeon is in government. Suffice it to say here that Lord Judge, ex-Chief Justice of England and Wales, said this year: "The objectives of unacceptable Stuart government are now achieved by delegated legislation… During the Covid pandemic our lives were redrawn and freedoms curtailed on the basis of over 500 Statutory Instruments… I venture to suggest that this reality would have been regarded by our ancestors [in the seventeenth century] as government by proclamation." (Lord Judge, Selden Society Inns of Court History Lecture, 2022, p. 5-6)

parliament.

That fact alone suggests a gross imbalance even in *legislative* power as between the parliament and the bureaugarchs. This must have been deliberate as members were as free to debate Statutory Instruments as they were reserved matters and general issues without any result (e.g. anti-social behaviour, nuclear weapons). The fact that they so often chose to poke their noses into House of Commons business while ignoring Scottish practical concerns speaks volumes for the culture of self-advertisement in Holyrood.

Sturgeon was not alone in ignoring the complexities of undebated regulation in favour of the sort of airy generalities that bring media attention. An example in this debate was her criticism of the government for awarding ferry-building contracts to foreign yards:

> I suspect that, like everyone else in Scotland, the Department of Trade and Industry is absolutely appalled that ministers are so incapable of protecting Scottish jobs that over the summer they awarded a public sector contract to a Polish shipyard that is under investigation for illegal subsidies rather than to a *Scottish yard* that plays by the rules and *delivers high-quality vessels on time and on budget.*[371] (emphasis added)

"Which yard might that be?" asked Hamish Gobson with a twinkle in his starboard eye. Answer came there none—though of course there were two: Govan/Scotstoun and Rosyth. But they were large, busy, privately owned and profitable, and they built warships rather than ferries, including two 65,000-ton aircraft carriers. Their main customer was the British, not the Scottish, government. Public sector project management was not a skill that survived devolution uncompromised.

Almost the only intelligent question posed in the whole debate came from "Snowstorm" Stevenson when he wandered "off piste" onto the unrelated subject of French sex crime:

> I want to draw on my experience from three years ago, when I visited Bapaume prison, which is some 50 miles [*sic*] north of Paris. Initially, I was told that the French prison service thought that there was a sexual component to the crimes of more than 50 per cent of male prisoners. The figure here is

---

[371] *Op. cit.,* cols. 18796-7

under 10 per cent. I challenged the French justice system on the matter on a couple of occasions and received entirely consistent responses. Are the figures explained by the French being more successful at finding sex offenders than we are? Is their culture totally different from ours, or is the power ratio between men and women different in France from that in our society?[372]

Once again, answer came there none. But it was an important question, far more important than the futile quibbling about court non-appearances for bailed criminal suspects, the endless calls for abolition of the Tory/Labour (delete as appropriate) council tax, or the perennial issue of ferry procurement failure. Stevenson managed to leave a wider thought hanging in the stale Holyrood air. How *does* the country of *l'amour* deal with sex crime? But that didn't last. He soon fell back on trusty trivia: "We have heard the old chestnut from the Tories—that if we lock up more people there will be less crime."[373] That was the end of the thirty-second, free-thought break. Now back to work…

The debate was wound up by Rob Brown in his capacity as Deputy Minister for Education and Young People. He repeated a point that was made regularly in the chamber, but which lost none of its force for that. Sturgeon was clearly getting under the government's skin:

> It is also disappointing that Nicola Sturgeon has come back from the recess with her usual ability to turn every subject into an argument about independence—we always seem to come to the end point that independence is the answer to everything.[374]

***

Though she did not contribute to any other debates between the first two Trident ones, Sturgeon did speak on the occasion of the Queen's 80th birthday. Little was said of interest, except the closing paragraph of Sturgeon's speech in which she appeared to devalue the monarchy by

---

[372] *Ibid.*, cols. 18837-8. In 2021, when tenders were opened for two new ferries, the only yards invited to bid were in Turkey, Poland and Romania.

[373] *Ibid.*, col. 18839

[374] *Ibid.*

saying she was congratulating not just the Queen, but everyone born in 1926:

> As we wish the Queen a happy birthday and send her our warm congratu-
> lations, we should take the opportunity to pay tribute to all those who will
> reach their 80th birthday this year, or would have reached it, had they still
> been alive. After all, it is thanks to them and the rest of their generation that
> we today enjoy the privileges and the freedoms that we do.[375]

Whether that was a deliberately inept insult to the dignity of Her Majesty, or just a ceremonial *faux pas*, it certainly introduced a sour note.
Maybe she thought it sounded egalitarian and "authentically" non-south-
of-the-border. A '26er's a '26er for a' that; nothing special, just one of
Jock Tamson's queens.

Alternatively, it might have been an example of Rhodes's point that
Sturgeon can empathise with the world more easily than she can with an
individual human being. The problem with her ostentatiously levelling
approach was that she appeared to be congratulating all the murderers,
terrorists, war criminals, fraudsters, wife-beaters, paedophiles, Nazis,
Unionists *and Tories* born in that year too. She had a close shave with
Margaret Thatcher who came into the world only ten weeks before the
1/1/1926 deadline.

But still, as Hamish Gobson has asked, who would begrudge Sturgeon's congratulations to '26-ers like Eric Morecambe, Jack Brabham,
"Alf Garnett", the 11th Duke of Marlborough, Kenneth Williams, Vladimir Putin's mother, Stalin's daughter, Jimmy Saville, Rev. Ian Paisley,
General Galtieri, the Argentine ex-President, Nelson Bunker Hunt the
silver hoarder, Marilyn Monroe, Hugh Heffner, Chuck Berry, the chap
who founded IKEA and Fidel Castro? However, Gobson also said that,
with all due respect to Sturgeon, one surely draws the line at Valéry Gis-
card d'Estaing the "pseudo-aristocratic French bureaugarch", Allen
Ginsberg the dead "beat" poet, and David Attenborough "the iguana"?

***

---

[375] 19 April 2006, col. 24691

The second Trident debate took place on 4 May 2006, fourteen months after the first. Sturgeon avoided this one too, as she did one on Nuclear Power, held on the same day. But the significance of the second most popular plank in the SNP platform, after destruction of the UK, is such that it should be mentioned briefly. Like most debates in Holyrood, the level of expertise in this one was lamentable, so the refusal to contribute on the part of a qualified expert in public international law was not helpful.

The motion was put down in the name of Chris Ballance (Green) who, it will be recalled, had said in the previous debate that Scotland should "give the world a lead" by preventing Britain deploying its nuclear weapons. His motion this time depended on the legal opinion of two London lawyers, which he appeared to think lent new respectability to an old argument. Once again, no action could result from this debate other than "sending a message" to the British government, which would not be likely to place Scottish interests higher than those of the United Kingdom as a whole. Yet that day three Statutory Instruments went into law undebated, probably unnoticed by the top tablers in their high castle.

Ballance moved:

> That the Parliament believes that the United Kingdom should not seek to replace the Trident nuclear missile system; notes that in 2005 the UK Government reaffirmed its commitment to all its obligations under the nuclear Non-Proliferation Treaty 1967 (NPT), including its legally binding obligation to negotiate nuclear disarmament in good faith; agrees with the legal opinion of Rabinder Singh QC and Professor Christine Chinkin of Matrix Chambers on 19 December 2005 that any replacement of the Trident system would constitute a material breach of Article VI of the NPT, and calls on the Scottish Executive to seek an early assurance from the UK Government that it will fully comply with our legal obligations in respect of the NPT and that it will not seek to replace the Trident nuclear missile system with another weapon system of mass destruction.[376]

Ballance began his speech with the sort of untestable conspiracy theory that kills productive debate:

---

[376] 4 May 2006, col. 25219, motion S2M-3866

The decision will be taken not at Holyrood or even at Westminster, but in the White House and at the Pentagon, with number 10 simply signing the cheque.[377]

Then came the nuclear Nimbyism:

Scotland must voice its opinion on a decision that would make us a target.[378]

Would nuclear war be fine between, say, India and Pakistan so long as Scotland were not a target? Ballance ended by saying:

Nuclear weapons are irrelevant against today's threats. What we need is greater respect for the United Nations, a strengthening of international law and action in support of our treaty obligations. The use of nuclear weapons, the threat of their use and the planned replacement of Trident are illegal and against our international treaty obligations. Let us today, in the Scottish Parliament, send a clear message to Whitehall that Scotland expects Downing Street to uphold the rule of law.[379]

The problem with saying "Scotland expects Downing Street to uphold the rule of law" is that what Scotland really needs to expect is that the *Kremlin* upholds the rule of law. But would President Putin be likely to abandon his gangsterish approach to international relations after being "sent a message" by an angry bookshop owner like Chris Ballance? As Gobson says: "I hae ma doots."

Jackie Baillie, for Labour, asked the right question:

What will the international context be in 20 to 30 years' time?[380]

Bruce Crawford spoke next and tried to destroy the debate for a second time by turning it into an argument about independence. He, too, thought that threats of force by major powers were "so twentieth century" that he could ignore them:

The collapse of the cold war has entirely removed any justification for the UK's possession of strategic nuclear weapons...

Should we replace Trident because two or three other nations now

---

[377] *Ibid.,* col. 25217

[378] *Ibid.*

[379] *Op. cit.,* col. 25219

[380] *Ibid.,* col. 25220

possess nuclear weapons? As far as I know, none of them has either the motivation or the capacity to attack the UK. Should we do it because of the threat of terrorism? Surely that cannot be the case… The truth is that the end of the cold war killed off any intellectual arguments that might have existed in favour of any UK requirement to retain weapons of mass destruction.[381]

Crawford tried to ridicule the original decision to buy the Trident system, saying: "It was the Jim Callaghan Government that struck the Trident deal in a beach hut in Guadeloupe." His condescension extended to misrepresenting the Tories too:

> It is quite clear—and no "facile argument"—to say that the only way and the best way to get rid of Trident on the Clyde and to rid Scotland of nuclear weapons is for Scotland to become independent. It is absolutely clear that all the unionist parties are wedded to the idea of continuing to have this weapon of mass destruction on the Clyde.[382]

Mark Ballard, another Green who spoke in the first debate, refused to look 20 to 30 years ahead as Baillie recommended:

> As for the idea that Trident is a deterrent, I pose the question: a deterrent against what? Osama bin Laden or al-Qa'ida? Perhaps it is a deterrent against bird flu. Nobody has a clue who this weapon is supposed to deter. The cold war is over. *There is no USSR and no more mutually assured destruction.* Like the generals of old, we are preparing ourselves to fight the last war, not the next one.[383] (emphasis added)

With the SNP it was back to independence:

Ms Sandra White (Glasgow) (SNP): Only an independent Scotland can rid Scotland and the British isles of nuclear weapons and it is imperative that we do so—[*Interruption.*] Members are laughing, but when Labour members say that nuclear weapons are a Westminster issue, I become even more convinced that only an independent Scotland can get rid of Trident.
Phil Gallie: Sandra White said that an independent Scotland could rid the British isles of nuclear weaponry. How on earth could that happen? An

---

[381] *Ibid.*
[382] *Ibid.,* col. 25223
[383] *Ibid.,* col. 25232

independent Scotland would have no influence over the rest of the British isles.

Ms White: I said that an independent Scotland would rid Scotland of nuclear weapons and could help to rid the British Isles of them—[*Interruption*].[384]

It is hard to imagine how a serious parliament can operate when exchanges like that are more than an occasional embarrassment. White says: "Only an independent Scotland can rid Scotland *and the British isles* of nuclear weapons." Gallie says an independent Scotland could not take decisions for the rest of Britain, and White says she did not say that, only that Scotland could *help* rid the British isles of nuclear weapons. But that is *not* what she had said. It is impossible to debate with people who deny their own assertions a few seconds after making them.

Revealingly, White copied one of Putin's lines when she said: "It is time that we realised that Trident is here to aid America in its aim of world domination."[385] This was not the only time White had displayed her tolerance of conspiracy theory. She was a Glasgow "list" MSP and, a decade later, was forced to apologise, as was the SNP as a whole, after she "highlighted a cartoon of piglets suckling a large pig with the word 'Rothschild' written on it and showing a bank with a Star of David. The smaller animals were emblazoned with flags of countries including Britain and Israel and also carried the words Al-Qaeda and Mossad."[386]

It was a relief to move from SNP medievalism back to rational opposition to the motion with Mike Rumbles, the democratically elected Liberal member for West Aberdeenshire and Kincardine:

> I wish that we could have had a real debate, because the few minutes that we have been given make a mockery of debate. Today's debate seems to have been designed to generate publicity for the Green party rather than as a genuine attempt properly to debate a hugely moral issue… I believe in the concept of a just war, or I would never have spent 15 years of my adult life in the Army. My war role was as a nuclear, biological and chemical warfare warning and reporting officer in the British Army of the Rhine. I trained to

---

[384] *Ibid.*, col. 25233

[385] *Ibid.*

[386] *Jewish Chronicle*, 9 November 2015

help to fight a conventional war on the north German plain, in which we always assumed a nuclear attack by the Soviet Union…

The theory of mutually assured destruction is indeed mad. However, I am not a CND supporter, because I draw a distinction between strategic nuclear weapons of mass destruction such as Trident, the use of which would be completely indefensible, and other tactical low-yield weapons that are designed for defensive use on battlefields.[387]

This was one of the few useful contributions to the debate. It was a nuanced criticism of an important government policy. It could have been answered, amplified or argued with by someone who had a training in public international law. But no such expert turned up for this debate, even if only to intervene.

Lord James Douglas Hamilton summed up with merciful brevity for the Conservatives. He quoted Churchill in words which apply directly to Ukraine today:

"Once you take the position of not being able in any circumstances to defend your rights against aggression, there is no end to the demands that will be made nor to the humiliations that must be accepted."

He ended with another quotation, this time from William Inge, who had been Dean of St Paul's Cathedral in the mid-twentieth century:

He told his congregation that it is no use for sheep to pass resolutions about vegetarianism when there are wolves about that like mutton. He was right because, for evil to succeed, it is necessary only for the good man to do nothing. I submit that the renewal of Trident is extremely regrettable but essential.[388]

Rob Gibson, a retired schoolmaster, summed up for the SNP, making the confusing point that "Britain's role as a world power with vital interests increases the threat for those of us who live in this country."[389] He did not say it in terms, but the implication was that the remedy against nuclear threat is to abandon all vital national interests and play dead, both morally and commercially. If true, that would negate his own

---

[387] *Op. cit.,* cols. 25235-6
[388] *Ibid.,* col. 25237
[389] *Ibid.,* col. 25238

Party's argument that nuclear weapons are useless.

John Home Robertson summed up for Labour, saying, "If we in this Parliament want to be taken seriously, we should not agree to silly motions."[390]

Patrick Harvie finished for the Greens but appeared confused. First, he said:

> We know that North Korea already has nuclear weapons, which is why no one proposes to invade it to dismantle its capabilities.

That seemed to justify British nuclear self-defence. It is certainly a point that President Zelensky of Ukraine would have made in relation to the Budapest Memorandum. Morality, Harvie implied, did not enter into it, only power. Then he said the opposite:

> I agree with one thing that Mike Rumbles said: this is a moral issue. I get bored and sick and tired of people who say that moral issues in politics are about finger wagging and who people go to bed with. That is narrow-minded nonsense. There are great moral issues of our age, for example the degradation of our environment, the treatment of refugees and asylum seekers in our communities and the treatment of prisoners. Retaining or replacing Trident is one of the great moral issues.[391]

With that, a view was expressed, a vote cow venerated and life moved on. Hamish Gobson wondered if anyone in Holyrood the social awareness to know that this debate was being held on Star Wars Day. That was a Hollywood marketing initiative whose slogan was: "May the 4th be with you…"

[390] *Ibid.,* col. 24241
[391] *Ibid.,* col. 25243

Chapter 8

The Wind Shifts

Something in the Scottish political air began to change in the summer of 2006. It seems to have started before the death of Margaret Ewing, which caused a by-election in Moray. Richard Lochhead won that, enabling his promotion from bureaucratic MSP to democratic one. He increased the SNP majority slightly, though Mary Scanlon, for the Tories, also increased her Party's vote very slightly. The Liberals also did well, recording a percentage gain that was twice that of the SNP's. Everyone's a winner! – except Labour, which halved its share of the vote, from over 19% to less than 10%. Ever since the second Iraq War, the Labour vote had been fragile. As evidence mounted that Tony Blair had taken the country to war on a false prospectus in 2003, support for Labour in Scotland began to drain away. Since the war never appeared to end, this was a long-term problem. The US did not finally leave Iraq until 2011, by which time the Labour "brand" was so badly tarnished in Scotland that it was unelectable for at least a decade.

The main beneficiary was the SNP. Well-known business figures began tentatively to explore the possible realities of an SNP government. Alex Salmond, though still not a member of the Holyrood parliament, began to pursue a smaller but significant Scottish imitation of the "prawn cocktail" circuit which Tony Blair and Gordon Brown had used in advance of the 1997 general election to convince City of London boards and banks that "New Labour" was fit for government. Sir George Mathewson, the recently retired Chairman of the Royal Bank of Scotland (now owned by NatWest), was an early convert to the newly "respectable" SNP, as were other "weel kent" local millionaires like Tom "Kwik-Fit" Farmer and Brian "Stagecoach" Souter.

Soon the follow-the-money element in the press was paying attention, and coverage of the SNP started to look friendlier. Almost as helpful, Tony Blair turned aggressive, describing Salmond as "so politically,
economically, historically and culturally ignorant that I find it scary."[392]
The occasion for that outburst was Salmond's claim that Scotland and
England could separate as easily as the Czech Republic and Slovakia had
done in the famous "velvet divorce" of 1993. The irony was that it was
Blair who had created the conditions for a "tweed divorce", by allowing
Dewar to devise a flawed parliamentary constitution for devolved Scot-
land.

However, there was a positive side to the SNP's rise in popularity.
There was no question that the impulse behind the formation of the
Holyrood parliament was a reasonable one in the minds of most Scots.
The United Kingdom was considered altogether too Anglocentric, and
Holyrood could have helped to redress the balance. Labour in Scotland
seemed to many to be going the same way as the Tories had, in that their
appeal was increasingly to a London-centred political mindset. As a
multi-national state, the UK was always at risk of damaging centralisation. But Blair left the SNP with an open goal when expressing contempt
for his own creation.

***

By September 2006, the bankruptcy of the Labour appeal was becoming evident. The first debate after the summer recess, on the First
Minister's programme, turned out to be an inconclusive colloquium
which demonstrated that. Curiously, the day's proceedings had been
opened by the Rev Roddy MacRae, of Glenelg and Kintail Parish
Church, speaking in the Time for Reflection. For some reason, he decided to quote Frederick the Great: "The Prussian army hero once said:
'The more I get to know people, the more I like my dog.'"[393]

---

[392] *The Herald,* 16 March 2007

[393] 6 September 2006, col. 27237. According to the *Hebrides News* (25 May 2011), Roddy
MacRae, a Lewisman, left the Church of Scotland for the Free Church in protest at its
"lifting a ban against homosexual clergy." Frederick the Great is considered by most
historians of the period to have been gay.

The First Minister opened the debate with a demonstration of "applied Aspiranto", reciting forgettable statistics and feel-good facts, of which the most important seemed to be the signing of an inter-governmental agreement with Malawi. That country had once been a near protectorate of Rev MacRae's church as a result of David Livingstone's exploration of central Africa in the 1860s. Now the Scottish government was trying to make political capital out of taxpayers' "generosity" (nobody had been asked) to the only country outside the UK with which Scotland had, due to its missionary past, an established link. To Hamish Gobson, boasting about charitable giving in this way was shameful and demeaning. In *Todday Today*, he quoted scripture: "Therefore when thou doest thine alms, do not sound a trumpet before thee, as the hypocrites do in the synagogues and in the streets, that they may have glory of men…. When thou doest alms, let not thy left hand know what thy right hand doeth: that thine alms may be in secret."[394]

McConnell was more of a trumpet man. He clearly felt his government's record was a cause for self-congratulation, and was not shy to tell the synagogue:

> Scotland is a far better place than it was before devolution and it is a better place than it was in 2003, too. Frankly, I do not believe for a second that the vast majority of that would have been delivered had anyone else been sitting in these Government seats. That record is the starting point for today's debate. Seven years into devolution, we are a stable and mature Parliament and Government.[395]

The First Minister said he wanted to concentrate on the future not the past, and this involved something he called a "futures project". Such was his passion for this idea that his Aspiranto jumped the rails:

> [The futures project] is not trying to predict the future with certainty; it is about Scotland's place and positioning [in the world]. To determine our place, we conducted a strategic audit to benchmark Scotland internationally…
>
> The strategic audit identifies the current target that we need to aim for:

---

[394] Matthew 6:2-4

[395] *Op. cit.,* col. 27243

eliminating poverty. However, the trends papers show that the target will be a moving one. We need to move with it. The project as a whole tells us to expect momentous change in the next 20 years, which indicates that we need to make choices now about how to ensure that Scotland can compete. That work has been widely published and is recognised as a model of its kind.[396]

The language seemed designed to baffle. What does it mean to "benchmark Scotland internationally"? What is a "strategic audit"? And why does a man in full-time political employment need "trends papers" to tell him that poverty is a big problem? Gobson wondered if McConnell were simply creating jobs for friends by handing out soft contracts for the production of anodyne flannel at taxpayers' expense in order to build a personal patronage network. More likely, he had managed to baffle himself. He was, after all, trumpeting a document which could see twenty years ahead but which failed to predict his own demise in eight months' time. Gobson thinks he would have been more reliably informed, and much more cheaply, if he had asked the Todday cailleach to read his tea-leaves by email.

McConnell went on to say that "Our ambition is to have the best education system in the world by 2020," and he ended with this gift to political satirists:

> The best small country in the world should have the best education system in the world.[397]

Sturgeon opened her reply by saying that the best future for Scotland is independence. Having got that routine incantation off her chest, she reverted to the lipless lippiness that was becoming her trademark:

> I do not think that Jack McConnell actually believes all the scaremongering rubbish that he has just spouted and has been spouting for the past few days. Let us remember, Mr McConnell is just following orders.[398]

She got in a reference to the Iraq war, but moved quickly on to money, which was to be the SNP's main theme until the referendum in 2014. Having said that McConnell's "orders" will be coming from

[396] *Ibid.*, col. 27244
[397] *Ibid.*, col. 27247
[398] *Ibid.*

Gordon Brown, who was shortly to visit Edinburgh, she went on:

> Before Mr McConnell next insults the intelligence of the Scottish people on the question of independence, he should reflect on some simple facts. Ireland, Iceland and Norway are all in the top six richest countries in the world. Devolved Scotland is 18th. Those countries all have higher growth rates than Scotland.[399]

Is it productive in public debate to insult a man by saying he insults the intelligence of others when he expresses his own point of view? This method of debate suppression will become more significant in volume 3, when the rules of free speech and open access to information became tighter in Scotland. I mention the subject now simply to mark it for the future. For the same reason, this unambiguous statement is important:

> *We* [the SNP] *will deal with the unfairness of the council tax*... We will do that not by way of a bribe in a pre-election year, as Labour is doing, but by introducing a fair system that gives pensioners in particular a better deal... People can also expect an SNP Government to stand up and be counted when it matters.[400] (emphasis added)

The phrase "unfairness of the council tax" was used in the SNP amendment to the motion under debate. Sturgeon must have wanted it to be highlighted. Yet it seems to have been for publicity only, not for action. At least Annabel Goldie seemed to think so:

> I listened with interest to Nicola Sturgeon's speech. She declared proudly that the Scottish National Party will "stand up and be counted when it matters", but the SNP has managed to oppose only six Executive bills in seven years—yet it calls itself the Opposition and masquerades as an alternative to the Government...
>
> The public will find it strange that the party that claims to have been the principle Opposition in this Parliament has been so weak-kneed and limp in opposing the Executive's proposed legislation.[401]

This was important in two ways. First, it revealed a divergence between the SNP's rhetoric and its actual record in opposition. Secondly,

---

[399] *Ibid.,* col. 27248
[400] *Ibid.,* col. 27250
[401] *Ibid.,* col. 27252, 27253

it highlighted once again the way in which its MSPs used Holyrood more as an electioneering platform than a parliament. Both were reflected in the Party's liberal use of abusive language in the chamber.

Abuse is incompatible with respect for "honourable Members". Erskine May, whose book has become the procedural reference for the House of Commons, has something to say about the "General requirement for moderate language" in debate. Paragraph 21.21 states: "Good temper and moderation are the characteristics of parliamentary language. Parliamentary language is never more desirable than when a Member is canvassing [i.e. analysing] the opinions and conduct of their opponents in debate. The Speaker will accordingly intervene in such cases and will also intervene in respect of other abusive and insulting language of a nature likely to create disorder. The Speaker has said in this connection that whether a word should be regarded as unparliamentary depends on the context in which it is used."[402]

The *Official Report* in those years has few instances of the Presiding Officer trying to intervene to control members' unparliamentary language, beyond that of Kenny "F-all" MacAskill. But the misuse of debate for electioneering purposes is not something that even good manners can control. When debates are simply displays of attitude, it is hard to see how electioneering can be avoided. But at a cost of £1 million and 3 unexamined Statutory Instruments per day, the Scottish voter is paying heavily to be sold to.

Goldie concluded:

> Most people do not want to be rid of the Scottish Parliament, but they want the problems of the past seven years to be fixed and they want Parliament to work better.[403]

The Greens had their own criticism, which is worth noting in relation to the Hate Crime Act, which will be discussed in volume 3. Shiona

---

[402] Thomas Erskine May produced the first edition of his *Treatise on the Law, Privileges, Proceedings and Usage of Parliament* in 1844. He was a clerk and lawyer who devoted his life to compiling a manual of parliamentary practice. Now in its 25th edition, it is known simply as "Erskine May" and is available online on the UK parliament website. The paragraph quoted was invoked as recently as 30 November 2021 by the Deputy Speaker in advance of the debate on a motion moved by an SNP MP, Ian Blackford.

[403] *Op. cit.,* col. 27253

Baird, a "list" member who did not survive the 2007 election, described a principle that her party supported at the time:

> The people of Scotland have the right to go about their business without Big Brother breathing down their neck, yet the Executive seems content to sit back while civil liberties are eroded. Greens will do everything in our power to ensure that our hard-won civil liberties are maintained and strengthened.[404]

Unfortunately, Baird did not press her "freedom" point. Her peroration began in Aspiranto and ended in pastiche:

> To build for Scotland a future that is fit for purpose is our challenge. It starts here and now. If we choose to, we can build a Scotland that is the most sustainable wee country in the world.[405]

The debate petered out after that, notable in its pointlessness only for a contribution that stands alone as an example of the type of language that was surely not what was envisaged by the promoters of the parliament in the 1980s and 1990s. Euan Robson, a democratically elected Liberal from the Borders who, like Shiona Baird, was to lose his seat in 2007, gave an exhibition of statements of the obvious which could hardly be surpassed:

> The future of Scotland lies in its people… Scotland's future depends on nurturing our children, on education throughout life for all, on health promotion and improvement, on treatment and care from cradle to grave, on the safety and security of all citizens and on their economic wellbeing in a clean, stable and sustainable environment.[406]

Apparently, Robson thought his country's future did not depend in any significant way on the world outside Scotland, or at least outside Britain, whose taxpayers funded a "clean, stable and sustainable environment". This was so myopic an outlook that it went beyond provincialism, bordering on parochialism. But nobody objected to his smugness.

This wholly unproductive debate lasted three hours and therefore

---

[404] *Ibid.*, col. 27256

[405] *Ibid.*, col. 27257

[406] *Ibid.*, cols. 27257-8

cost the country about £600,000, or twelve police officer years, and two unexamined Statutory Instruments. Gobson asked aloud for how long such an extravagant waste of taxpayer funds can be called "sustainable" in English rather than just in Aspiranto.

***

Since so many of the debates in the parliament had so little practical value, it is a relief to turn to one that at least had *moral* value—that is if Roseanna Cunningham is to be believed. On 26 September 2006 the third of the Trident-related debates took place. Once again, Roseanna Cunningham proposed the motion, and once again the SNP's expert on public international law made no speech, and indeed contributed nothing to the debate beyond a few interventions.

This time the motion was simpler:

> That the Parliament believes that there is no justification for the renewal or replacement of the Trident nuclear weapons system.[407]

Cunningham began with the oddest argument in the whole nuclear debate:

> **Roseanna Cunningham (Perth) (SNP):** If we are not using nuclear weapons, why do we continue to buy them? ...
> **Phil Gallie (South of Scotland) (Con):** Roseanna Cunningham says that we never used Trident, but we used it as a deterrent and it worked. There were no major wars between the major countries, and Russia collapsed because of the arms race. Surely it was a success.
> **Roseanna Cunningham:** I apply that logic to buying shoes that then sit in the wardrobe and never get worn. I consider it a waste of money.[408]

Can it *really* be that the SNP frivolity about nuclear weapons extends to discussing them in the same breath as women's shoes? That makes a mockery of the genuine moral argument about when and why a nation might decide to use them. Yet, despite the lame footwear analogy, Cunningham said she recognised the *moral* character of the debate:

---

[407] 28 September 2006, col. 28055, motion S2M-4864
[408] *Ibid.,* col. 28053

I say to Jackie Baillie in particular that it seems craven and cowardly to state the obvious point that nuclear weapons are a reserved matter with the implied criticism that we should not be debating the issue despite her call for "the widest possible debate" in the country…

Either the Parliament is part of the national debate or it is not, and that national debate is profoundly moral.[409]

Cunningham moved on to the practical argument she was making. Like many other MSPs, she wanted to belittle her own country by parroting the traditional Soviet/Putin line that the United Kingdom was not an independent agent but a compliant tool of the United States.

Whom do we contemplate using the weapons against? It is surely not enough to say that we must have them as a deterrent. During the cold war, the Union of Soviet Socialist Republics was *the target of choice*. Which nation or nations now fulfil that role for the UK, or is an independent UK nuclear capability simply to be seen as part and parcel of the USA's nuclear capability at one remove? Recent international events might lead us to that conclusion, so is our target really whoever the USA decides is its target? Are we to spend £76 billion on weapons that really only exist to fit into the USA's strategic interests?[410] (emphasis added)

Ignoring the trivialising phrase, "target of choice", Cunningham's argument was self-defeating. If the decision about using Trident was not being taken in Westminster but in Washington, then the entire debate was pointless—unless the US Congress studies the *Official Report* of the Scottish parliament, which seems unlikely.

Jackie Baillie ignored the "craven and cowardly" insult and spoke directly about the pointlessness of the debate:

I approach the debate with a sense of déjà vu: another SNP debate, another reserved matter. I will digress for a second to point out to the SNP that, in a seminal piece of work, the Electoral Commission identified that almost 60 per cent of people in Scotland were critical of the Parliament because it spent too much time talking about issues over which it has no power. The

---

[409] *Ibid.*, col. 28054,5
[410] *Ibid.*, col. 28055

SNP might want to reflect on that.[411]

She then alluded to the criticism I have mentioned above, namely that the SNP seemed curiously uninterested in improving the govern-ance of Scotland, only in destroying that of the United Kingdom:

> **Jackie Baillie:** I will give a friendly warning to the SNP: the people of Scot-land will soon begin to wonder whether there is any point in having SNP MPs at Westminster. Are the sorrowful six [i.e. the six SNP MPs then serv-ing] incapable of making the case there, where—let us not forget this point—the decision will be made? Let us consider that for a minute. I looked back at *Hansard* and found that Angus Robertson [an SNP MP] asked a question in December 2005. That was nine months ago. There was also a question in June 2005, six months earlier, but I had to look back to 2002 before I found anything else.
>
> Perhaps my research is not that great, but it is interesting that, in the place where the SNP can influence matters and argue for change, it just does not bother. It prefers instead to work through this Parliament, which is not the body that will be responsible for the decision. Of course—wait for it— the SNP believes that independence is the answer to all ills.
>
> **Nicola Sturgeon (Glasgow) (SNP):** Hear, hear.
>
> **Jackie Baillie:** I say to Nicola Sturgeon that I am genuinely curious to know whether, in a brave new independent Scotland, the SNP would view Trident as an asset or a liability in its negotiations with Westminster? Would it hang on to it for a bit in order to barter it away and trade it for something else? What would its approach be? We deserve to know, because I am not con-vinced that Nicola Sturgeon has thought that through. In that policy vacuum lie uncertainty and instability.
>
> **Bruce Crawford:** Will Jackie Baillie give way?
>
> **Jackie Baillie:** No, I will only give way to Nicola Sturgeon if she wants to answer the point.
>
> **Nicola Sturgeon:** I will ask Jackie Baillie a simple question: are weapons of mass destruction right or wrong?
>
> **Jackie Baillie:** The point is simple: I posed Nicola Sturgeon a question but she is unable to answer it, and the record will reflect that.[412]

Two points arise from that exchange. The first is the SNP's

---

[411] *Ibid.*

[412] *Ibid.*, col. 28056

reluctance to engage in productive political action in the House of Commons where decisions on reserved matters are taken. Part of the reason for that must have been the Dewar Constitution, which made negativity and sniping much easier in Holyrood than at Westminster.

Secondly, Sturgeon's question about the morality of nuclear weapons—presuming that is what she meant by "right or wrong"—was seriously saloon bar (quite aside from its being a way to avoid answering Baillie's question). No inanimate object can have moral qualities. Morality can exist only in sentient beings—and not all of those, as any ex-law student ought to know. The rules of criminal responsibility, for example, vary for the sane (sentient) and the insane (inadequately sentient). The idea that a *weapon* can be "right or wrong", rather than its *use* by a sentient being, is so juvenile in an adult assembly that it deserves notice. Were the non-nuclear bombs that fell on Dresden in February 1945, killing many more civilians than troops, "right"? What about the "Clydebank blitz" in March 1941? Was Sturgeon happy with that because the Germans used "right" bombs rather than "wrong" ones? Did she think "right" incineration was nicer for the victim than "wrong" incineration?

Much of the rest of the debate was a rehearsal of the "arguments"—"opinions" would be better word—presented in the previous Trident colloquium. To an extent this must have been because it is hard to develop an argument of any substance in four minutes, which was all the time the Presiding Officer allowed for speeches from the floor. A few are worth noting.

Maureen Watt, an SNP bureaucratic member for North-East Scotland, lashed out at Baillie with *ad feminam* aggression, apparently forgetting the subject of the debate:

> Jackie Baillie's amendment is a typical fudge. Her hypocrisy beggars belief. Her speech was full of nice, soppy words, but nobody was fooled. Labour here and in the other place is morally bankrupt. After hearing Jackie Baillie's speech, I doubt whether she would recognise a moral or an ethic if it hit her in the face.[413]

Watt also argued that war in Europe is not worth preparing for since

---

[413] *Ibid.*

it is never going to happen.

> Nobody has suggested that Iran and North Korea seek to develop weapons
> with a wish to attack us, yet Britain—at the same time as keeping and even
> talking about replacing Trident nuclear weapons—tells us that those coun-
> tries should not develop their own arsenal. What blinds the politicians who
> tell us that with their attitude of do as I say, not as I do? They must be
> persuaded that that superior and patronising attitude has no place in the
> world of the 21st century.[414]

Tommy Sheridan made the interesting, and as far as I can see accurate, point that: "All the political parties in Scotland that are committed
to independence are also committed to unilateral nuclear disarmament."[415]

John Swinburne of the Scottish Senior Citizens Unity Party adopted
a less thoughtful approach. He was the American-born but Scottish-ed-
ucated Director of Motherwell Football Club who was campaigning at
the time for the re-introduction of corporal punishment in schools. He
sounded very sure of his position as a disarmer, though on an interesting
ground:

> The MOD is the ministry of donkeys—I am talking not about the politicians
> but about the civil servants and the military people who drive them on and
> tell them what to say. The civil servants are so thick that they cannot face
> the reality that the cold war is over. It is a dead cold war. It no longer ex-
> ists.[416]

The most interesting contribution to the debate came from Mark Ballard (Green). It will be remembered that he said in the previous debate
that nuclear weapons were useless because: "Like the generals of old, we
are preparing ourselves to fight the last war, not the next one." So, it
appeared, was he. He included Ukraine in the examples he gave of countries that have *successfully* disarmed *unilaterally*:

---

[414] *Ibid.,* col. 28064

[415] *Ibid.,* col. 28068. With hindsight, it is relevant that the Dean of the Faculty of Advocates, Roddy Dunlop QC, recently noted that the majority of social media posts denying Russian war crimes in Ukraine today come from pro-independence supporters or
lobbyists. (*Daily Express,* 9 April 2022)

[416] *Ibid.,* col. 28068

Multilateralism has not worked for the past 50 years, but South Africa has unilaterally disarmed, and Ukraine has unilaterally disarmed. I look forward to a future in which the UK and Scotland join that list. Unilateral disarmament is the only way we will be able to get rid of these illegal and immoral weapons. Let us take that step.[417]

Ballard was wrong about one important thing he did *not* say, but which is implicit in his remarks and which is now clear in connection with Ukraine. Nuclear weapons *do* deter. Specifically, they have deterred both NATO and the United States from intervening too openly against the Russian invaders of Ukraine. Possession of nuclear weapons can put a country beyond the reach of normal international restraints. This was emphasised recently when, in connection with allegations of Russian war crimes in Ukraine, former President and prominent member of the country's Security Council, Dmitri Medvedev, pointed out that the idea that Russia might be punished for war crimes is *illogical*.

The idea of punishing a country that has one of the largest nuclear potentials is absurd. And it potentially poses a threat to the existence of humanity.[418]

Ballard's point about unilateral nuclear disarmament was accepted by the anti-nuclear speakers. They seemed to have no idea of the realities of international relations in a nuclear-armed world. The entire debate was premised on ignorance.[419]

That raises serious questions about the wisdom of letting members of a "provincialized" parliament express opinions on subjects of national importance that they know so little about. Gobson points out that even bus drivers have to pass tests which include knowledge of road signs and

---

[417] *Ibid.,* col. 28071

[418] *New York Times*, 6 July 2022

[419] The only prominent UK politician ever to have argued plausibly in favour of unilateral nuclear disarmament was Enoch Powell, who did so in the House of Commons on 28 June 1983 (*Hansard*, vol. 44, col. 494). His argument was that to use such weapons, Britain would have to act irrationally. He said, "The question we must ask is whether we can protect ourselves against [Soviet] insanity by ourselves acting in an irrational manner." In the end, he conceded that if disarmament involved the United States but not the Soviet Union that would be risky. "I do think it can be argued," he said in closing, "that it is better to have two major nuclear powers in the world than only one." So, even Powell conceded that Mutually Assured Destruction worked.

the Highway Code before they are allowed to start work. Surely MSPs, who are paid more than bus-drivers, should be expected to display an equivalent level of basic knowledge of fields they choose to debate?

***

Given Sturgeon's fervour on the anti-nuclear subject, it is relevant that the eighteen words I quoted above were the only ones she spoke in that debate. She was, however, in full flow later in the day when she asked McConnell a question which is interesting in a different way in the light of more recent events:

> Last October, the Minister for Finance and Public Service Reform set up an independent budget review to look at whether "taxpayers' money is being spent wisely". Why is the finance minister refusing to let taxpayers, not to mention the Parliament, see the findings of the review?[420]

After a lot of quibbling about the status of the review, there was this significant exchange—significant in the light of attempts to control information after the SNP came to power:

> **Nicola Sturgeon:** The question is very simple. Do the Scottish public not have the right to see an independent report on the Government's financial competence and management before rather than after next year's election? I remind the First Minister that he said in the chamber just a few weeks ago, and has repeated today, that he wants to be judged on his record, but when he has an independent assessment of his record, what does he do? He suppresses it and runs away and hides in a corner. Does that not say it all about the Government's record? The Scottish people will draw their own conclusions from the Government's secrecy and will conclude next May that it really is time for change.
>
> **The First Minister:** The Scottish people will draw their conclusions from the fact that, every week in the chamber, the Scottish National Party promises £100 million for this, that and the next thing and suggests that it can spend that money and make tax cuts at the same time. That is nonsense and trivial budgeting from the SNP.[421]

---

[420] *Ibid.,* col. 28113
[421] *Ibid.,* col. 28115

But let us not detain ourselves with issues about secretive government—there will be quite enough of that in volume 3 to keep any citizen investigator happy for years. Instead, let us return for one last time to nuclear weapons. Amazingly, the parliament found time for a *fourth* debate on the subject, just three months after the previous one. Mercifully, it did not last long as it had to be crammed into a day on which the chamber also debated knife crime, the budget process and the operation of post offices. The special interest in this case is that the motion was proposed by Sturgeon herself.

***

Sturgeon's motion was:

That the Parliament notes the publication by the UK Government of its White Paper on the future of the Trident nuclear missile system on Monday 4 December 2006; recognises the need for a full debate to explore the military, economic and political consequences of Trident renewal and believes that a convincing case can be made, in military, economic and political terms, for the non-replacement of Trident, and calls on the UK Government not to go ahead at this time with the proposal in the White Paper.[422]

Speaking now as Leader of the Opposition, she started by saying that "a recent opinion poll" found that 61% of the people wanted the Holyrood parliament to have the power to decide whether Britain's nuclear deterrent should be sited in Scotland. She wanted to stress at the outset:

The case against Trident is not just moral; it is also about how to make this world of ours a safer place to live in. We live in uncertain times, but the replacement of Trident risks making the world more dangerous, not less. It will not help the process of disarmament and non-proliferation; it will hinder that process.[423]

The reason she gave for saying nuclear defence makes the world a more dangerous place has been shown since to have been murderous nonsense:

---

[422] 21 December 2006, col. 30779, motion S2M-5355

[423] *Ibid.*, col. 30777

The white paper's central premise is that a country is safer with nuclear weapons than without. That argument is fundamentally wrong. *Eight countries in the world have nuclear weapons; 180 do not—and they are no less safe because of it.* Being nuclear free is the international norm, and we should be striving to make it even more so and to make Scotland normal in that regard.[424] (emphasis added)

One of those 180 "normal", "safe" countries was, of course, Ukraine. It was made "normal" when it handed its nuclear weapons over to Russia in 1994 in return for the security guarantee mentioned above. Death, torture, mass kidnapping of children, poisoning, rape, the bombing of hospitals (including maternity hospitals), looting and massive physical destruction, including wrecking power and clean water supplies, have all been the direct consequence of Sturgeon's idea of being "safe". Gobson is not the only one to hope that Scotland never has to rely on her judgement in such matters.

She wagged a patronisingly ignorant finger at Tony Blair who had argued in favour of renewing the Trident system:

> This may come as news to Tony Blair and the supporters of a new Trident, but that treaty [i.e. Nuclear Non-Proliferation Treaty][425] does not give the privileged nuclear club carte blanche to do whatever it likes. That treaty was a bargain. Countries that did not have nuclear weapons promised not to develop them and in return the five nuclear states, including the UK, promised that they would negotiate in good faith to achieve disarmament…
>
> Like my colleagues in the Scottish National Party, I have always been opposed to nuclear weapons, but at least, during the cold war, they had some sort of rationale. We knew who they were pointed at and what they were designed to deter. The threats in today's world are entirely different. Nuclear weapons will not deter suicide bombers. In an uncertain world, where would

---

[424] *Ibid.*, col. 30778

[425] The Treaty on the Non-Proliferation of Nuclear Weapons opened for signature in 1968 and entered into force in 1970. To date, 191 countries have signed, including the original five nuclear powers. Gradual reductions of nuclear stockpiles have been achieved since the end of the cold war. The global stockpile reached a peak of 70,300 weapons in 1986, and has now declined to about 12,700, with the US and Russia holding 90% of those between them. Russia has significantly expanded its nuclear force since the first invasion of Ukraine, in 2014.

Trident be targeted?[426]

Where indeed? Despite her limited international experience, Sturgeon was confident enough in her own righteousness to end on a distastefully personal note.

> The suspicion lingers that the decision to replace Trident is more about building monuments to Tony Blair than it is about national security.[427]

Maureen Macmillan replied for Labour saying: "This should be a debate not about the constitution, but about Trident," to which Alex Neil made an important reply in terms of future conduct on the part of the SNP.

> Maureen Macmillan makes the point that we are supposed to be having a debate. What does she think the chances are that, at the end of that debate, Tony Blair and his Government will agree to get rid of nuclear weapons?[428]

The implication was that debate is pointless unless the change the SNP wanted comes about. This was one of the early examples of the Party refusing "losers' consent" to parliamentary or other democratic decisions. This was an essentially "Bolshevik" approach to democracy and is always destructive. As it was, and remains, the premiss of all SNP debates on reserved matters (and referendums), the Bolshevik invention of this practice is worth noting briefly.[429]

Before the coup d'état in Petrograd in November 1917, the Russian Provisional Government had planned to convene a Constituent Assembly which would draw up a new, non-Tsarist constitution for a democratic, federal government of Russia. Nationwide elections to the Assembly had already been organised. Despite the November coup, they went ahead in December as planned, and on a reasonably fair basis. The

---

[426] *Ibid.*, col. 30779

[427] *Ibid.*

[428] *Ibid.*, col. 30780

[429] An earlier example on a different level which illustrates the consequences of a lack of "losers' consent" was the American civil war. The South preferred to fight than to accept any democratic or legal verdict against slavery. The North came round to the opposite position after the *Dred Scott* case in 1857. This is analysed in some detail in *The Justice Factory (op. cit.* pp. 207-213).

Bolsheviks received only 24% of the vote. When the delegates assembled, they were defeated by the other parties on key proposals like who should be chair of the assembly. Lenin immediately understood that democratic procedure would not work in the Bolsheviks' favour, so he waited until all the delegates had gone home for the night, then called in armed Red Guards and had the building sealed. When the elected delegates returned the next day to continue their deliberations, they found they had been locked out. Lenin then formally dissolved the Constitutional Assembly. That was the end of democracy in Russia until 1991. The Bolshevik leader saw no point in permitting votes which he expected to lose. Neil was making an analogous point in questioning the point of a debate which did not produce the result the SNP wanted.

Macmillan raised another relevant issue:

> I am concerned that the Scottish National Party wishes to withdraw Scotland from NATO. SNP members say that they do not wish to be beholden to the American bomb for their defence. That, of course, would not save them from nuclear fallout if there was a nuclear war, because it is no respecter of boundaries. The SNP policy of leaving NATO would have serious repercussions for Scotland.[430]

Phil Gallie for the Conservatives asked Sturgeon why they were debating this issue yet again. Her answer was this:

> We are having the debate because it deals with a vital issue for people in Scotland—*let us remember that Trident is based in Scotland.*[431] (emphasis added)

It is hard to imagine what relevance Sturgeon could have seen in the precise location of the British submarine base. Did she imagine that a nuclear war could be fought elsewhere and not affect Scotland? Was she ignorant of the effect in *Scotland* of the Chernobyl explosion in Ukraine in 1986? Was she unaware of the predictions for *global* starvation due to food shortages resulting from soot-cloud-induced global cooling that would follow a major nuclear exchange *in any part of the world*? Was this nuclear Nimbyism again?

Not long before, Sturgeon had insolently mocked the First Minister

---

[430] *Op. cit.,* col. 30781

[431] *Ibid.,* col. 30782

for apparently failing to understand that "fish can swim across borders".[432] Now she was making McConnell's mistake herself. Gobson reckons that even bus drivers know that nuclear fallout drifts with the wind, and that explosions cause smoke—and big ones big smoke.

Jim Wallace, the leader of the Liberals, made Jackie Baillie's point in another way when he said:

> Few today would be so bold as to identify with any certainty what future threats the United Kingdom is likely to face.[433]

Of course, the pro-independence parties *were* so bold, especially Sturgeon with her ideas about how safe countries that imitated Ukraine would be if they too handed their nuclear weapons to Russia in return for security guarantees.

Roseanna Cunningham made perhaps the most childish contribution in any of the nuclear debates:

> I endorse everything that Nicola Sturgeon said in her opening remarks, but I might have been slightly more scathing about what I see as an international example of men with mid-life crises worrying about whether theirs is bigger than the others'.[434]

She ended by saying that the nuclear debate was also connected with the attempt to deny climate change, a theme which, even then, was emerging as a weapons-grade Aspirantism.

> What is happening in the middle east could be well described as oil wars, with the USA's main interest being in a continued supply of oil, instead of in addressing the issue of scarcity of non-renewable resources. In that context, nuclear weapons become a way of ignoring the reality of climate change or, at least, of allowing the West to ignore that reality.[435]

Christine May for Labour had a different idea of the SNP's hidden motivation for this debate:

> Phil Gallie wonders why we are having this debate—I think we know why.

---

[432] 24 April 2004, col. 7850

[433] 21 December 2006, col. 30785

[434] *Ibid.,* col. 30786

[435] *Ibid.,* col. 30787

We are having it for reasons of avoidance. We are avoiding a debate on any aspect of SNP policy on matters that are within the competence of the Scottish Parliament. Are we surprised? No, we are not…

Defence policy is properly the responsibility of SNP members at *Westminster*. My party uses its Westminster members to reflect our views on such matters and to lead the debate. It is illuminating that the debate is being held here because of how little impact the ineffectual and confused whingeing of the SNP's members in Westminster is having. [436] (emphasis added)

For the Conservatives, Bill Aitken made Jackie Baillie's point again, which provoked Sturgeon to intervene to make her "Ukraine" point a second time:

Bill Aitken: In her opening speech, Nicola Sturgeon talked about the moral dimension to the argument. I think that we all agree on aspects of what she said. She must realise that SNP members do not have a monopoly of concern about the possible consequences of the launch of a Trident missile. However, to suggest that the country is not safer because we have had nuclear weapons during the past 60 years or so is to deny the lessons of history.
Nicola Sturgeon: Does Bill Aitken think that the 180 countries throughout the world that do not have nuclear weapons are less safe because of that?[437]

Aitken gave a prescient reason for his view of Sturgeon's potentially lethal complacency about risk:

Bill Aitken: The fact is that members are part of a cosseted generation in that none of us has had to go to war. My father had to go to war, as did his father, but that has not happened to us because of the deterrent effect of nuclear weapons. To suggest that there is a lack of candidates who might cause trouble in the world is to demonstrate a degree of naivety that I find astonishing. We need look no closer than the middle east, where one country has built up significant conventional and nuclear forces and is led by a president whom we might kindly describe as a megalomaniac—
    [*Interruption.*]
The Deputy Presiding Officer (Murray Tosh): Order.
Bill Aitken: It is irresponsible to suggest that we should not retain our nuclear deterrent in such a climate…

---

[436] *Ibid.*, col. 30787, 30788
[437] *Ibid.*, 30797

Jim Wallace is right that the threat that we faced changed completely in the 1980s. Of course it did: the cold war ended as a result of the firm line that was taken by President Reagan and Mrs Thatcher. However, who can say that the threat will not change again? History shows that events are always fluid and we must acknowledge that.[438]

Bruce Crawford closed the debate for the SNP. He did so in language which would be ruled out of order in a proper indaba, or in a parliament with stricter rules for relevance. He started by trying to embarrass John Home Robertson: "I wonder whether his loyalist speech was his application to get into the House of Lords." Next was Tony Blair, whose intention of renewing the Trident fleet was characterised like this: "'Please, George [Bush], can we be in your gang?'" When Jackie Baillie tried to intervene after he had questioned her multilateral disarmament policy, Crawford said peremptorily: "Sit down. The member has had her chance to speak."[439]

When Crawford refused yet again to accept an intervention, it got too much for one member:

> **Sarah Boyack (Lab):** Will the member take an intervention on that point?
> **Bruce Crawford:** I want to make some progress on the issue of Trident being a deterrent.
> **Michael McMahon (Hamilton North and Bellshill) (Lab):** This is not a debate, it is a lecture.
> **Bruce Crawford:** Michael McMahon is right to say that a debate is not happening in the country.[440]

To respond to the point that *parliament* is not having a debate by saying there is no debate in the *country*, was both contemptuous and aggressive. Taken all together, the SNP attempt to focus every controversy on the independence issue, and then to ridicule, abuse and/or trivialise the contributions of all other parties (and ignore most other issues) had uncomfortable echoes of Lenin and the Red Guards in January 1918.

Before he sat down, Crawford even managed to embarrass *himself!* Ignoring the Baillie/Wallace/Aitken/Gallie argument that future threats

[438] *Ibid.,* cols. 30797-8
[439] *Ibid.,* cols. 30800, 30801
[440] *Ibid.,* col. 30801

are unpredictable, the former human resources manager in the Scottish Office drew on his accumulated experience of international politics and showed how little he knew about the history and affairs of the country which possessed half the world's nuclear weapons:

> In the past, an intellectual argument was made for having Trident as a deterrent. People who held that view said that the Russian bear was a problem and that the Soviet bloc posed a threat. I never accepted that argument, but at least it had some intellectual rigour. Today, however, we should be asking ourselves who the Trident weapons are aimed at. The answer is no one. Who will they be aimed at in the future? No one really knows. Occasionally, when Blair, Brown or other Labour members get into a hole, they start trotting out the names of Korea or Iran or *even suggest that the Russian bear might return*. That is no way in which to properly formulate foreign and defence policy.[441] (emphasis added)

---

[441] *Ibid.*

Chapter 9

Victory!

With fixed term parliaments mandated in the Dewar Constitution, everyone knew when the next general election would be. The result was that electioneering started in parliament immediately Christmas was forgotten. Gobson would go further and say that the nature of the parliament was such that it never stopped, which was one reason why the body was so ineffective when it came to what members were actually paid for: namely administering Scotland. Like most of Dewar's attempts to achieve "a new way of doing politics", this one did more harm than good.

Between the New Year and the election, which was scheduled for 3 May, Sturgeon did not speak in any major debate. However she was a persistent thorn in Jack McConnell's side at First Minister's Question Time (FMQT). Due to the lack of practical reciprocity in Scottish government, these short weekly sessions achieve little beyond political grandstanding. This is "selfie politics" on a grand scale, and it works extremely well for attention seekers.

At FMQT, the leader of the Opposition can take a "question area" in which he or she can ask more than one question about a specific subject for the First Minister's immediate personal attention. At the first session after the holidays, on 18 January 2007, Sturgeon chose drugs policy. However, for electioneering purposes she tried to take the focus away from parliament, and re-locate it in the media directly, where she could expect wider exposure.

After bandying figures with McConnell, Sturgeon drew attention to a "Government decision, reported by the BBC this morning, to

withdraw funding from a drug addiction project in Aberdeen."
McConnell replied coldly:

> [Ms Sturgeon] should be wary about repeating in the chamber claims that
> are reported elsewhere without checking her facts. It is simply not true that
> the Executive has withdrawn funding from the Incite Project in Aberdeen.
> The project was funded, as promised, from 2003 to 2005, and all the funding
> was delivered… It was not the Executive but the local drug action team in
> Aberdeen that made decisions about that funding. It is absolutely right that
> such decisions are made locally. To repeat such a claim, as Ms Sturgeon did,
> without checking the facts demeans the debate and this discussion—we
> should check our facts first.[442]

In criticising McConnell for his unwillingness to play the publicity
game *outside* the chamber, Sturgeon mirrored Tony Blair's habit of making key announcements outside parliament and thereby undermining its
role as the nation's supreme political decision-making body. Personal
media projection seemed more important than constitutional propriety.
Reporters listen and write notes, but members of parliaments talk back
and ask inconvenient questions, as herself was doing.

> I remind the First Minister that he had two opportunities in the past week
> to debate live on television with the Scottish National Party and pitch his
> policies against ours. On both occasions, he ducked the opportunity. I also
> remind him that this is First Minister's question time: it is his opportunity
> to answer questions about his record, not to repeat untruths about the SNP
> that he does not have the courage to back up in debate. Is it not the case
> that, on drugs, the Government has been long on promises and very short
> on delivery? … After eight years of broken promises, do not the communi-
> ties that live with drug addiction and drug-related crime day in and day out
> now need a new Government with the drive, energy and commitment to
> tackle this massive national challenge?[443]

Sturgeon's willingness to put self-promotion ahead of informed debate about public policy shows an impressive singleness of purpose,

---

[442] 18 January 2007, cols. 31356-7

[443] *Ibid.,* col. 31357. It is worth noting that, in the absence of any other publicly recognised achievements, it was only because she was a parliamentarian that Sturgeon would
have invited to appear on TV in the first place.

given the rise in actual drug deaths. According to National Records of Scotland (NRS) figures, the total in this country was 291 in 1999 but had risen to 421 by 2006, the last reporting period before this debate. The following period illustrated the consequences of the SNP approach. Once the Party was in government, Scotland suffered a catastrophic *increase* in the problem of lethal drug addiction. By 2020, the NRS figure had risen to 1,339. The situation now is that Scottish drug-related deaths are about 250 per million, while England and Wales both have about 50 per million. Scotland has by far the highest figure in Europe. The second and third-highest are Norway and Sweden, with about 70 per million (about 30% of the Scottish rate), which are followed closely by Ireland and Finland. The all-EU average is around 10 per million, just 4% of the Scottish rate.

Even in 2007, it was clear that Scotland had a serious problem, yet Sturgeon preferred to lift up her eyes unto the polls, from whence she hoped would come her future strength. In the light of that, Jack McConnell's withering response was understandable:

> It is the outputs that matter; not the party politics that we witness regularly in the Parliament from the SNP.[444]

***

At the following week's FMQT, Sturgeon turned to the voting rights of prisoners:

> Today is Burns day. The bard said that we should "see oursels as others see us" because that would free us "frae monie a blunder". Talking of blunders, I refer the First Minister to yesterday's court ruling on prisoners' voting rights.[445]

This would hardly be worth mentioning but for the fact that, once in power, Sturgeon legislated to do more or less the opposite of what she argued for in this debate. The "court ruling" she referred to was from the European Court of Human Rights which was then trying to force all

---

[444] *Ibid.,* col. 31358
[445] 25 January 2007, col. 31567

countries to give voting rights to prisoners. This raised an "inverse de-volution" issue, of a judicial rather than political sort. Decisions along these lines from the Strasbourg court were later to be sharply criticised, for example by Lord Sumption, a retired Supreme Court judge. In the 2019 Reith Lectures on the BBC he expressed the view the Court was taking decisions on issues which were political rather than legal. Such issues should be decided, he said, by elected, national parliaments rather than by appointed judges in Strasbourg ruling for the whole continent.[446]

Sturgeon made her view plain on prisoners' voting rights even though the conduct of elections in the UK, of which this issue is one aspect, is the responsibility of the UK government.

> Is it not the case that most people in Scotland, me included, do not think that prisoners should have any right to vote…
>
> We believe that prisoners should not have the right to vote, but that if change is necessary it should be kept to an absolute minimum… Is it not the case that this is the second time in a week that the Westminster Government has been shown to disregard completely Scottish interests and the Scottish Executive has been shown to sit back and let it do that? Is it not time that instead of a pack of cowran, tim'rous beasties for an Administration, Scotland had a real Government that would stand up for the Scottish interest?[447]

McConnell's response revealed his exasperation with Sturgeon's re-fusal to take Holyrood seriously *as a parliament* and her preference instead for political grandstanding, even on as serious an issue as voting rights:

> The reality is that Nicola Sturgeon does not want to talk about devolved issues in the Parliament because the SNP does not have the policies on education or health, or any consistent policies on transport… That is why, week after week, Ms Sturgeon brings to the chamber issues that are the responsibility of another Parliament. She does not want to debate the issues that matter here in the chamber. When she does, she will get far more respect from everybody else.[448]

---

[446] See BBC Radio 4 Reith Lectures, part 1 "Law's Expanding Empire"
[447] *Ibid.,* cols. 31568, 31570
[448] *Ibid.,* col. 31570

In 2020, Sturgeon's government passed the Scottish Elections (Franchise and Representation) Act, which gave prisoners the right to vote in Scottish and local council elections, providing they were serving a sentence of less than twelve months. Perhaps because the Act also conferred voting rights on refugees and those granted asylum, the relevant minister, Michael Russell, said it was a "radical and progressive bill."[449]

***

Next week, it was schools. Borrowing procedure from Westminster, it was customary at FMQTs to ask an anodyne question first, followed by the real one. Thus:

Nicola Sturgeon (Glasgow) (SNP): To ask the First Minister when he will next meet the Prime Minister and what issues they will discuss.
The First Minister (Mr Jack McConnell): I have no immediate plans to meet the Prime Minister.
Nicola Sturgeon: Perhaps that is wise, given the breaking news that Tony Blair has been interviewed by the police for a second time in relation to the cash for peerages investigation. Why has the First Minister failed to deliver on his promise to improve school discipline?
The First Minister: That is not the case at all. The reality throughout Scotland is that there are improved teacher numbers, improved school buildings—which the nationalists oppose—and improvements in facilities for dealing with troublesome pupils...[450]

McConnell, the ex-teacher, revealed that he had at least one thing in common with his adversary:

I taught in Scotland's schools when the kids in them were demotivated and felt that they had no hope and no future outside school because of a Conservative Government's economic actions.[451]

Sturgeon had been one of "the kids" who were apparently "demotivated" and felt they "had no hope". But far from being demotivated by

[449] BBC News, 20 February 2020
[450] 1 February 2007, col. 31806
[451] *Ibid.*, col. 31808

Tory neglect, she regularly claimed that her own spectacular motivation had come directly from Mrs Thatcher herself. McConnell's idea seemed to be that if people experience difficulties they are likely to abandon the attempt to help themselves. Sturgeon was not so spineless, though she refrained from expressing the contempt she must, quite justifiably, have felt for the First Minister's limp approach to leadership.

McConnell did have another point though:

> **Nicola Sturgeon:** The First Minister says that education is his top priority, but he said that at the previous election and the election before that, and has failed to deliver... I suggest to him that education is vital and that Scotland has huge potential but, to fulfil that potential, we need less rhetoric from a failing First Minister and real action from a new Government with fresh ideas and the will to deliver.
>
> **The First Minister:** Members from across the parties will notice that, in four statements from Ms Sturgeon, which partially included questions, there was not one policy, initiative, idea or grain [*sic*] that might inspire Scottish youngsters, teachers and parents or improve their lot... Ms Sturgeon and the Scottish National Party have a completely different priority for Scotland, which *puts separation before education*.[452] (emphasis added)

***

In the third session, Sturgeon asked a question which has not been answered to this day by any government, including her own: "What are the Executive's plans to reform the council tax?"[453]

McConnell answered that he and his Liberal coalition partners had different policies, so they were "studying the issue". Presumably not wishing to imply that coalition government, which the Dewar Constitution was designed to encourage, can paralyse executive decision-making, he relapsed into Aspiranto. Studying issues rather than acting on them was, he said, "an open and transparent way in which to conduct ourselves." He contrasted that with the Opposition in an exchange which, even reduced as here, is worth quoting at some length since it illustrates

---

[452] *Ibid.,* cols. 31808, 31809
[453] 8 February 2007, col. 32038

the problem for democracy when opponents do not give each other the respect that comes from recognising that they have honestly-held but reasonable differences of opinion on important matters of common interest.

> **The First Minister:** The SNP runs and hides from the figures every time, making promises that it cannot possibly keep. The SNP will say anything to try to win votes in Scotland but, increasingly, it is being exposed for that approach...
>
> **Nicola Sturgeon:** I yet again explain to the First Minister the concept of First Minister's questions: they are his opportunity to answer questions about his policies and about his record. I am delighted that the First Minister seems so keen to talk about SNP policies—it makes me wonder why he runs a mile every time he is asked to have a head-to-head debate with Alex Salmond. The reason why, *five years after promising to reform the council tax, the First Minister still has not delivered on that* is that he knows that *he cannot make the council tax fairer...* It is *inherently unfair* and it is not based on the ability to pay... If the First Minister cannot or will not say how he will make council tax fairer, *is it not time that he let someone else get on with scrapping the unfair council tax* and putting in its place a fair system that is based on the ability to pay?
>
> **The First Minister:** The truth is that the SNP would put in place a system that would cut £1 billion from local taxation and local services in Scotland...
>
> **Nicola Sturgeon:** Is it not the truth that, after that bluster and waffle, the First Minister still does not have the guts to debate with Alex Salmond and is running scared? However, on council tax, the First Minister can run but he cannot hide... I can understand why the First Minister wants to divert attention from that, but his bluster will not hide that hard reality. Is that not why people in Scotland now want to see the back of the First Minister, the back of Labour and the back of the *unfair council tax* and want a new SNP Government that will put fairness back into local taxation?[454] (emphasis added)

***

A week later, we were back to Trident, which was now spiced up with the issue of Alex Salmond's absence from Holyrood.

---

[454] *Ibid.,* cols. 32037, 32038

Nicola Sturgeon: When the First Minister took office, he said that he would always listen to the people of Scotland. When he meets Tony Blair later today, will he tell him what the former First Minister, Henry McLeish, had to say—that Scotland is sick of Labour's "negative", "extreme" and "London-based" approach to politics?

The First Minister: It beggars belief that Ms Sturgeon is prepared to come here and talk about leaders from London. There is only one group in this Parliament that is led from London, and that is the Scottish National Party.

Nicola Sturgeon: Is it not the case that the First Minister still does not have the courage to say those things to Alex Salmond's face?[455]

In *Todday Today*, Gobson speculated on the intimidating nature of Alex Salmond's face. Could it really be so frightening that a seasoned politician might be unmanned by speaking to it?

Sturgeon went on to argue that if Trident were to be replaced by more powerful weapons "the United Kingdom will lose all moral authority to tell other countries to disarm or to desist from developing nuclear weapons." Though he mocked the oddity of a nationalist trying to save the moral authority of the country she wants to destroy, Gobson discussed Sturgeon's implied point that the only useful purpose of possessing nuclear weapons is to persuade others not to possess them— rather than persuading others not to *use* them, which is the official view.

The Leader of the Opposition had got her MADs mixed up, Gobson said. Mutually Assured Destruction has worked for seventy years, while Mutually Assured Disarmament has not worked once. It failed with conventional weapons in the 1920s, and was a major cause of the war in Ukraine a century later. Given that the US and Russia held more than 90% of the world's nuclear arsenal between them, Sturgeon's implied question could have been put more clearly: what was the likelihood of persuading both the United States and Russia to disarm bi-laterally as a result of Britain's doing so unilaterally? If that did not work and Sturgeon still got her way, Gobson argued, Britain would have nothing to fall back on in the event of global apocalypse but the terrifying qualities of Alex Salmond's face.

At first, McConnell avoided Sturgeon's question and talked instead

---

[455] 15 February 2007, col. 32258

of Scotland's marvellous economic performance, which was totally off the subject. But he pulled himself together and made an important practical point in relation to Sturgeon's sentimental one about defence spending. He started with possibly the most extravagant boast in Holyrood's history to date, then went on more realistically to kick the chair out from under SNP cohesion on nuclear policy:

> **The First Minister:** The *dynamism, innovation and power of the Scottish Parliament* is making a difference here in Scotland, *which is leading* the UK and, in some areas, *the rest of Europe.*
>
> **Nicola Sturgeon:** I am sure that the First Minister will be happy to tell the Prime Minister what he wants to hear; the question is whether he will have the guts to point out some hard realities in Scotland. I hope that the First Minister and I agree on the need to give every child the best possible start in life. For that reason, if for no other, will he tell Tony Blair in no uncertain terms that when 250,000 Scottish children still live in poverty, a decision to spend £25 billion on weapons of mass destruction would be absolutely indefensible? Will the First Minister speak up for Scotland when he meets Tony Blair, or will he just go along to listen to his master's voice?
>
> [*Interruption.*]
>
> **The First Minister:** I do not want to return to a theme, although I realise that members are enjoying it, but it is a bit rich for a member of the party that is led by the Dick Whittington of Scottish politics—someone who goes looking for the bright lights of London at every chance he gets—to talk about her master's voice. What Nicola Sturgeon says about the money that she claims would be saved by not having Trident is contrary to her party's stated position. Angus Robertson [MP]—in London—who is her party's spokesperson on defence and foreign affairs, made it clear last October, on behalf of Alex Salmond and the whole Scottish National Party, that *all the savings the SNP claims would arise from not having Trident would be spent on conventional defence forces.* If the party that flip-flopped on a Scottish currency, flip-flopped on a deficit and an oil fund, flip-flopped on public-private partnerships and tried to flip-flop on higher education expenditure is now flip-flopping on defence expenditure, Nicola Sturgeon needs to be more honest in the chamber and say so.[456] (emphasis added)

Sturgeon was, for once, left flat-footed by McConnell, and could

---

[456] *Ibid.,* cols. 32259, 32260

offer nothing more than a version of Tommy Sheridan's astute observation about separationists being anti-nuclear: "If Trident is a benefit of the union," she said, "it is no wonder that more and more people in Scotland support independence."[457]

***

After that there were three weeks of indifferent performances by Sturgeon. On 22 February, she took as her subject class sizes in schools; on 1 March airguns; and on 8 March the fact that "rail commuters across Scotland are today enduring a second day of travel chaos and misery" due to a strike by the nationalised railways, whose daily subsidy was the same as that of the parliament. Sturgeon's approach to strikes was not marked by ostentatious tolerance:

> I remind the First Minister that the railways are his responsibility and that Network Rail is *funded by the taxpayer to the tune of £1 million each day*. Is not that reason enough for the First Minister to have been in there before the strike started in order to knock heads together in the interests of the taxpayer and the travelling public?[458] (emphasis added)

After these weaker performances it was hardly surprising that, with only two further FMQTs to go before parliament rose for the start of the official campaigning period before the election, she returned to sure-fire vote-winners in her choice of question. These were Trident, the vote cow, and the council tax, the hardy perennial. (The last FMQT was overshadowed by a short debate about The Future of Scotland—again!)

First was Trident. Sturgeon chose to concentrate on the complaint that the Westminster government imposes "policies on Scotland against our will", as if each of the component parts of the United Kingdom ought to have a veto on central government decisions. Gobson wondered whether Sturgeon was aware of the parallels with the Polish *sejm* in the eighteenth century when Catherine the Great dismembered the country by exploiting the weakness of its central authority which allowed

---

[457] *Ibid.*, col. 32260
[458] 8 March 2007, cols. 32965, 32967

parliament to veto executive decisions. Once again, the discussion was futile. Sturgeon was not debating but simply repeating the Party's election message.

> **The First Minister:** The debates about the Tories imposing policies on Scotland against our will were about the poll tax… No attempt by the SNP to distract attention away from that and on to issues that are decided elsewhere will succeed. The people of Scotland know that the SNP now stands for poll tax 2. The SNP will pay for that at the polls.
>
> **Nicola Sturgeon:** Never before has one man talked so much utter nonsense in one answer. I remind the First Minister that the Tories paid a heavy price in Scotland for imposing the poll tax. Labour will pay a heavy price for imposing Trident. Is it not the case that what we have is Labour disunited and in disarray, depending on Tory votes to steamroller Scottish opinion? Instead of standing up for Scotland, the First Minister backs up the unholy Labour-Tory alliance every step of the way. Is it not just as well that, seven weeks today, people in Scotland will have the chance at the ballot box to reject those—Labour or Tory—who would impose Trident, and the chance to vote instead for peace and public services?[459]

The phrase "peace and public services" in connection with savings in the defence budget due to de-nuclearization had already been shown by McConnell not to be SNP policy. But she ignored that—and why not? Who remembered what Angus Robertson said in the House of Commons four months earlier? Indeed, who remembered what she herself had said on this subject in Holyrood three weeks before? Who cares what the policy is, anyway? We are only here to sell ourselves. This was recreational politics at its irresponsible extreme.

Jim Wallace for the Liberals recognised this when he commented immediately afterwards on that exchange:

> Does the First Minister agree that, regardless of what view one takes on nuclear weapons, they are a serious issue that should not be reduced to constitutional point scoring?[460]

---

[459] 15 March 2007, cols. 33277-8
[460] *Ibid.,* col. 33278

***

For the final FMQT before "end of term day", Sturgeon chose the "unfair council tax"—again. In this, she went beyond constitutional point scoring to a level of deceptiveness that corrodes public discourse.

Since Elizabethan times, the law has differentiated between "innocent puffery" in advertising and pre-meditated fraud. In the first case, everyone's geese are swans, which is only human. In the latter, the customer is deliberately misled so the seller can make sales which a more honest advertiser would not have made. The border between puffery and fraud is policed by the criminal law. The political world has not yet found an equivalent legal boundary.

Part of the problem lies in the televising of parliament. It is hard to imagine Sturgeon talking in manifesto bullet points to a forum where only those present and readers of the *Official Report* would be directly aware of what she said and how she said it. But with televised parliaments, electioneering becomes an obstacle to productive debate. So long as the cameras are rolling, few parliamentarians seem able to resist the temptation to perform for a waiting world. Being a goal-orientated self-promoter, Sturgeon grasped that opportunity with both hands.

She started with a question that is worth recording since it could just as validly be asked today:

> A few weeks before the previous election, the First Minister promised to devise "a fairer council tax" system. Now that we are just a few weeks from the next election, can he finally tell us exactly how he will do that?[461]

That was an entirely reasonable request, especially since McConnell retreated into Aspiranto, saying his government had commissioned "an independent review of local government finance". He then turned to attack the SNP proposal, repeating his line that it was a "poll tax". But that was not accurate. Sturgeon was right to call it a "smear", since "poll tax" is a loaded term in Scotland. In fact, the SNP proposal was for a local income tax, which they said was based on "the ability to pay".

The Party's manifesto for the imminent election made three

---

[461] 22 March 2007, col. 33498

mentions of council tax:

> "Local taxes can be fairer. The SNP will scrap the Council Tax and intro-
> duce a fairer system based on ability to pay. Families and individuals on low
> and middle incomes will on average be between £260 and £350 a year better
> off. Nine out of ten pensioners will pay less local tax." (p. 6)

> "Scrapping the unfair council tax and replacing it with a system based on
> ability to pay. The local income tax rate will be set at 3p." (p. 9)

> "We will scrap the unfair Council Tax and introduce a Local Income Tax
> set at 3p. This will apply at both the basic and higher income tax rate and
> will not be levied on savings income." (p. 20)

In the chamber, Sturgeon told those who watch parliamentary television at noon about the SNP's electoral promise on this subject. She did
this five times before she finished:

> *My party will abolish the unfair council tax.* Nine out of 10 people will be better
> off and most pensioners will pay nothing. In other words, there will be a tax
> cut from the SNP, instead of a tax con trick from Labour.

> I ask again, what is his policy to *reform the unfair council tax*?

> I am happy to talk about SNP policy. I will announce it from the rooftops
> if that is what the First Minister wants. *The SNP will abolish the unfair council
> tax.* The First Minister might not like that, but the question for him—four
> years after he promised to make the council tax fairer—is what he will do
> instead. He will not answer that question because he has no plans to change
> the council tax. Is it not the case that if Mr McConnell gets his way, the
> people of Scotland will continue to be punished by the *unfair, ever rising council
> tax*? Is it not about time he had the guts and the honesty to stand up and say
> so?

> Can I remind the First Minister that the *SNP's plan to abolish the unfair council
> tax* represents the biggest tax cut for middle Scotland and for pensioners in
> a generation?

> Can I remind the First Minister that people want a fair local tax and a lower
> local tax? That is why more and more of them are backing the *SNP and our
> policy to abolish Labour's council tax.*[462] (emphasis added)

---

[462] *Ibid.,* cols. 33499, 33500 (all Sturgeon quotes)

These essentially electoral commitments were all made in the space
of a couple of minutes in what was supposed to be First Minister's *Question* Time. Not unreasonably, McConnell objected:

> Ms Sturgeon would have more credibility if she asked questions rather than
> read out prepared speeches.[463]

With that, Sturgeon sat down and Annabel Goldie had the chance to
put an actual question to the First Minister.

McConnell had been right to make the point he did, even though he
ought to have answered Sturgeon's question about Labour policy which,
as his own Party's election manifesto later revealed, was limited to the
unambitious one of keeping council tax rises to the minimum.[464]

A more fundamental point concerned the manner of delivery. Debates in Holyrood are dull, poorly attended and seem to lack interest for
the general public. Look, for example, at the tiny number of views on
the Scottish parliament's official YouTube channel where debates and
FMQTs from 2017 onwards are all saved for posterity. Viewing figures
for some debates often fail to reach 100 after five years, and FMQTs
rarely more than a few thousand.[465]

The reason for the general indifference is Holyrood's evolution from
a debating chamber to a self-advertising portal. Sturgeon understood this
better than anyone else at the time. That was her competitive advantage
in Scottish politics, right from the start. She seems never to have been
freighted with any "reciprocity" baggage, or even the conventional courtesies of human interaction with those she thought she did not need in
her own crusade—as Dorothy-Grace Elder's comments about their time
sharing a room together implied (see above).

In this, Sturgeon was typical of Scottish parliamentarians, who are
mostly indifferent to constituents' concerns. The average voter will

---

[463] *Ibid.,* col. 33501

[464] Local government finance was confined to p. 99 of the 103-page document. The only
unambiguous statement was this: "We are firmly opposed to any form of local income
tax."

[465] For comparison, the House of Commons YouTube channel gets *per capita* three to
ten times as many views as Holyrood, and even the House of Lords is substantially
higher, proportionally, than Holyrood.

struggle to get a reply to questions which do not offer advertising possibilities. Constituency surgeries are largely a thing of the past. Like apparatchiki in the Soviet Communist Party, most MSPs seem deaf to all but their master's voice, and *that master is not the electorate*.

Reciprocity in government is the basis of the rule of law. It implies a two-way interaction between those who make the laws and those who have to obey them. The aim of devolution was to bring government closer to the people through institutional reform, which meant *increasing* reciprocity. However, Holyrood has *reduced* it. The reason is partly the Dewar Constitution, but more importantly it is due to the *character* of the people involved. No constitution can mandate empathy or generosity of spirit from those not capable of them.

A real parliament encourages collective interaction within a clearly defined and publicly acceptable set of rules and conventions for decision-making. It should not be a disguised instrument for imposing a single, dominating will on a roomful of weaker ones and, through them, on the country as a whole. Genuine debate is not about projecting personal power; it is a chance to bring reason and informed opinion to bear on controversial subjects of political importance about which there is genuine disagreement. The general preference in Holyrood for contemptuous hostility over respectful rivalry presents a systemic threat to the rule of law.

***

The final parliamentary debate before the election took place on 29 March. Perhaps redundantly in the circumstances, the subject was, once again, "The Future of Scotland". McConnell led off with a rather unconvincing attempt at electioneering, far weaker than Sturgeon's abrasive performances in the last few FMQTs. This prompted Alex Neil to intervene with a question that Labour should have been asking the SNP since Christmas:

> On a point of order, Presiding Officer. Is Mr McConnell speaking as the First Minister or as the leader of the Labour Party? He has been billed to speak as the First Minister, but he is speaking as the leader of the Labour

Party.[466]

Sturgeon soon started electioneering again in connection with the "unfair council tax", presumably for the benefit of those who had missed her last broadcast. No Labour member intervened to try to stop her, and the Presiding Officer sat mute, inglorious, unMiltonic:

> We will deliver fairer and lower local tax. Unlike Labour, we will not defend the unfair council tax. An SNP Government will abolish the unfair council tax. We will cut bills for nine out of 10 taxpayers. That is a real tax cut from the SNP, not a tax con from Labour.[467]

Then she moved on to another policy area which featured strongly in the SNP manifesto, namely the health service, whose inadequacies she had so often blamed the government for.

> We will treat patients as human beings, not dump them on hidden waiting lists and pretend that they do not exist. We will introduce a patients' rights bill to give every patient an individual waiting time guarantee based on need.[468]

In saying that, she was paraphrasing the SNP manifesto which said:

> Individuals sometimes need to be treated more quickly than the national waiting time guarantees. To ensure this happens we will introduce a Patients Rights Bill to give every patient a legally binding waiting time guarantee appropriate for their condition.[469]

After references to issues like Trident, nuclear power stations and the war in Iraq, she made an important election "promise" which met an unexpected challenge:

> **Nicola Sturgeon:** A democratic referendum will put the decision on independence firmly where it belongs—in the hands not of politicians but of the Scottish people.
> **Karen Gillon (Clydesdale) (Lab):** If the SNP wins the election, we will have a referendum in 2010. What happens if the people of Scotland say no?

---

[466] 29 March 2007, col. 33694

[467] *Ibid.,* col. 33698

[468] *Ibid.,* col. 33699

[469] *It's time,* p. 35

Nicola Sturgeon: The difference between Karen Gillon and me is that I want to give the Scottish people the right to choose and she wants to deny them that right. If she wants to put her point to the test, she should back the right of the Scottish people to a referendum. Let me make this promise: when the time comes, my party will win the argument for independence by building the confidence of the Scottish people, not by trying to scare them into submission like Labour.[470]

Notice how Sturgeon skipped round Gillon's perfectly reasonable question. Why would she not give details of her policy in the event of a "No" vote? Did she *really* "trust the Scottish people to decide Scotland's future"?

There were some other contributions which are worth recording in part to give context to future debates. Sturgeon's opponent in Govan, Gordon Jackson, raised the perennial issue of shipbuilding:

Gordon Jackson: I have asked this question repeatedly and no one has answered me: how will a shipyard that is largely and crucially dependent on United Kingdom Ministry of Defence orders survive, never mind prosper, under a Government that intends to produce an independent Scotland? Nicola Sturgeon said when she was in the chamber—she is away now that we are talking about Govan—that we are scaremongering and she calls what we say a negative rant. I do not think so. It is not scaremongering; the question calls for an honest, straightforward answer, but nothing is offered.

Alex Neil: I will deal with that bit of scaremongering. As the member knows, the policy of the UK Government is, and the policy of an independent Scotland and a London Government would be, to have a single market in shipbuilding. That is Gordon Jackson's Government's policy—if he does not know that, it is his problem. I tell Gordon Jackson that *under an SNP Government our shipbuilders would be able to compete more effectively because they would pay corporation tax at a much lower rate than at present.*

Gordon Jackson: That is simply not true. The truth of the matter is that no European Government gives its defence orders outside its own borders.[471]

---

[470] *Op. cit.*, cols. 33699-33700

[471] *Ibid.*, col. 33708. Jackson's point was true for all *major* countries, like Britain, France, etc. Small ones, like Ireland, have no option but to buy defence equipment from abroad. Neil's claim that "independent Scotland and a London Government would… have a single market in shipbuilding" seems questionable. Certainly, there was not a word about shipbuilding in either the SNP or the Labour Party election manifestos.

(emphasis added)

Jackson was treating parliament as a sort of court, but the expert advocate—he had been a QC for fifteen years by then—seemed not to realise that he was competing in a televised game-show called Scotland's Got Political Talent.

The most common technique for refusing to answer a question was diversionary, Aspirantish flannelling, as Sturgeon did with Gillon. Next came sneering at the questioner, as Neil had just done with Jackson. Neither engages with the issue in point, and both produce better headlines than the dull facts of any individual issue. Opacity was the inevitable consequence of unregulated advertising in the chamber.

Robin Harper said in his spot for the Greens: "Addressing climate change must be the top priority policy driver for a sustainable Scotland," adding: "We will work constructively to create a greener, fairer country... A great deal more needs to be done on renewables and energy efficiency..." He ended with a clarion call. He wanted a government that would "address climate change—which, after all, is the biggest issue that has ever faced the world."[472]

About the only surprise came from the tousled-haired socialist in the Sheridan camp, Colin Fox. His hero is Tony Benn. He had participated in the miners' strike in Ayrshire; had picketed the Ravenscraig steelworks when it was threatened with closure; and had participated in the occupation of the Caterpillar factory in Uddingston after it had actually closed. Once peace descended on industrial Scotland, he moved to London to work with the Militant Tendency in Hackney. His views may not have been mainstream but, unlike Sturgeon's point about the referendum, he at least had an internally self-consistent argument derived in part from personal experience. After mentioning "the affront that the rich are to poor people", he said:

> As a young accountant, I worked on firms' books when corporation tax under Mrs Thatcher was at 52 pence in the pound. Labour reduced it to 40, then 30 and, last week, it was reduced to 28 pence in the pound. I have even heard my friends in the independence movement, the SNP, demanding that

Had anyone asked London if that was its policy?
[472] *Ibid.,* cols. 33709, 33710

it be cut to 12 pence in the pound.[473]

Where is the logic in seeking to entice businesses here to allow them to pay less tax? The corporate elite is already spoiled and does not give a damn where it sets up businesses, where it goes for cheap labour or where it gets cheap rent and government loans. It does not give a damn about the countries it goes to; it goes where it can get the lowest level of corporation tax. That is blackmail. Let those companies go elsewhere.[474]

John Home Robertson seemed more interested in personal status than public policy. He "pulled moral rank" rather as Sturgeon had tried to do with Mohammad Sarwar before her first defeat in Govan. Unlike those lost souls who go into politics "to become important", Home Robertson said, he was one of those who work "for the benefit of the people we represent." He wanted the chamber and those watching parliamentary TV to know that, though he was not standing for re-election, he had once been a contender:

I have been a foot soldier in the long fight to achieve Scotland's Parliament... I was the young delegate for Berwick and East Lothian at the 1976 Labour Party conference who moved the motion that committed my party to home rule for Scotland. I was then one of the die-hards who never let go of the issue through the Thatcher years. It took a long, long time, but the achievement of the Parliament was all the sweeter for that.[475]

Sturgeon came back for another bite of the electioneering cherry when she interrupted Bill Aitken, a Conservative:

Once upon a time in Scotland, George Mathewson, Tom Farmer, Bill Samuel, Brian Souter and their ilk would have supported the Conservative party. Why does Bill Aitken think that those people today support the SNP? Does he agree that it is because successful Scots want a successful Scotland and

---

[473] At 12%, this would have been even lower than the Irish corporation tax rate of 12.5%, then the lowest in the EU. The OECD average is about 25%. Neil's point to Gordon Jackson about shipbuilding being assisted by lower corporation tax in an independent Scotland was based on this rate. The SNP plan presumably was to attract US and other multinationals who wanted to be inside the EU. Their strategy was to beggar the Irish in a race to the bottom on business tax rates.

[474] *Ibid.,* col. 33725

[475] *Ibid.,* col. 33729

they know that the way to achieve that is to vote SNP?[476]

The debate was wound up for the Nationalists by an unexpectedly persuasive speech from Kenny MacAskill. Despite being a member of the fundamentalist wing of the Party, and therefore committed to supporting full independence with no shilly-shallying, he managed to begin with what passed in Holyrood for a light touch:

> The debate started off with the First Minister, who was reminiscent of Harold Macmillan, saying that we have never had it so good… Mr McConnell delivered his text with an ease that was almost like Harold Macmillan's and he failed to deliver [*sic*] any passion or commitment. That contrasted with Nicola Sturgeon, who made it clear that the coming election offers a clear choice between instilling fear and promoting confidence; between looking backwards and going forwards into the future; and between failure and fitness to govern. It is time for Scotland to take responsibility.[477]

Now that Sturgeon and MacAskill are political opponents, it is worth recording that even then he deliberately offended Sturgeon's most sacred cow by taking a measured view of Margaret Thatcher and the "18 long years of malevolent Tory maladministration".

> The fact is that *not all of Scotland's social problems can be placed at the door of Margaret Thatcher or London rule*, and our people and Government need to accept responsibility for tackling issues such as domestic violence and alcohol abuse. As a result, we need to take political, economic and social responsibility if we are to drive Scotland forward in the 21st century.[478] (emphasis added)

He, too, was advertising, but without Sturgeon's contempt for the competition. MacAskill managed to sell his product without belittling anyone. This was rare among the Nationalists. He came across as more mature and officer-like in his call for Scots to take responsibility for themselves and their future. Yet he did so while still weaving the Party's manifesto slogan into his peroration:

---

[476] *Ibid.,* col. 33734. She omitted to say whether Souter, Farmer *et al* were supporting the SNP in the hope of a significantly lower corporate tax rate. Aitken did not ask.

[477] *Ibid.,* col. 33735

[478] *Ibid.,* col. 33736

At the end of the day, we have a choice in this election. This morning, we have heard all about the apocalypse and catastrophe that will happen if people vote for the SNP... The fact is that Scotland is looking for a change. We have had eight years of an Executive that has failed to move Scotland on. The *time has come for the people of Scotland not to apportion blame or to say, "It's all the fault of 18 years of Thatcherism* or the eight wasted years under this Executive." *We must take responsibility*, improve our economy, act internationally in a way that allows us to adhere to our moral values and change our society for the better. It is time to move Scotland on. It is time for the SNP.[479] (emphasis added)

***

MacAskill was right. It *was* time for the SNP. By now the polls were showing a trend that must have worried Jack McConnell profoundly. On the day before the debate, YouGov/*Daily Telegraph* published a survey which put Labour on 29%, as against the 35% which it had achieved in the 2003 election. By contrast, it gave the SNP 35% as against 24% in 2003. Those figures were for the democratic seats (constituencies), but those for the bureaucratic vote ("list" seats) were not very different. That should not be surprising as it was the same voters who were counted. The different *outcomes* in the two types of seat arise only because of computer-based gerrymandering.

The result was that Labour went into the official campaigning period as underdogs. These were the years in which the Labour vote was eroding across the United Kingdom and, as already noted, collapsing in Scotland, largely as a result of the Iraq war. But that cannot have been the only factor. There must have been a more positive attitude towards the SNP as well because support for *independence*, at 24%, was significantly lower than support for the *Party*, at 35%. Independence was less popular than at any time since surveying started in 1999. It was to sink further, to 23%, by 2012.[480] Clearly, not all SNP supporters wanted to break up the United Kingdom. Many believed in devolution only. Others were

---

[479] *Ibid.*, col. 33737

[480] *Scottish Social Attitudes Survey* (2017), ScotCen, John Curtice, p. 2

simply sick of New Labour or bored of McConnell's smart, successful vacuity.

The SNP manifesto for 2007 was called "It's time" and, like most such documents, was long and largely unreadable. It was presented as a joint programme on behalf of Salmond and Sturgeon. The introductory pages had the lady smiling, with her shoulder against the man's chest, and he looking sober, responsible and husbandly, standing with his hands in his pockets, as if jingling the family coppers. The impression is hyper-bourgeois. The seventies had been left far behind—no more sunless, Central Belt shit-kickers with guitars strapped to their backs heading for the hills in drink-laden vans for "freedom ceilidhs" in remote Highland bothies. Runrig was out; "project Nicola" was in. The look was anodyne, bland and very *Daily Mail*. Gobson felt that the couple's body-language "style-checked Noddy and Big Ears". At any rate, there was not a hint of Scottishness in the pictures, the design or the presentation. The mood was political Toytown.

The strapline was: "It's time to move forward." Any readers still awake after that would have learned that Scotland had suffered "8 years of low ambition and low achievement". The remedy was predictable: "It's time for a Scottish government that cares about success for our nation. Nicola Sturgeon and I are ready to take Scotland forward. It's time for the SNP."

There was another 75 pages of that sort of stuff. The length was partly caused by repetition, as if the target reader was unlikely to be paying full attention. I have already quoted the "unfair council tax" and Sturgeon's promises to replace it with a "lower and fairer local tax leaving more money in peoples [*sic*] pockets at the end of every month." (p. 5) Other examples included the idea, which was more closely associated with Salmond than Sturgeon, of trying to turn Scotland into a version of Ireland, whose low corporation tax rate had helped transform a horse-and-cart economy into one of "ambition and high achievement". This offered a non-British example for Salmond-Sturgeon to emulate:

> We can do as well as independent Ireland, now the fourth most prosperous nation on the planet. (p. 7)

> We only have to look around us at similar nations – Ireland and Norway to

name just two – to see the levels of success Scotland should be reaching. (p. 14)

Scotland is surrounded by an Arc of Prosperity. In Norway, Iceland and Ireland we have three of the six wealthiest nations in the world. (p. 18)

For Scotland to become more like Ireland, it was necessary to destroy the United Kingdom. Salmond-Sturgeon said they preferred a democratic approach to that, implying that they did not understand the importance of the "physical force" tradition in modern Irish history (i.e. violence). However, the democracy that the SNP was promising was to be limited to Scotland. Though it was not said explicitly, it is clear from the text as a whole that the fate of the United Kingdom was to be decided in Scotland only.

We will trust Scots to take the decision on Scotland's future in an independence referendum. The choice will be yours. That is the fair and democratic way. (p. 5)

Together we can build a more prosperous nation, a Scotland that is a force for good, a voice for peace in our world… The SNP trust the people of Scotland to decide on independence in a referendum. The choice will rest with you – that is the fair and democratic way. (p. 7)

Priorities include… publication of a White Paper detailing the concept of Scottish independence in the modern world as part of preparations for offering Scots the opportunity to decide on independence in a referendum, with a likely date of 2010. (p. 8)

Referendums had never been mainstream policy in the SNP. The country would simply—somehow—achieve independence, and most thoughts were either on the benefits of that or, in the nastier individuals, on the pain they hoped a separate Scotland would cause to those Scots who thought the Union a good idea.

Before Holyrood there had been no way to achieve an "Irish" result. Without a physical force tradition of its own, at least since the battle of Culloden in 1746, and with no practical plan for separation, the old SNP was really just dreaming. But the new breed of nationalist dreamt of different approaches. Thus there were two distinct sorts of dreamer.

The older type was dominated by people like Hugh McDiarmid, who simply hated England and waited with bilious passivity for something to turn up—like the Germans in the 1930-40s, or the Soviets in the 1950-60s.[481] Their idea was borrowed from Irish nationalists: England's difficulty was Scotland's opportunity. It was a lazy-minded, parasitical approach. McDiarmid and his cronies sat in Milne's Bar in Hanover Street singing "Scotland the Brave" while waiting with drinks in hand for the Wehrmacht or Red Army to arrive and not shoot any of *them*. Like the Irish rebels two generations earlier, they were trading on the tolerance of the British state. Even the founder of the SNP eventually got angry at their presumption.[482]

By the time Sturgeon was emerging from her adolescent political chrysalis, all that was already history. By the 1980s most SNP members had the decency to be embarrassed about their Party's semi-racist past. Alex Salmond was one of the "new brooms" who did not feel tainted by his Party's history. Sturgeon joined around the time he was first elected as the MP for Banff and Buchan, but she was half a generation later. While Salmond was swearing allegiance to the Queen, she still dancing to Duran Duran at the ice-rink in Ayr.

The Salmond-Sturgeon generation and a half represented the second type of dreamer. In the 1970s and '80s, "home rule" for Scotland was a faint hope due to the broken promise of a half-cocked "Scottish Assembly" under Jim Callaghan's government. But Tony Blair and Donald Dewar changed everything. Holyrood gave the dreamers salaries, expense accounts and free publicity without end or limit. The Dewar Constitution failed to structure the new parliament in such a way that it was obviously subordinate to the national parliament on larger, all-Union issues like defence. Since Dewar was a lifelong Unionist, this was presumably not a deliberate attempt to give sectarian nationalism the oxygen of

---

[481] See, for example: "'The Man is a Menace': MacDiarmid and Military Intelligence", Scott Lyall, *Scottish Studies Review* (2007), vol. 8, p. 37

[482] John MacCormick, the main founder of the SNP (see further in the Appendix), wrote about McDiarmid in his autobiographical history of modern Scottish nationalism saying, "I am certain that [McDiarmid] has been politically one of the greatest handicaps with which any national movement could have been burdened. His love of bitter controversy, his extravagant and self-assertive criticism of the English...." *The Flag in the Wind: the Story of the National Movement in Scotland*, John MacCormick (1955, 2008), p. 35

publicity. But he and the civil servants who reported to him did not write the Scotland Act with the same care and vision that the Framers of the US Constitution drafted their founding document.

The Americans in the 1780s were conscious of the Polish problem of promiscuous vetoing. For that and many other reasons, they were determined to have a strong central government and no secessionism. They managed this while building the world's first stable democracy, partly because they were able to establish a multi-level system of civic responsibility. For 250 years it has provided for different categories of controversy to be treated at different levels of government. New Labour was not so wise. Holyrood's democratic deficit is ultimately the fault of Westminster as it made the rules. It is unfair to blame Sturgeon and others—personal rudeness excepted—for taking advantage of Dewar's "new way of doing politics".

The problem for the SNP in the run-up to the 2007 election was how to sell a pro-independence party to a country that was not particularly enthusiastic about independence. In 1997, 74% of Scots voted for a parliament of some, as yet undefined, sort. In 1999, the first Social Attitudes in Scotland survey revealed support for independence at 27%. Although the figures are two years apart, most political historians accept that there was a massive difference between support for *devolution* and support for *independence*. That could have been a serious problem for the SNP. But it hit upon a brilliant solution: offer a *referendum*.

That was a clever device as it could distance the Party from the cranky ego maniacs and English-haters, while still attracting legacy "old dreamers" since they had no other option if they were ever to achieve the emotional gratification they sought. At the same time, promising a referendum *only* did not directly threaten those who preferred devolution to independence. As Karen Gillon tried to remind Sturgeon, it is possible to lose a referendum.

Covering all bases, the manifesto enabled the Party to appeal to those for whom the sight of Jack McConnell sent them to sleep. It could be a "conviction" party to those who had convictions, and it could be a "competence" party to those who simply wanted good government. The manifesto undoubtedly suffered from the attempt to be all things to all voters, but the election result showed it to have been a clever tactical device.

***

For the detached observer of the political snake pit, there is a more fundamental point to make about the SNP manifesto. Floating high above all the salesmanship was the question of style. Was the electorate likely to understand its language in the same way as those who wrote it? The 2007 manifesto was written half in sentimental clichés and half in modish Aspiranto. Each on its own can be deceptive; together they make clarity almost impossible. The former appealed to the old dreamers and the latter to the disappointed McConnellites who wanted "smart, successful Scotland" to "raise its game".

Both cliché and Aspiranto were used to make some important points. Thus: "The 300-year old Union is no longer fit for purpose. It was never designed for the 21st century world. It is well past its sell by date and is holding Scotland back." (p. 6) Other exhortations used Aspiranto only: "Increase Scotland's profile world wide." (p. 8) But there were lapses. The next group of words, presented as a sentence, is not even grammatical: "Taking the right choices to ensure best value on capital spending." (p. 8) And this one is unintelligible: "Ensure that Scotland is making progress across the full range of policy portfolios so our nation becomes healthier, safer and fairer." (p. 8) Can anyone attach a concrete meaning to that? And why does government policy need someone to "drive [it] forward"? (*passim*) Surely policy is "implemented" by the civil service, who do not need to be "driven forward" like a mutinous army?

And all that is just in the first eight pages. There were another *sixty-eight* to go. Even on page 63 we are still being told that "government will *drive forward* this important area of reform." I will spare the reader any more linguistic pain. It is a phenomenon which afflicts all mainstream parties. Perhaps for that reason, the Green Party manifesto did not use the phrase "drive forward" once. It was a more literate effort than the others and, by the graces of God and Robin Harper, *shorter*, being a mere 28 pages.

Tommy Sheridan's Socialists produced a document that was longer (57 pages), and which contained some preposterous ideas. But at least it conveyed the impression of having been written by educated people rather than by corporate froth salesmen. Most of the sentences began with the nominative, went on with the verb and ended with the accusative, as Lord Palmerston once said Foreign Office cables should. More importantly, it presented coherent *arguments* that the sentient voter could consider. If you ignore the actual policies, it was a more serious political document than any of the others. It certainly treated voters as intelligent adults with whom the authors were genuinely trying to connect. Perhaps that is why the Socialists did so badly in the election.[483]

Another serious presentation of "off-consensus" views came from UKIP, the United Kingdom Independence Party. It was the new kid on the block, catering to the anti-bureaucratic wing of conservative Britain. They won the manifesto stakes with an offering which was neatly presented, literate and *only four pages long*! This was their key point:

Sack all 129 Members of the Scottish Parliament and replace them with MPs. Most Scots agree devolution has been disappointing and expensive. Scotland has 59 members of the British parliament (MPs), 129 MSPs, 7 MEPs and 1000s of councillors. Scotland doesn't need all these costly politicians. Our policy is to have the British Westminster parliament meet for three weeks out of four to debate law that applies to the whole of Britain. Then, in the fourth week, the 59 Scottish MPs come home to attend to Scottish-only business in the Scottish Parliament – with the Welsh and Northern Irish doing similarly, and English MPs staying in Westminster to debate law that only applies to England in an "English Parliament". We will sack all 129 MSPs and replace them with our Westminster MPs, sitting in Edinburgh on Scottish matters. This will solve the "West Lothian" question, and streamline the Scottish Parliament, with the potential to save millions of pounds each year. (emphasis in original)

By contrast with UKIP, the Labour manifesto was as robotically written as the SNP one. It was just as repetitive, just as meretricious and even longer (103 pages). Hamish Gobson discussed the phenomenon of

---

[483] Another factor might have been the "swinging sauna" case which was by then in the news. The allegation was that Tommy Sheridan had visited expensively exotic establishments in Manchester which no Scottish socialist should have any desire to spend money in. Party strife erupted after the puritans revolted. Sheridan was sacked from his own organisation and has not managed to make a successful return to politics.

verbal "more-ism" in *Todday Today*. He thought there might be two reasons for this. The Labour-SNP diarchy might have fallen for the Goebbels method of propagandising, which is to take a simple message and say it over, and over, and over again hoping to browbeat the electorate. Alternatively, they understood the salesman's timeless motto: "If you don't know what you're talking about, keep talking." Whatever the reason, the result was that, unlike the Greens, the Socialists and UKIP, the two main parties were selling a predictable mix of fake principle (Aspiranto), false hope (sentimental cliché) and modish hot air (the over-designed package).

Retrospective evidence for that view and, incidentally, for the intelligence of the average Scottish voter, came on election day when turnout was a dismal 52%—far below the average of around 70% which is normal for UK elections in Scotland (though it was generally lower under New Labour). This was not far above the sham, fully-bureaucratic elections held for the European Parliament. For those, the turnout in Scotland is closer to 30%.[484]

***

The election has been well covered elsewhere, and in any case is peripheral to this story except for the result, which is central. In short, the SNP won a close contest, beating Labour by one seat, though without achieving anything close to an overall majority.

Sturgeon finally managed, at the third attempt, to take Govan from Gordon Jackson. Now she was a fully democratic member of the parliament, not just a bureaucratic also-ran, admitted to the chamber by the grace of Donald Dewar's losers' lifeline. The fact that her majority was slender (744, about 3%) did not make any difference. It was an important result for Sturgeon personally. This was her first outright victory in a public election. Now that she had real constituents she was no longer at the mercy of the men in grey kilts.

---

[484] Turnout in Holyrood elections in this period were: 1999 – 59%; 2003 – 49%; 2007 – 52%; 2011 – 50%. The turnout for European Parliament elections in this period were: 1999 – 25%; 2004 – 31%; 2009 – 29%.

Labour won 46 seats as against the SNP's 47 (of 129). That was ago-nisingly close for McConnell, but sweetly significant for Salmond-Stur-geon. The agony for Labour was compounded by the fact that in the "democratic" seats, they won 37 to the SNP's 21. *It was the computer which changed the picture.* The d'Hondt formula was applied to "list" or party votes and the computers awarded Labour 9 such seats, and the SNP 26. The popular vote for these seats favoured the SNP over Labour, but only by a tiny margin. The SNP won 31% of the vote in "the bureau-cratic handicap", while Labour won 29%. The computer took that 2% difference and transformed it into 15 seats, or nearly 30% of the 56 "list" seats. That was not proportional representation, which would have taken a 2% difference in party votes and turned it into a 2% difference in seats, giving victory to Labour. It was a form of vote theft, organised by Don-ald Dewar in the hope of keeping Labour in power in Scotland forever.

The fact that Labour won the constituencies, of which there were 73, but lost in the party-managed seats, of which there were only 56, yet lost the election overall, shows how flawed the Dewar Constitution was, even in its own terms: it devalued voters' choices but without either cre-ating consensus or shutting out the Nationalists. The voting system un-dermined the parliament by devaluing individual constituency represen-tation in order to achieve what might be called a "national party plebi-scite". In both categories of seat taken together, Labour received a total of 1,242,789 votes (constituency plus "list"), while the SNP received 1,297,838 on the same basis. The SNP won a quasi-referendum on which party should govern, albeit very narrowly.

This was a "presidential" approach, which meant that there was *only* a national issue. Constituencies were down-graded, and local issues bur-ied. In terms of the founding principles which Dewar wanted to embody in his new parliament—access and participation, equal opportunities, ac-countability and power-sharing—the past was the past. Smart, successful Scotland was moving into one-dimensional politics—are you "yes" or are you "no"? Subtlety, shades of opinion, measured disagreement and the freedom to reserve judgement were all victims of this new, cartoon-ish reality. The only position which mattered was that of the First Min-ister. Parliament, as the body which chooses the government then mon-itors its performance in office, was becoming passé and increasingly

powerless. Scotland was being reduced to a constitutional binary in a
concealed betrayal of those who voted for the parliament in 1997 in
hopes of reducing the "democratic deficit". The Dewar Constitution has
actually *increased* it.

***

Despite the questionable result, the Queen's business had to continue, so a government needed to be formed. Though the SNP was the
largest party, it fell 18 seats short of an overall majority. A deal had to be
done. Salmond tried to form a coalition with the Liberals, but that fell
apart on their absolute refusal to agree to an independence referendum.

The Greens were more biddable, perhaps because they were so much
weaker. The Party had received 4% of the bureaucratic vote, and 0.1%
(2,971 votes in total) in the democratic seats. But the computer had
awarded them 2 seats (down from 7 in 2003) so they were in a position
to offer some limited co-operation in government. Their manifesto was,
due to its literate style, admirably clear on the independence issue: "The
only way to determine Scotland's constitutional future is by referendum,
because only a referendum allows a clear choice on a constitutional matter that often crosses party divides." (p. 24)

The SNP decided they would try to form a minority government in
partnership with the Greens. Parliament reconvened on 9 May for what
is formally referred to as the "third session" of the parliament (2007-
2011). All members swore their oaths of allegiance, or made non-religious "affirmations" to that effect. Roseanna Cunningham held to the
radical line and made her solemn affirmation "under protest".[485] Elaine
Smith, a Catholic pro-lifer from Lanarkshire who objected to same-sex
marriage on the ground that it would open the way to polygamy, made
a longer statement:

> Before taking the oath, I state that I believe that the people of Scotland
> should be citizens, not subjects, and hold firmly that my allegiance should
> be first and foremost to them. However, I recognise that to serve my con-
> stituents in the Parliament I must meet the legal requirement of taking the

---

[485] 9 May 2007, col. 2

oath and will, therefore, do so.[486]

However, what had been a torrent of constitutional questioning before the oath-taking four years earlier had almost completely died down. It is notable that the breaker of nations did not repeat her protest of 2003.

On 14 May parliament assembled to elect a Presiding Officer. George Reid, as the outgoing incumbent, made a farewell speech and then held the election for his successor. There were two candidates, Alex Fergusson and Margo MacDonald. MacDonald was well known nationally, while Fergusson less so. He was a largely a-political, Old Etonian Tory, originally from Wigtownshire, who farmed in the hills of south Ayrshire and was the democratic member for Galloway and Upper Nithsdale.[487]

He must have been widely trusted as he won by a large margin, beating the ex-SNP firebrand by 108 votes to 20. More than half of the Nationalist members must have voted for him (the ballot was secret and therefore could not be monitored by the party whips). If so, it shows the spirit of vengefulness which the SNP shares with President Putin. People who change their minds are not renegade old comrades but *traitors* who "betrayed" the Party. They would rather elect a Tory enemy than a strong sympathiser who had successfully defied their clannish authority to sit as an Independent. Gobson thought it made them look more like gangsters than politicians.

The new Presiding Officer made a speech of acceptance, in which he said he would "reluctantly suspend my party allegiance for as long as I serve in this office". All the party leaders made handsome speeches of congratulation.

---

[486] *Ibid.,* col. 6. The only other entertainment came from Brian Adam, Maureen Watt and Dave Thompson, who took the oath and then repeated it in "Doric". Thompson also repeated it in Gaelic, as did Alastair Allen, Rob Gibson and John Farquhar Munro. Bashir Ahmad repeated it in Urdu, and Michael Russell repeated it in Gaelic and "Scots". All were SNP except Munro, a Liberal. Significantly, he was the only one of the Gaelic repeaters who was a native speaker. For the others, it was a political affectation as they were more at home in English than the language of saints and scholars.

[487] Fergusson was the son of a Colonel in the Argylls who became a Church of Scotland Minister in later life. First elected in 1999, he was one of the proposers of the non-denominational Time for Reflection, which begins each parliamentary week. He retired from politics in 2015, was knighted in 2016 and died in 2018.

Two days later, the election was held for First Minister. The nominations, in alphabetical order, were Annabel Goldie (Conservative), Jack McConnell, Alex Salmond and Nicol Stephen (Liberal). They each made a short speech. Though she had no realistic hope of being elected, Goldie still said something substantial, concentrating on the dangers of consensus politics.

> For the past eight years, the political regime has been characterised by a condition that some may argue was consensus, but which, to others, was cosiness. It was an incumbency where the ruling politicians felt in control, unchallenged in their political administration. Consensus had become complacency.[488]

After mentioning "the charade of a contrived consensus", Goldie made a plea for reciprocity in government which is even more relevant today than it was in those distant days when MSPs still routinely answered constituents' letters and treated them as legitimate stakeholders in national politics.

> Every MSP in this Parliament must respect the voters, who have had enough of posturing, politicking and process and who, instead, want policy, purpose and progress.[489]

McConnell spoke next, still officially being the First Minister. Unfortunately, his speech concentrated on the achievements of the Labour Party, and which policies he would support or otherwise in the new parliament. It was not much of an improvement on his election manifesto.

Then Salmond had his chance. He took a generous line, praising Donald Dewar—a Unionist!—but observing that this was the first election Labour had lost in Scotland in fifty years. Then he made a point which, like Goldie's, is even more relevant today than it was then:

> This is not Westminster. This Parliament is a proportional Parliament. It is a Parliament of minorities where no one party rules without compromise or concession. The SNP believes that we have the moral authority to govern, but we have no arbitrary authority over this Parliament. The Parliament will be one in which the Scottish Government relies on the merits of its

---

[488] 16 May 2007, col. 20
[489] *Ibid.,* col. 22

legislation, not the might of a parliamentary majority. The Parliament will be about compromise and concession, intelligent debate and mature discussion.

That is no accident. If we look back, we see that it is precisely the Parliament that the consultative steering group—the founding fathers of this place—envisaged…

The days of Scottish Government imposing its will on the Parliament are behind us… My commitment today is to reach across the parties and try to build a majority, issue by issue, on the things that matter to the people of Scotland. I will do so through necessity, certainly, but also through a genuine belief that it is the right and best way to govern Scotland.[490]

Nicol Stephen talked politics rather than principle. He started off with the rail line to Edinburgh airport, as if that was relevant to the business of the day, then got onto business rates, university funding and renewable energy. Seemingly, no party controller had thought to flick the switch that told him that the election was over.

Goldie and Stephen were eliminated in the first ballot, and Salmond beat McConnell in the second. However, he won narrowly, by 49 to 46, as there were no fewer than 33 abstentions. Depressingly, *every* vote was cast along party lines. All the Conservatives and Liberals abstained, as did Margo MacDonald, and the two Green members voted for Salmond. If party allegiance really was the only determinant, the election was pointless. They might just as well have done the arithmetic on the back of an envelope and retired to the pub for the afternoon.

After due congratulations from Goldie, McConnell and Stephen, Salmond made a short victory speech returning their good wishes in statesmanlike terms. The new First Minister reminded Goldie that he had recently proposed a toast to her at the Glasgow Scouts and Guides Burns Supper and commented on the "excellence" of her reply. It was so good that he said, "I was sorely tempted to vote for her today—tempted, but not seduced." He thanked Stephen for a "typically gracious" speech of congratulation and wished Jack McConnell and Bridget, his wife, "every good wish for the future".

He also introduced a personal note:

---

[490] *Ibid.,* cols. 24, 25

As Annabel [Goldie] pointed out, my wife Moira and my wee sister Gail are
in the gallery today—I say to Annabel that it is a good job that my big sister
is no here—and I thank them and the rest of my family for their support.
My dad is also here. My father has never seen me in a parliamentary chamber, because he has always refused to set foot in the Palace of Westminster.[491]

Then he referred to the election of Scotland's first Asian member of
parliament:

In 1961, Bashir Ahmad came to Glasgow to drive buses. In 1961, the very
idea of a Scottish Parliament was unimaginable. In 1961, the idea of a Scots
Asian sitting in a Scots Parliament was doubly unimaginable, but Bashir is
here and we are here. That part of the community of Scotland is now woven
into the Parliament's tartan and we are much stronger as a result. We are
therefore diverse, not divided.[492]

Salmond ended on a generous and constructive note which nonetheless appeared to acknowledge the fell power of the bureaugarchy:

All of us in the Parliament have a responsibility to conduct ourselves in a
way that respects the Parliament that the people have chosen to elect. That
will take patience, maturity and leadership on all sides of the chamber. My
pledge to the Parliament today is that *any Scottish Government that is led by me
will respect and include the Parliament in the governance of Scotland* over the next four
years.[493] (emphasis added)

The same day, Sturgeon was appointed Cabinet Secretary—a new
formulation, replacing that of "Minister"—for Health and Wellbeing.
Far more importantly, she became Deputy First Minister.

Twenty years earlier, she had still been at school. It was a meteoric
rise. She was soon to overtake Dunlop as the most famous old Dreg-
hornian. Despite her private reticence, she had developed a hard shell
and effective camouflage. Her unbendable resolve was reinforced by
success. Though she still hated the Iron Lady and all she stood for, the
Iron *Woman* now had her hands—Gobson would say "claws"—on the

---

[491] *Ibid.,* col. 34
[492] *Ibid.,* col. 35
[493] *Ibid.,* col. 36

levers of power. Would Scotland be the main beneficiary, or would she?

Either way, Gobson hoped in print that she would rise to the challenges of high office and "transcend her genre", in a way that the early SNP had never been able to do. At least, that was the view of Compton Mackenzie who helped found the Party. In the early 1940s, when Europe was descending into the bloodiest war in its history, the future author of *Whisky Galore* viewed events from the music-filled library of his large house above the Traigh Mhor on the isle of Barra. He realised that he had lost interest in the SNP. The reason is relevant to this story:

> The politicians had pushed aside the dreamers… The clash of utopian aspiration was silenced, and for a generation Monty [i.e. Mackenzie] watched the party he had helped to found become *a platform for the ideas of small-town politicians*. Henceforth he would restrict himself to Barra affairs.[494] (emphasis added)

Was Sturgeon's future as Deputy First Minister to be "small-town", or would she retain some trace elements of the "utopian aspiration" which had attracted her to politics as a schoolgirl in 1987?

---

[494] *Compton Mackenzie: a Life*, Andro Linklater (1987), p. 282

Appendix

Popular *versus* parliamentary sovereignty

For nearly a century, the most important constitutional claim of nationalist politicians in Scotland has been that Scotland is superior to England in that it has an ancient tradition of "popular sovereignty" which is fundamentally different from the principle of "parliamentary sovereignty" that is the basis of Westminster governance. Such ideas lay at the root of both the Constitutional Convention, which cleared the ground for establishment of the Holyrood parliament, and the SNP's campaigning arguments for ridding Scotland of the curse of an allegedly alien approach to national decision-making. Nicola Sturgeon made the point herself while being sworn in as an MSP for the 2003-7 session of parliament (see above). It will therefore be helpful to clarify the issue by rehearsing briefly the relevant history. But first, some clarity on the word "sovereignty" is needed.

Sovereignty

Before sovereignty there was ownership, which evolved when settled communities of agriculturalists replaced hunter-gatherers and nomadic pastoralists. Powerful men took land into their possession and control, along with the people who lived on it, augmented by enslaved war captives. Ever larger societies evolved, culminating in the Roman Empire. Rome achieved peace through conquest and exercised what we now call sovereignty, though it took over a thousand years for the word to be used commonly in a constitutional context.

After Europe was invaded by semi-nomadic "barbarians" in the Dark

Ages, it reverted to ownership, control and proto-empire-building. In the middle ages, however, it was the Church which established quasi-imperial authority over the "civilised" world. It tried to apply the principles of Christianity by using the moral and spiritual authority of the Pope to arbitrate between the competing "owners" of different parts of Catholic Europe (i.e. excluding the Orthodox world, Islamic colonies, pagan states, etc.). Often this failed and war broke out. The principles of Christian chivalry sometimes mitigated the savagery of conflict, but rarely to any great extent. However, the Papacy's attempt to bring peace through an early form of international law had a cultural effect that was not only important for Europe at the time, but was to provide a template for more recent efforts world-wide to limit the destructiveness of warfare, especially industrial or nuclear. It laid the foundation for public international law.

In the early sixteenth century, Martin Luther challenged the moral authority of the Papacy, focussing on the corruption resulting from the monetisation of the spiritual authority. The Church routinely charged for the "forgiveness of sins" and privatised the resulting revenue stream, from which it built St Peter's Basilica in Rome. Luther's protest sparked a series of revolts which ultimately destroyed the Church's "universal" (i.e. pan-European) authority during the Reformation. The result was more warfare than ever before due to the fracturing of the Papal jurisdiction. In one sense, Luther was the original nationalist.

During the subsequent wars of religion, Catholic and Protestant rulers fought one another over both territory and religious affiliation. This culminated in one of the most destructive conflicts in human history, known as the Thirty Years War (1618-1648). Perhaps a third of all Germans died; it was a disaster comparable with the Black Death three centuries before. The war reached a bloody climax at the siege of Magdeburg in central Germany in 1631. Of the 30,000 inhabitants only 5,000 survived the artificially-created firestorm after the largely wooden-built city was set alight by forces of the Catholic League, led by Prince Tilly from Flanders. Those who escaped the inferno were killed by the besiegers as they fled. Tilly wrote afterwards to the Holy Roman Emperor, for whom he was fighting: "Never was such a victory since the storming of Troy or of Jerusalem. I am sorry that you and the ladies of the court were not there to enjoy the spectacle."

Proportionately speaking, the massacre of Magdeburg was more lethal than the infamous firebombing of nearby Dresden by the British and American air-forces in February 1945, and at least as murderous as the sack of Constantinople in 1204 by Christian knights during the Fourth Crusade. If civilisation were to survive the aftershocks of the Reformation, an accommodation would have to be reached between rulers willing to kill their opponents' subjects indiscriminately, equipped as they by then were with gunpowder-based technology.

This was not exclusively a "continental" phenomenon. Oliver Cromwell massacred the inhabitants of Wexford and Drogheda in 1649 almost as ruthlessly as Prince Tilly had the Magdeburgers. The governor of Drogheda, the one-legged Catholic, Sir Arthur Aston, a veteran of the Polish-Swedish wars, surrendered his town but earned no mercy thereby. He had his brains beaten out with his own wooden leg. That was only two years after Scottish government forces had massacred the defenders of Dunaverty Castle in Kintyre, who had been promised quarter if they surrendered. Of the 300-odd, largely Catholic, royalists who took the Covenanting general, David Leslie, at his word, not one appears to have survived.

Ironically, both the English and the Scots were trying to impose peace by rooting out what they saw as heresy. After the Thirty Years' War, the new idea for the avoidance of war in Europe was that rulers should be allowed to differ in their religions, but also allowed to enforce conformity at home. "Cuius regio, eius religio" was the formula which, loosely translated, means: "his region; his religion". Thus, when Scotland changed religion in the 1560s, the new king changed with it. James VI was born a Catholic and crowned a Protestant.[495]

Power was now concentrated within states due to the demise of the Papacy as the international arbiter between Christian princes. This power was supposed to be inviolable by other rulers, all of whom were

---

[495] Being the son of Mary, Queen of Scots, James was baptised a Catholic in 1566 at an extravagant ceremony in Stirling Castle. At his coronation seven months later, following his mother's forced abdication, John Knox preached the sermon in a more modest ceremony in Stirling Parish Church. A Protestant country was to be ruled by a Protestant monarch.

considered juridically equal. That is what came to be meant by the word "sovereignty". It was the idea behind the Peace of Westphalia (1648), which brought the Thirty Years' War to an end, and it influenced European diplomatic practice for three hundred years.

Before the Reformation, there had been no "sovereignty" of any recognised, *national* sort, whether popular or parliamentary. But with sovereignty came the opportunity for absolutism. Without Papal oversight, and with the ancient feudal "bargain" between liege and lord decaying, rulers like Henry VIII in England had a much freer hand, both at home and abroad. Parliaments came under threat all over Europe. The Estates General in France last met in 1614. Reciprocity was in retreat as a principle of government. The feudal world of theoretical chivalry and universal morality was replaced by a more modern one inhabited by the likes of Machiavelli and Cardinal Richelieu.

James VI and I saw himself as a moderniser, on the European pattern. He did not accept medievalism, with its Christian ideal of reciprocity between man and God and, by implication, between ordinary men and powerful men. He preferred a more absolutist, top-down concept of governance. He went so far as to write a short book of advice for his son, entitled *Basilikon Doron* (1599), about the proper conduct of monarchy. In it he emphasised the dangers of reformed religion in terms which reveal his attitude to democracy. Whereas the Catholic Church had been prone to "pride ambition and avarice", James said, the new Protestant churchmen, "clogged with their own passions", ran riot because the Reformation was not implemented by their own "Prince's order" as happened under Henry VIII in England. Instead of submitting to the principles of modern absolutism, they preferred Presbyterian ideas of quasi-democratic government in the church. As James put it in his book:

> Some fierie spirited men in the ministrie got such a guiding of the people at that time of confusion [i.e. Reformation], as finding the gust of gouernment sweete, they begouth to fantasie to themselues a Democraticke forme of gouernment... [They] settled themselues so fast vpon that imagined Democracie, as they fed themselues with the hope to become *Tribuni plebis*: and so in a popular gouernment by leading the people by the nose, to beare the sway of all the rule.

The most dangerous people that Protestantism threw up were the Puritans, who James described as being worse than Highland "thieves":

> Take heede therefore (my Sonne) to such Puritanes, verie pestes in the Church and Commonweale, whom no deserts can oblige, neither oathes or promises binde, breathing nothing but sedition and calumnies, aspiring without measure, railing without reason, and making their owne imaginations the square of their conscience. I protest before the great God... that ye shall neuer finde with any Hieland or Border-theeues greater ingratitude, and moe lies and vile perjuries, then [i.e. than] with these phanaticke spirits.

After the Union of the Crowns, James and then his son, Charles I, attempted to rule England without parliament, and Scotland by proclamation. Charles eventually provoked civil war in the British Isles. In January 1649, he was put on trial by parliament in Westminster Hall for high treason.

The essence of the charges was that he had broken pre-existing law, often medieval in spirit and therefore less tolerant of absolutism, in his manner of administering the country.

Charles refused to plead, for an important reason that is directly relevant to this story. The issue he raised was of sovereignty under law. The opening exchange between the King and the Lord President of the *ad hoc* court made this plain.

> **King**: I would know by what power I am called hither... by what Authority, I mean, lawful; there are many unlawful Authorities in the world, Thieves and Robbers by the highways: but I would know by what Authority I was brought from thence, and carried from place to place, and when I know what lawful Authority, I shall answer [i.e. plead]. Remember, I am your King, your lawful King... I have a Trust committed to me by God, by old and lawful descent, I will not betray it to answer a new unlawful Authority, therefore resolve me that, and you shall hear more of me... Let me see a legal Authority warranted by the Word of God, the Scriptures, or warranted by the Constitutions of the Kingdom, and I will answer.
> **Lord President.** Sir, you have held yourself, and let fall such Language, as if you had been no ways Subject to the Law, or that the Law had not been your Superior. Sir, the Court is very well sensible of it, and I hope so are all the understanding people of England, that the Law is your Superior, that you ought to have ruled according to the Law... *Sir, as the Law is your Superior;*

so truly Sir, there is something that is Superior to the Law, and that is indeed the Parent or Author of the Law, and that is the People of England.[496] (emphasis added)

The last sentence is a statement about the location of ultimate sovereignty, though at the time more in theory than in practice. Charles was found guilty and beheaded. Six weeks later, parliament passed an Act "abolishing the Office of King". Two days after that, a similar one abolished the House of Lords.

However, the Restoration, at which Charles's son, Charles II returned as King in 1660, recomplicated matters by attempting to reconcile the Crown and parliament, ultimately without success. It was not until 1688 that the "Glorious Revolution" solidified practical sovereignty in a compromise with elite reciprocity that came to be referred to as "the Crown in parliament".

Soon afterwards, for reasons connected with the desire for peace and prosperity in Britain and defiance abroad of the autocratic pretentions of Louis XIV, Scotland and England decided to bury the blunderbuss, so to speak, and abolish themselves in order to create a new state called Great Britain.

Unlike the Peace of Westphalia, the Treaty of Union between England and Scotland allowed for religious diversity *within* a single state. The Church of Scotland was entrenched in the constitution as the established church in *part* of Great Britain, while the English were left to the more exotic mercies of the Church of England in *another part of the same state*. Few complained when the Welsh subsequently embraced Methodism.

This level of internal diversity was unique at the time, and made possible only by the Union. For the first time, peace reigned in Britain *despite national differences*. The Enlightenment subsequently gave theoretical backing to the common desire to live and let live. It was in order to destabilise that mutual tolerance that twentieth century nationalists tried to invent a distinction between parliamentary and popular sovereignty.

---

[496] There are innumerable accounts of the trial. One of the most illuminating analyses, because it balances the constitutional issues with the autocratic but dignified character of Charles, is the radio discussion in the In Our Time series on BBC Radio 4, available online.

Parliamentary sovereignty

The prevailing view of sovereignty in *England* at the time of the Union became the *British* view because Scotland had less developed traditions of constitutional law. That was due to the almost continually disturbed state of the country from the death of Alexander III in 1286 to the defeat of Bonnie Prince Charlie in 1746. Scotland had no tradition of formal, systematic reciprocity in post-medieval government (and even the medieval heritage was questionable). That was what both parliamentary and popular sovereignty are said to facilitate. The two points are related, as the Stair Society's expert has noted:

> Before 1689 there were few developments of significance in Scottish constitutional law… The *Scottish parliament*, unlike the English *never represented popular opinion*, which found its expression in General Assembly [of the Church of Scotland] and in the Convention of Royal Burghs.[497] (emphasis added)

The Crown in parliament meant the monarch plus most of what we would today call the "executive". It was "the spending department", so to speak, while it was parliament which raised much of the money the Crown spent. It consisted of the "first estate", made up of churchmen, and the "second" of nobles. They sat together in the House of Lords. Finally there was the "Commons", sitting in a separate House. MPs were elected on an outdated franchise by people who owned enough property that they paid tax on land. The whole arrangement was disorganised and inconsistent, but it did allow for the expression of public opinion in a crude way. That was not part of the Scottish parliament's function. It was never, until its last decade, the centre of public life in the capital. It was not an institution seen to be of central national significance.

The over-riding principle of the English parliament was that those who paid the taxes should have a say in how they were spent. After

---

[497] "The Transition to Modern Law, 1532-1660", J. Irvine Smith, in *Introduction to Scottish Legal History* (1958), p. 31. The Stair Society, founded in 1934, is Scotland's leading legal history society. It is named after Viscount Stair (James Dalrymple, 1619-95), the original systemiser of Scots civil law. His son, the Master of Stair, was the principle instigator of the massacre of Glencoe.

Charles I, it came to be accepted that the king could no longer impose taxes directly on the population (unlike, say, excise and customs duties which arose indirectly as a result of trade). Direct taxation impacted most significantly on land, and the owners of taxable assets felt it right they were represented in the only body which had the power to grant or withhold revenue to or from the Crown. This was reciprocity of an "entry-level" sort. It differed from the feudal bargain which had originally been the result of conquest, latterly mitigated by Christian reciprocity at a personal level (especially in connection with the moral duty to observe contract commitments, both commercial and legal, which had been freely entered into).

Principled opponents of reciprocity, including James I and Charles I, promulgated the theory of the Divine Right of Kings which allowed for autocratic rule under a different level of "contract"—this time with the Almighty. That was a theory which emerged with the Reformation as sovereigns in Protestant countries assumed the "divine" functions which had previously been exercised by the Pope. Charles said at his trial: "I have a trust committed to me by God". But the gentry in the House of Commons and their allies in the City of London's huge and wealthy merchant community (something Scotland significantly lacked), still wanted to know how their money was being spent.

Between them and Oliver Cromwell's New Model Army, they revived the medieval idea of theoretical reciprocity, though in a seventeenth century form. The blow of the anonymous executioner's specially sharpened blade on the back of King Charles's neck on 30 January 1649 outside the Banqueting House in Whitehall sent a shockwave all round Europe. Absolutist monarchs were appalled. At a stroke, they were faced with reciprocity, red in tooth and axe. It was the first time a reigning monarch had been put on trial for his life *by his subjects*. As far away as Russia, Tsar Alexis imposed punitive trade sanctions by expelling the entire English merchant community from Moscow.

A century later, Sir William Blackstone, the famous legal scholar, wrote in his *Commentaries on the Laws of England* (1765) that reciprocity has, in effect, been the core principle of the British constitution all along. It originated in feudal times, in a different form, when loyalty was given in return for protection. The corollary was that such subordination was conceded in terms of the feudal bargain. The king could rule, but only according to the law of the free (i.e. not enserfed) people, an idea that was expressed in the Magna Carta and which returned at King Charles's trial in different form. That idea had been ignored by monarchs who wanted to be above the law in a period when feudalism was decaying into absolutism.

Blackstone described a balance of power between the three components of sovereignty, only one of which was even partly democratic. It was a system which required a certain amount of mutual tolerance. In that sense it reflected the principle of accommodation which had been established between England and Scotland in 1707 on church matters:

> With us the executive power of the laws is lodged in first, the sovereign; secondly, the lords spiritual and temporal, which is an aristocratical assembly of persons selected for their piety, their birth, their wisdom, their valour, or their property; and, thirdly, the House of Commons, freely chosen by the people from among themselves, which makes it a kind of democracy. As this aggregate body, actuated by different springs, and attentive to different interests, composes the British parliament, and has the supreme disposal of every thing, there can no inconvenience be attempted by either of the three branches, but will be withstood by one of the other two, each branch being armed with a negative power, sufficient to repel any innovation which it shall think inexpedient or dangerous.
>
> Here then is lodged the sovereignty of the British constitution; and lodged as beneficially as is possible for society. For in no other shape could we be so certain of finding the three great qualities of government so well and so happily united. If the supreme power were lodged in any one of the three branches separately, we must be exposed to the inconveniences of either absolute monarchy, aristocracy, or democracy, and so want two of the three principal ingredients of good polity—that is, virtue, wisdom, and power... The constitutional government of this island is so admirably tempered and compounded, that nothing can endanger or hurt it, but destroying the equilibrium of power between one branch of the legislature and the rest.[498]

The phrase "sovereignty of parliament" is shorthand for the

---

[498] *Commentaries on the Laws of England*, William Blackstone, ed. James Stephen (1874), p. 32

sovereignty of the Crown in parliament. The House of Commons was never sovereign in isolation—and still is not completely so; e.g. it has to obey decisions of the courts[499]—but as the eighteenth century wore on the Commons' power grew at the expense of the Crown and the aristocracy. At the same time, the Enlightenment reduced the influence of the "Lords Spiritual", whose moral authority wafted away like incense in the high roofbeams. That left the King, the Lords Temporal only and the Commons to rule collectively, with none having absolute power.

Though the Commons was increasingly important, it was not sovereign on its own, even in the early nineteenth century. An important illustration of that was King George III's refusal to permit his government to honour William Pitt the Younger's promise to the Irish that the Act of Union between Great Britain and Ireland, which was legislated for in 1800 in an attempt to emulate the success of the Scottish union in 1707, would be accompanied by Catholic emancipation. The King said that to do so would be to violate his Coronation Oath to uphold the Protestant religion.[500]

That prevented the implementation of a sensible, humanitarian reform which had been promised by the Prime Minister and which was critically important in the context of both war with Napoleon and the disturbed state of Ireland. The King's refusal was an act of "sovereign assertion". His most recent biographer says:

> Principles were involved. George's objection was ultimately bound up with his Coronation Oath, a solemn promise he felt he had made to God on that day, and therefore simply not susceptible to the hopes or promises of prime ministers, however loyal, long-standing and talented.[501]

---

[499] There are also voluntary derogations of sovereignty, like the relics of EU control, commitments to the United Nations or NATO and internal devolution, all of which could in principle be reversed quite lawfully. Even the European Court of Justice's superiority to parliament was (largely) reversed by Brexit.

[500] The text of the "post-Revolution" oath had been written in 1689 for William and Mary. It included this question to future monarchs: "Will you to the utmost of your power maintain the laws of God, the true profession of the Gospel, and the Protestant reformed religion established by law?"

[501] *George III: the Life of Britain's Most Misunderstood Monarch*, Andrew Roberts (2021), p. 588

A parliament that was sovereign in isolation from other branches of government would not have had to bow to the King's will on so important a matter in the middle of a major, Europe-wide conflict. But the British parliament did. Catholic emancipation was not enacted until 1829, nine years after George's death. Sovereignty was still shared between the Crown and parliament.

It was only in after the middle of the nineteenth century that the Crown ceased to have any significant executive power. The Lords Temporal likewise succumbed to developing democracy. The Upper House yielded primacy to the Commons in 1911 when the Parliament Act removed its power to reject money Bills, and hence their Lordships' control over revenue raising (including from themselves). The end for both came in 1928 with the Equal Franchise Act, which mandated the same voting rights for men and women in elections for the House of Commons.

Full democracy meant that it is the British electorate *alone* which hires and fires the members of the House of Commons. Those members then choose the government and supervise its behaviour, without having to defer to either the Crown or the Lords. The people are in charge through their representatives *in parliament*. That is *popular* sovereignty in the real sense, including that meant by the President of the court which tried Charles I. There is no difference, *of any sort whatsoever*, between Scottish citizens of the UK and English ones in this respect.

Difference between political and legal sovereignty

There is, however, an important distinction to be made between what the first modern constitutional authority, A.V. Dicey, described as "political" sovereignty and "legal" sovereignty.

There are things that the *legal* sovereign cannot do, for essentially *political* reasons. No monarch is omnipotent. That applied even to the most undemocratic regimes. Dicey quoted the Ottoman Empire: "The Sultan could not abolish Mahommedanism." Even Louis XIV had limits to his practical power. He could revoke the Edict of Nantes (1685), Dicey says, thus banning Protestantism from France, but he could not have done the opposite as he could never have forced the whole French people to become genuine Protestants. Louis may possibly have said "L'état c'est moi", but his power over his *état* was never unlimited. Some aspects of life are always going to be beyond the reach of any ruler that is not, like Stalin, prepared to kill as many of his subjects as it takes to silence the rest. Without mass murder, reciprocity can rarely be denied for any length of time in societies in which the people are politically conscious.

Dicey described how this distinction operated in Britain:

> What is true of the power of a despot... is specially true of the sovereignty of Parliament; it is limited on every side by the possibility of popular re-sistance. Parliament might legally establish an Episcopal Church in Scotland; Parliament might legally tax the colonies; Parliament might without any breach of law change the succession to the throne or abolish the monarchy; but everyone knows that in the present state of the world the British Parlia-ment will do none of these things. In each case widespread resistance would result from legislation which, though legally valid, is in fact beyond the stretch of parliamentary power... These examples show the extent to which the theoretically boundless sovereignty of Parliament is curtailed by the ex-ternal limit to is exercise.[502]

Perhaps Dicey's most striking illustration of the difference between legal and political sovereignty concerned the United States: "Before the War of Secession [i.e. the Civil War] the sovereign power of the United States could not have abolished slavery without provoking civil war." (p. 33) There can be no arguing with that.

There always has to be a single, publicly identifiable bearer of the *legal* sovereignty if a state is to operate within the international community as a coherent entity. Even if the whole people are sovereign, there has to be a representative, or bearer, of that sovereignty, in other words a head of state. That could be a hereditary monarch who was born to the job, or it could be a politician, as in the United States or Russia, who has fought for it.

The *political* sovereign is harder to define, though equally important as it reflects day-to-day reality.

> The electorate is in fact the sovereign of [Britain]... The object is to secure

---

[502] *Introduction to the Law of the Constitution*, A.V. Dicey (1885, 1914 ed.), p. 31-2. We have seen an example of that in our own day with the Poll Tax riots in London in 1990.

the conformity of Parliament to the will of the nation… Our modern code of constitutional morality secures, though in a roundabout way, what is called 'the sovereignty of the people'.[503]

Democracy is a system for establishing reciprocity between the legal sovereign and the political sovereign. When it works properly; there should be no significant difference between the will of the people and the will of parliament.

We all know that no large system ever works properly, but some work better than others. Many think the Dewar Constitution works less well than the British constitution of which it is an ill-fitting subordinate extension. That may or may not be true. But what is certainly *not* true is that there is in Scotland a "constitutional tradition of the sovereignty of the people" which is different from the English/British tradition in that respect.

Before the civil wars of the 1640s, the *legal* sovereign in Scotland was always the Crown, just as it had been in England for centuries. From the execution of Charles I in 1649 to the installation of William and Mary as joint monarchs in 1689 sovereignty was disputed between the Court and parliament. Thereafter parliament was paramount (though far from omnipotent).

When the legal sovereignties of Scotland and England were abolished in favour of the new legal sovereign, Great Britain, there was no tradition of purely *political* sovereignty, as distinct from *legal* sovereignty, in Scotland. In that situation, there could be no popular sovereignty.[504]

That is what Sturgeon failed to grasp when, at the opening of the new parliament in 2003, she refused to affirm allegiance to her legal sovereign because she claimed to be loyal only to the Scottish part of her country's political sovereign. In a reasonably well-governed state, the political sovereign and the "popular" sovereign are to all intents and purposes the same thing. That was never the case in pre-Union Scotland.

---

[503] *Ibid.,* p. 286

[504] After 1690, when the Crown was knee-haltered by the Glorious Revolution, there was a period of semi-sovereignty of parliament in Scotland. But this was never complete and, in any case, lasted only seventeen years.

Popular sovereignty

The "sovereignty of the *Scottish* people", Sturgeon-style as something separate from that of the *British* people, is a line of constitutional argument that emerged only after the SNP was founded on 14 December 1933.[505] That was a year of nationalist upsurge throughout Europe. In Germany, a new party had come to power intending to reassert the political sovereignty of "das Volk", while in the Soviet Union Stalinist nationalism was replacing Bolshevik internationalism. Heroes like Peter the Great came back into favour at the expense of Marx and Engels. As in the new Germany, the Soviet idea was that a single all-powerful leader would represent the united and homogenous entity referred to as "the narod" ("the people") and, since everyone except "enemies of the people" agreed on everything in the political realm, the will (i.e. vote) of one was the will, or vote, of all. Elections were redundant and, in both countries, held only for form's sake. German nationalism has moved on since then; Scottish and Russian nationalism has not. Like President Putin, the SNP is still fighting battles which have their roots in the 1930s.

In order to justify their political claims, Scottish nationalists invented a constitutional theory based on a misinterpretation of the Declaration of Arbroath (1320). That was what Swinney, Sturgeon *et al* battened onto sometime between 1999 and 2003. Their claim was essentially a marketing one, and it has been rejected by almost all serious historians. Like Putin, the SNP wanted to misuse history for its own ends. It wanted to persuade the non-expert citizen that there has always been a constitutional difference between the English tradition of "parliamentary sovereignty" and the alleged Scottish one of "popular sovereignty".

These populists have a "sacred text". Just as English (and many

---

[505] This was the date of the amalgamation of the right-wing Scottish Party and the left-wing National Party, to form the Scottish National Party. The first conference was held on 14 April 1934, under the leadership of Sir Alexander MacEwan, a craggy-faced, Gaelic-speaking lawyer from Inverness who had been born in Calcutta and was originally a Home Rule Liberal. A month before the SNP was formed, MacEwan had fought a by-election in Kilmarnock, where he came last. He was soon replaced as leader by Andrew Dewar Gibb, the Regius Professor of Law at Glasgow University (1934-58), who had stood as a *Unionist* in by-elections in Hamilton (1924) and Greenock (1929), in both of which he too came last.

American) legal supremacists have the Magna Carta, Scottish "popular sovereignty" nationalists have the Declaration of Arbroath. They argue that this document provides evidence of reciprocity in government because a group of barons said that if they found they had a king who was not prepared to defend the country from the English, they would replace him. As a result, the Declaration has become "perhaps the best-studied document in Scottish history."[506] The Swinney-Sturgeon argument that there is a difference between Scottish democracy and English democracy depends on the Declaration for its authority. There is no other important document which corroborates their claim.

The background is reasonably well-known. In 1320 a group of Scottish barons petitioned the Pope to intervene with the English King, Edward II, the loser at Bannockburn in 1314, as he still wanted to incorporate Scotland into the English kingdom. That was an entirely reasonable request in the diplomatic circumstances of the time, and it was the sort of petition that many other groups of nobles had made in other countries, from Lithuania to Ireland and including both England and France. Given the importance of the Papacy to every monarch in Latin (i.e. western) Christendom at the time, this should not be surprising. The Scottish example of this practice was nothing out of the ordinary at a procedural level.[507]

At a textual level, the Declaration was derivative. The most quoted passage was adapted from the account of the Catiline conspiracy in 63 BC written by the Roman historian, Sallust. That was convincingly demonstrated seventy years ago by an Edinburgh lawyer who was, like many of his sort in those days, a fluent Latin reader.[508]

---

[506] Laura Harrison, "'That famous manifesto': the Declaration of Arbroath, Declaration of Independence and the power of language", *Scottish Affairs*, (2017), vol. 26, p. 435

[507] The fact that such letters to the Pope were common in Europe at the time has been emphasised by Grant Simpson in "The Declaration of Arbroath revitalised", *Scottish Historical Review* (1977), vol. 56, p. 11 at 22: "At least a dozen are said to have been sent [from England] between 1220 and 1320." Scots too did this, including one such letter in 1237 at the time of the signature of the Treaty of York which defined the Anglo-Scottish border. According to Simpson, this was done because of "Papal concern for peace" (p. 24). That was also the issue in 1320.

[508] "Sallust and the Declaration of Arbroath", Randall Philip, *Scottish Historical Review* (1947), vol. 26, p. 75

The relevant passage describes what the barons said might happen if they found themselves serving a king who refused to continue defending their country against the English. The forty-odd barons who attached their seals to the Declaration wanted, for obvious reasons, to put the Scottish case in a way that would appeal most easily to his Holiness, so they copied the famous classical author:

> Yet if he [our king] should give up what he has begun, seeking to make us or our kingdom subject to the King of England or the English, we should exert ourselves at once to drive him out as our enemy and a subverter of his own right and ours, and make some other man who was well able to defend us our King; for, as long as a hundred of us remain alive, never will we on any conditions be subjected to the lordship of the English. *It is in truth not for glory, nor riches, nor honours that we are fighting, but for freedom alone, which no honest man gives up but with life itself.*[509]

The italicised sentence is the main one which the lawyer found in Sallust in almost identical form. It implies selflessness and sacrifice, and conveys an apparently noble defiance of a bullying enemy in terms as exalted as some of Winston Churchill's wartime speeches. Not unnaturally, it has been recruited to the nationalist cause by those who want to present the destruction of the UK as an act of heroic resistance to alien tyranny. The reality, however, was rather different from the rhetoric in two critical respects, both of which relate to the idea of "popular sovereignty".

The most common argument for Scottish independence based on the "Arbroath letter" (as the Declaration has also been called[510]) is that

---

[509] Translation by the National Records of Scotland. Philip (*ibid.*) speculates that the author was Abbot Bernard of Arbroath Abbey, since the Abbey was likely to have a copy of Sallust in its library. However the tone was aggressive, which might be why the writer wanted to remain anonymous. Philip says: "The quotations from Sallust would be recognised in the papal Chancery, and the writer may have thought that if his identity came to light this appeal to classical authority would afford him some protection." (p. 78)

[510] It was only since the Second World War that the word "Declaration" has been commonly used, and that was largely due to the nationalists' attempt to make a connection with the American Declaration of Independence. For a while, some commentators suggested that it was the Arbroath letter which inspired Thomas Jefferson to write his Declaration. No prominent scholar who now holds that view. The only book still arguing it, and also taking the Swinney-Sturgeon constitutional line, is Edward Cowan's:

the barons who sent it were representing *the people of Scotland* when they said that any king who did not defend the country against the English would be replaced. That is the crux of the nationalist argument. However, not even the *barons* claimed that. They said *they* would replace the king, presumably by means of a palace revolution. Such revolts were common in the middle ages, when the political history of many states was a cycle of tyranny, revolt, anarchy and back to tyranny. The Arbroath barons did not mention "the people", or even the "community of the realm" except in the preamble which listed the people who sent "devout kisses of [the Pope's] blessed feet". In any case, the idea that the Scottish people had any influence over noble and gentry politics in Scotland, much less regal succession, was as absurd as it would have been in England at the time.

Lowland politics in the fourteenth century was feudal, with the underlying bargain being service in return for protection. No feudal lord tried to establish the opinion of his liege peasants or his bonded serfs (which is what many Scots still were) before going to parliament to speak (which most were reluctant to do because travel was so time-consuming and expensive).[511] In the Highlands, the idea of the proto-democratic representation of clansmen was even more far-fetched. They comprised about half the country and half the population. There, even feudalism was limited to the charters which the great chieftains held of the Scottish Crown (and many of those were disputed, lost, obsolete or had never

---

The Declaration of Arbroath: for Freedom Alone (2003). Curiously it was published in the same year that Swinney led the charge for popular sovereignty. Might there have been a connection? Cowan's approach can be gauged from this sentence in the preface to the 2020 edition: "Some commentators seem unwilling to acknowledge the letter's essentiality, paramountcy and eminence, while appearing quite relaxed about the primacy of *England's much inferior and now mainly redundant Magna Carta*." (p. iv, emphasis added) So Scotland is superior to England in terms of medieval constitutional law, and the Declaration is "the supreme articulation of Scottish nationhood and constitutionalism." (p. 39)

[511] Because most of the barons would have been tenants-in-chief of the Crown, and therefore summoned to all meetings of the parliament, it could be argued that Arbroath actually represented the indirect exercise of *parliamentary* sovereignty. The Scottish parliament was peripatetic before the seventeenth century, and in 1320 it met at Arbroath. I have been unable to establish whether or not there was any connection between the meeting and the letter, but on so important a matter it would be surprising if there were not.

been written down). Beyond that, public power was exercised by the clan chiefs and their households. The idea that a chief would consult his ordinary clansmen on major foreign policy or dynastic issues was absurd.

Without a reliable flow of information, *popular* sovereignty was impossible. The legal sovereign has to have a means of ascertaining the will of the political sovereign—i.e. the people. The maximum reasonable inference might be to add all who fought at Bannockburn to the list of those who could be said to have supported the anti-English cause. But that would exclude those, like the MacDougalls of Lorne, who occupied large territories in the Hebrides and on the adjacent mainland but who had refused to fight on behalf of Robert the Bruce. That was partly for personal reasons (Bruce had murdered the chief's wife's brother) and partly due to the way in which he had favoured their local competitors for "imperial" expansion in the west, the MacDonalds of Islay, who did fight.

In 1320, it would have been physically impossible, and politically inconceivable, for any form of reciprocity to exist between people like the Arbroath barons and the MacDonald clansmen of Kintyre, or the tenants of cattle reivers from the Borders. Popular sovereignty at the time of the Declaration simply did not exist—nor could it until democracy arrived in the late nineteenth century as a consequence of improved communications.

Scotland in 1320 was not so united as the "popular sovereignty" boosters would have modern voters believe. The country was too varied and disordered for that. Worse still, it seems that not even the *barons* could be relied on. Within four months of sealing the Declaration, many of them were in open revolt against the King, which raises the question: can a "community of the realm" exist when there is disagreement about fundamental issues, or is permanent unanimity required?

Many scholars have remarked that the apparent national unity of the Declaration had been shattered before the year 1320 was ended: the Soulis conspirators, including *five barons who had sealed the letter, planned to kill the king.* Men who had shared the Declaration's noble cry in April had turned traitor by August. Conversely, several of those named in the letter had been at some time, like Robert Bruce himself, on the English side.[512] (emphasis added)

Add to those considerations the fact that until the Treaty of Perth in 1266, the whole of the Hebrides including the Western Isles, plus Kintyre, Arran and Bute were not even part of Scotland. They were ruled from Norway, as were Orkney and Shetland, which stayed that way until 1468.[513]

The barons' letter was largely forgotten after 1320. It is disputed whether the Pope ever received his copy as no trace of it has been found in the Papal archives. It was not rediscovered until the late seventeenth century, when it was republished by Sir George ("Bluidy") Mackenzie of Rosehaugh, the first major systematiser of Scottish criminal law. He was also the founder of the Advocates Library in Edinburgh (now the National Library). In the 1670s he was one of the main persecutors of the Covenanters on behalf of King Charles II and the Scottish parliament. He was a Royalist who was opposed to reciprocity in government. As Lord Advocate, he sanctioned the judicial torture of recalcitrant subjects using "thumbikins" or "boots", and the despatch overseas of those convicted but not executed. Many were sold into slavery in Virginia, the Caribbean or Tangiers. Mackenzie was also an assiduous antiquarian, and it was he who was responsible for the first published reference to the Declaration in 350 years.

Even then, it was not issued in English translation, the only form the Lowland "populus" could have understood, until after the Revolution of 1688. It was not published in Gaelic either, since few Highlanders were literate, and few of those who were spoke much English. It was

---

[512] Simpson, "Declaration of Arbroath revitalised", *op. cit.* p. 29

[513] One of the early acts of the Scottish Privy council after taking possession of the Northern Isles was to abolish Norse law and replace it with Scots. This was the sort of measure to be expected from a victorious "conqueror", and valid in the circumstances. But it suggests that "the community of the realm" had little, if any, practical meaning in the sense of protecting the king's subjects from the excesses of powerful men. A list of penalties the new courts imposed included some Scottish innovations: "Hanging, branding, drowning, strangling followed by burning, scourging, banishment, ducking in the sea, fines, standing in the kirk door, in the pillory, the jougs [an iron collar chained to a wall or post] or the branks [a metal contraption fitted to the mouth and head and intended to prevent speech: the wearer was led around in public for added humiliation]." (*A Legal History of Scotland, vol IV: The Seventeenth Century*, David Walker (1996), p. 198)

rarely mentioned in the eighteenth century and in the nineteenth was usually quoted in order to buttress the "nationalist-unionist" story in terms of a vanished past. Sir Walter Scott's account in his *History of Scotland* describes the Declaration fairly except that he omits the anti-English point, which is, of course, the nub of the matter. This aspect of Scotland's past was uncontroversial until the nationalists discovered they needed ancient authority for their attempt to falsify constitutional history in the 1930s.

History rewritten

This "creative reinterpretation" of history was mainly the work of John MacCormick who had helped found the National Party of Scotland while he was studying law at Glasgow University in the 1920s. He claimed democratic superiority over England because Scotland had always been a freer country than its neighbour. He put it this way in his political autobiography:

> In nearly two thousand years no conqueror has ever brought in his train a new and alien ruling class to subjugate the common people... The practice of democracy came naturally to the people of Scotland since in the fundamental sense of family all men were equal in blood and dignity if not in power or wealth... Scotland had no need for a Magna Carta ... The king was not a supreme ruler standing above all law but was the head of a family, *primus inter pares*, who had to obey the law like anyone else.[514]

Every sentence of this passage is nonsense. Scotland was conquered by invaders from Ireland who established Dalriada, then proceeded to drive out the Britons and exterminate the Picts, as the Declaration itself explicitly boasts. The only "law" the Declaration asserts is the right of barons to change kings if the reigning one is not sufficiently hostile to the English. The suggestion that the king was subject to law more generally was ludicrous in a state which had very little law of any sort, even in the Lothians which were the only really "settled" part of Scotland at the time in a civic sense.

---

[514] *The Flag in the Wind, op. cit.*, p. 47

Reflecting the thinking of the 1930s when the SNP was formed, Mac-Cormick justified the separation of Scotland from England on the basis of the different "history and *racial origins* of the two nations." (p. 46, emphasis added) Race-based history, being the product of warped brains, is confused. MacCormick's was no exception. Early in his story he says: "All too often the crimes of crude violence which come to the notice of the courts in places like Glasgow are committed by people with recognisably Irish names." (p. 53) Later he says: "I think that these islands [i.e. including Ireland] have given more to the world than any other conglomeration simply because we have here learned the meaning of give and take… I would rather be in a minority in these islands than anywhere else on the world." (p. 136) The beginning of the give and take that Mac-Cormick appreciated was, as mentioned above, the religious tolerance established by the Acts of Union, which is what he spent most of his life trying to undo.

Perhaps most importantly, the superiority of law over the Crown that MacCormick claimed ran right back into the Dark Age mists of Scottish history had been specifically denied by James VI. The King believed that he was descended from the conquerors of the land north of the Tweed and so had the same right to rule there as the heirs of William the Conqueror had south of it after 1066. James argued that he therefore was, like any imperial victor, not bound by native law. As triumph in battle was a sign of God's favour, he ruled by "Divine Right", the theory that was to be the underlying cause of the civil wars in the British Isles in the 1640s-50s. James's quasi-imperial history was deeply suspect, and in part ludicrous, but it was closer to the truth than MacCormick's race-based fantasy.

Between the Wars of Independence (i.e. Bannockburn, 1314) and 1532, when the College of Justice (i.e. Court of Session) was founded, there was not much law in Scotland, even in theory. What we now call Scots civil law had to wait for Viscount Stair in the 1680s, which was when Mackenzie also published his foundational text on the criminal law. Other than treason, most law further afield than the Lothians was delegated to the owners of regalities, sheriffdoms and other heritable jurisdictions—i.e. to the lairds—since the Crown was usually too weak to make its writ run in the Highlands and Islands. Much the same was true in the Borders and the far north. For centuries, justice was, in effect, franchised out to the most powerful men in the disputed areas. The Treaty of Union in 1707 explicitly preserved these jurisdictions as *rights of property* (in Article XX).[515]

Those courts were owned for the most part by people who sat or were represented in the Scottish parliament since it was, right to the end, a *feudal* assembly. They were in a similar position to the lords of English manors from the time of the Conquest to the 1160s when Henry II introduced the beginnings of the common law (meaning law common to the whole kingdom). That slowly but steadily superseded manorial courts and local custom. Scotland did not achieve an equivalent level of internal consistency until the Heritage Jurisdictions (Scotland) Act (1746) abolished them all in the aftermath of Culloden. For the first time, the whole country had the benefit of uniform law applied by independent, (semi-) professional sheriffs.

Before 1707, most members of the Scottish parliament were either direct tenants of the king or officers of state he appointed to sit *ex officio*. As a body, it did not even pretend to express public opinion which, as noted above, was largely unknowable outside the capital. The idea of popular control of the sovereign in medieval Scotland was either a Nigel Tranter-ish confection of the sort Sturgeon read as a girl, or it was fake history for the purposes of political destabilisation.

MacCormick-style "Arbroathists" argue that the barons represented the people of Scotland through "the community of the realm".[516] This sounds proto-democratic, but in fact it was the opposite. In the Declaration the barons claimed authority—as James VI later did—from the

---

[515] In his *Basilikon Doron*, James VI said these rights were "the greatest hinderance to the execution of our Lawes in this countrie." To the lairds, these rights of property were important as courts, due to each sheriffdom's territorial monopoly, generated a substantial income in fees, fines, etc.

[516] A joint university group, called The Community of the Realm (COTR), has produced an exceptionally informative website with podcasts about the Declaration and its context. It stresses its centrality and political utility *at the time* but mercifully refrains from drawing any self-congratulatory constitutional conclusions for Scotland today. (See: www.cotr.ac.uk) It is particularly interesting on the differences between the various versions of the Declaration that were made by medieval copyists. By contrast, the full issue of the *Scottish Historical Review* (vol. 101) which was devoted to the Declaration in 2022 is minutely detailed but curiously uninformative, as if written only for academics.

fact that their ancestors had *conquered* Scotland. The text justifies the barons' control by quoting their ancestors' "ethnic cleansing" (to use the modern phase). Referring to the Kingdom of Scots, it says: "expulsis primo Britonibus et Pictis omnino deletis." The National Archives of Scotland translates that as: "The Britons it first drove out, the Picts it utterly destroyed." The barons' letter from Arbroath has been taken as a statement of popular liberty when it was in fact an imperial claim by the descendants of an invading elite which wanted to be spared the sort of treatment (by the English) they boasted of having meted out to those (Britons and Picts) they had conquered.

MacCormick's claim that "in two thousand years no conqueror has ever brought a new and alien ruling class to subjugate the common people" is not therefore supported *even by the Declaration itself*. Had he not read it? The barons based their argument for Papal protection from "people south of the border" on the claim that they *themselves* were *descended from conquerors*. How could they have conquered a land which is supposed to have been unconquered?

The history of MacCormick's "history" is interesting in itself. It came to be accepted by many Scottish exceptionalists in the 1950s. But that did not last long. The expansion of Scottish history studies from the 1960s on has doomed it to oblivion, at least in academic circles. Too much is now known to take it seriously anymore as a statement of national political principle, either in fact or in embryo. Constitutionally speaking, Swinney-Sturgeon were stuck in nostalgia for a world which never existed outside the covers of romantic historical novels or the imagination of a journeyman lawyer with a grudge against the country that tolerated him. They had been suckered by "tabloid" history—another illustration of the skills shortage in Holyrood.

History re-corrected

The only apparent support for the "popular sovereignty" view from a "respectable" source that is regularly quoted by nationalists is the Opinion of Lord Cooper—then Lord President of the Court of

Session—in *MacCormick* v *Lord Advocate* in 1953.[517]

This was the case in which two nationalists, the same John MacCormick plus Ian Hamilton, then a law student at Glasgow University, went to court to argue that the newly crowned Queen Elizabeth should be known in Scotland as Elizabeth I because there was no previous Scottish monarch called Elizabeth. It was a trivial issue, and MacCormick had trivialised himself in 1945 by joining another party (the Liberals) after, like Compton Mackenzie, he abandoned the increasingly cranky SNP. His co-petitioner, Ian Hamilton (later Ian Hamilton QC) had helped steal the Stone of Scone from Westminster Abbey on Christmas Day, 1950. (They returned it to the public domain by leaving it later in Arbroath Abbey—a deliberately symbolic location.) Their suit was more of a jape than a serious constitutional challenge.[518]

Nonetheless, being the courteous judge he was, Lord Cooper took the case seriously and, while finding against MacCormick and Hamilton, said *obiter* in his Opinion: "The principle of the unlimited sovereignty of Parliament is a distinctively English principle which has no counterpart in Scottish constitutional law." This sentence has been seized on by some nationalists as justification for the "Arbroath" theory that the barons who claimed to speak "for Scotland" actually did so.

A better-informed reading of Cooper's Opinion has been given by Colin Kidd, Professor of History at St Andrew's University, who has written extensively about Scottish constitutional development. He emphasises the invention of the myth by MacCormick, and its transformation into apparently serious constitutional theory by his son, Professor Sir Neil MacCormick, who called the Declaration of Arbroath an "iconic text".[519] Professor Kidd writes:

---

[517] *MacCormick v Lord Advocate* (1953) Session Cases, p. 396

[518] Ian Hamilton himself implies in the Foreword to MacCormick's book that what he calls "the Queen's Title action" was conceived informally: "We dreamed it up one spring day on the banks of Loch Lomond." (*Flag*, MacCormick, *op. cit.,* p. v)

[519] Professor MacCormick (1941-2009) was the Regius Professor of Public Law and the Law of Nature and Nations at the University of Edinburgh, and a European MEP for the SNP. The Leverhulme Trust describes him on its website as "the SNP's greatest intellectual." One of the senior Court of Session judges I interviewed for *The Justice Factory* (*op. cit.*) said of him: "I never knew John MacCormick, though I knew his son, Neil—everyone did. He is a genius. He's got a knighthood, though why I have no

Lord Cooper's argument has subsequently enjoyed a wider political salience, and this line of thinking features in the justifications advanced for a Scottish parliament from the Claim of Right for Scotland right through to the devolution referenda in 1997. Indeed the fascinating point of constitutional law raised by Lord Cooper has helped consolidate one of *Scotland's most enduring political myths—the myth of Scottish political sovereignty*.[520] (emphasis added)

Lord Cooper's words were true on their face but to say that Scotland does not have a tradition of the unlimited sovereignty of parliament does not mean that it had any tradition of *limited* sovereignty. As I have tried to show above, the Scottish parliament did not have *any* tradition of sovereignty, limited or unlimited. Only the Crown had that, and its sovereignty was as *un*limited as that of any other monarch of the time.

Lord Cooper said nothing about "popular sovereignty". All he said was what was *not* the case, not what *was* the case. As Cooper's most distinguished successor has pointed out, though criticising English practice the Lord President "did not deign to say what the Scottish position was."[521]

Without going into the argument in detail, it is enough to say that all sovereignty is limited, even that of "the Sultan" or Louis XIV. Given the confused state of Scottish constitutional thought in the sixteenth and seventeenth centuries, Professor Kidd's main point surely stands: "There was no national consensus on the location of sovereignty in pre-Union Scotland."[522]

---

idea. He's been a law professor at Edinburgh University since he was 32, but none of us can understand any of his books. Perhaps the Queen does." (p. 161)

[520] "Sovereignty and the Scottish Constitution Before 1707", Colin Kidd, *Juridical Review* (2004), p. 230. The opposing argument was that the original king from whom James VI claimed descent, Fergus MacFerquard, is said to have been *elected* in 330 BC. (p. 228) Presumably, since then Scottish monarchical conquests had been legitimised by that original election—for which, of course, there is no evidence, even if any such custom were not invalidated by desuetude.

[521] *The Courts, the Church and the Constitution: Aspects of the Disruption of 1843*, Lord Rodger of Earlsferry (2008), p. 6. Lord Rodger's brief discussion of the case is especially authoritative given his past, not only as Lord President of the Court of Session, like Lord Cooper, and membership of the UK Supreme Court, but also as a prolific writer on academic (especially Roman) law.

[522] *Ibid.*, p. 230. Professor Kidd characterises Coopers' *dictum* as "constitutional kite-flying". He prefers another judge's formulation in the same case: "There was little to suggest that [by 1707] the framework of government in Scotland had been so

Prior to 1690, the Scottish parliament never played an independent part in government, unlike the English one, which did but which shared it with the Crown. With the exception of the Reformation decade, and the period from 1690 to 1707, the Scottish parliament almost always acted as a rubber stamp for royal measures decided elsewhere. From the reign of James III (1460-1488) to the rustication of James VII (1688) the parliament was almost completely controlled by an elite body called the Lords of the Articles. That operated with most of the privileges of a modern Cabinet, but with greater powers and almost no accountability to anyone other than the king. Reciprocity did not feature in its approach to government. With few exceptions, the parliament's role was limited to approving or rejecting legislation drafted in secret by the Lords of the Articles.

That committee was usually selected indirectly by the Crown from the membership of the parliament and empowered to draft, debate and finalise most legislation. It was then presented in finished form for acceptance (and occasionally rejection) by the parliament as a whole, which was forbidden from meeting to discuss the government's measures. By the seventeenth century the king was in complete control over the committee of "Articulars" as they were sometimes called. The first important authority on the subject has written of this period:

> Along with royal control over selection of the Lords of the Articles, we find a large increase in the control of the committee over the parliament. It obtained the sole power of initiating business, and the House was prevented from meeting except for the election of the Articles and for the receipt of their report; members of the parliament who were not "Lords Articulars" were *forbidden either to consult together in their separate Estates or to attend, as onlookers, the meetings of the committee.* Under James VI and Charles I, the whole report, covering the entire business of the parliament, was presented in a single day.[523] (emphasis added)

---

consolidated that the Scottish parliament enjoyed unchallenged sovereignty." (p. 236)

[523] *Parliaments*, Rait, *op. cit.*, p. 8. Prof. Rait's history of parliamentary impotence can be summarised in a few quotes: "The medieval parliament [tended] to act as a mere court of registration for the actions of the party in power." (p. 33) "No opposition is ever traceable in parliament. The party in power had it in complete control and it registered their deeds automatically." (p. 34) Re. James V: "Parliament was a tool in his hands,

The relationship between the "Lords Articulars" and the Scottish parliament was not dissimilar to that between the European Commission and the European parliament today. Neither had/has any power to initiate legislation, only to accept or reject laws drafted by others. Both were/are procedurally incapable of representing the people's interests to the powers in the land.

Part of the problem in Scotland was ignorance at the centre of opinion at the periphery. Communications were poor, as roads were almost non-existent. Often large areas of the Highlands and the Borders were dangerous for unarmed lowlanders. More significantly, *the Scottish parliament had hardly any electors.* Even at the time of the Union, there were only 4,000 voters, which for a country of more than a million people did not represent "popular sovereignty". Indeed it was not until the application in Scotland of the Reform Act in 1832, which was largely (and often inappropriately) copied from the English Act of the same date, that Scottish voters gained meaningful representation in any parliament.

From 1707 to 1832, the franchise for Scottish seats in the House of Commons was the same one used for the pre-1707 parliament in Edinburgh. While the Reform Act increased the electorate in England by 35% (to about 650,000), in Scotland it went up by 1,200%, from 5,000 to 65,000. Before the Reform Act, the entire electorate in my own county, Argyllshire, was about *fifty*. Every MP from 1707 to 1832 was chosen by the Duke of Argyll and his family, who controlled most of the votes. With one brief exception, every Member sent to Westminster was actually called Campbell.

Seldom were elections before 1832 even contested. There was little point. The electorate was tiny, and the ballot was not secret. So if you voted against the Duke and held land from him, even indirectly, he would know about it. That was enough in a situation in which the Sheriffdom of Argyllshire was *owned* by the Duke as a heritable jurisdiction.

---

and passed only what he approved." (p. 43) Queen Mary: "Up to the Reformation, the parliament of the Three Estates cannot be said to have exercised any decisive, or even any influential, voice upon the determination of national policy... There was no parliamentary opposition... The rule of law was not recognised." (p. 46) James VI: "The king's party summoned parliament rarely, and usually for the purpose of ratifying what had been done in their self-chosen Conventions." (p. 51) And so on until the turbulent times of the civil wars and the abolition of the Lords of the Articles in 1690. (p. 389)

The court usually sat at Inverary, just down the hill from his castle. Most of the sheriffs were relatives of his. Professor Rait summed up the situation like this:

> Both in shire and in borough, the Scottish system of representation was superbly qualified to lend itself to the corrupt parliamentary methods of the eighteenth century.[524]

In order to persuade their target audience that Scotland had been more "democratic" before the Union rather than less, the nationalist boosters had to create a myth of the past that might deceive voters on that point. They had a model to hand in the form of the Irish nationalist claims of a golden age before "England" invaded in 1171. From the 1880s on, Irish republican activists published material almost as remote from the facts as MacCormick's historical bubble-blowing. They did this knowing that mythologies can provide important justification for the violence they wanted to encourage.

Irish writers like Yeats and the "Celtic Twilight" school—mocked by James Joyce but imitated by many Scots writers—invented a version of Celtic mythology which could be used to justify the future they were planning to impose on their countrymen. The Irish academic who wrote the Introduction to the centenary re-issue of *Ulysses* put this clearly:

> Claiming to be upholders of the past, they were anything but. They knew that they must *creatively misinterpret the past if they were to shape the golden future.* Such a future would be less a revival than a birth, a project of self-

---

[524] *Parliaments, op. cit.*, p. 123. Dicey and Rait quote a 1788 report which gives some figures for the oligarchic control of votes, through the misuse of feudal superiorities. "In Aberdeenshire, out of a total of 178 votes, 44 were controlled by the Duke of Gordon and 33 by the Earl of Fife; in Banffshire, out of a total of 122 votes, 37 were controlled by the Duke of Gordon and 50 by the Earl of Fife; in Inverness-shire out of a total of 103 votes, 31 were controlled by the Duke of Gordon and 55 by one or other of six landowners; in Kinross-shire, out of a total of 26 votes, 16 were controlled by Mr Graham; in Lanarkshire, out of a total of 124 votes, 43 were controlled by the Duke of Gordon and 12 by Mr Lockhart of Castlehill...." (*Thoughts on the Union*, Dicey and Rait, *op. cit.*, p. 366) From 1707 to 1832, the MP for Edinburgh was chosen by just *thirty-three* people and *all* the other MPs for the Scottish burghs, fourteen of them, had a *total* electorate of 1220 between them. (*Parliaments*, Rait, *op. cit.*, p. 268) Restrictive though that was, it was better than the situation pre-1690, when general elections on modern lines were unknown in Scotland. Parliament was summoned by the king when, and for as long as, it suited him.

invention.[525] (emphasis added)

Fortunately for Scots, John MacCormick's invention has not (yet) had to collide with reality the way the Irish dream had to in the fifty years after independence. In the course of half a century, the country became so poor and illiberal that there was an almost uncontrollable emigration of young people from the new Free State to the prosperity and actual freedom of Britain, the United States and elsewhere. While Russians point out that 40% of all males born in the Soviet Union in 1923 did not survive the Great Patriotic War, the Irish can claim that "four out of every five children born in Ireland between 1931 and 1941 emigrated in the 1950s."[526]

Half a million people from a country of under three million left between 1945 and 1960. And that was after the end of the War, during which around a sixth of Ireland's working age population went to Britain to take jobs in war industries or to join the armed forces. They preferred to work in factories that were being bombed by enemies of parliamentary sovereignty rather than live in a country at peace where they had to accept supervision from the local priest, who represented the Irish "community of the realm" in its most oppressive form. Most rural areas were without electricity and running water. Life on small, unmechanised family farms was exhausting, lonely and so boring, especially for women, that the near-slums of a Midlands industrial town in wartime seemed, by comparison, to be colourful, affluent and above all *free*. Most of the non-combatants never went back home to live.[527]

These emigrants were glad to escape the fairy-tale illusions that were promoted by the Taoiseach, Eamon de Valera, after he came to power during the nationalist upsurge in the early 1930s that MacCormick had battened onto. De Valera made a radio broadcast on St Patrick's Day 1943 which has become famous for its Yeats-style illusionism. Significantly, he delivered it on the day after the largest "wolf-pack" submarine

---

[525] Declan Kiberd in *Ulysses* (2011), p. lxxvi

[526] *Ireland 1912-1985,* J.J. Lee (1989), p. 379

[527] For further reading on this sad but fascinating topic see Clair Wills: *That Neutral Island: a Cultural History of Ireland During the Second World War* (2007) and *The Best are Leaving: Emigration and Post-War Irish Culture* (2015).

attack on an Allied convoy in the War sank 22 merchant ships for the
loss of only one U-boat, and the day before the Wehrmacht retook Kharkov in savage fighting in eastern Ukraine. But Irish minds were on higher
things.

In his talk, de Valera described the "national dream" of Ireland which
had been in the minds of Young Irelanders a century ago as it had the
later revolutionaries whose core mission had been the promotion of the
"creative misinterpretation" of Irish history. The Taoiseach referred to
St Patrick's "land of saints and scholars" while avoiding saying that its
present calm repose was possible only because the Royal Navy had, despite grievous losses, successfully kept the Germans out of all the British
isles, including Ireland. Neither did he admit that his freedom to broadcast depended indirectly on the fact that there were so few saints or
scholars still alive in the wreckage of Kharkov—or, for that matter, of
Kiev, Minsk, Leningrad or Stalingrad (where the Germans had surrendered just six weeks before). Ignoring the rest of the world, as introverted, crab-like nationalism usually does, De Valera spoke of Ireland in
terms that were halfway between German "blood and soil" and Soviet
Realism. It was

> the home of a people who, satisfied with frugal comfort, devoted their lei-
> sure to the things of the spirit - a land whose countryside would be bright
> with cosy homesteads, whose fields and villages would be joyous with the
> sounds of industry, with the romping of sturdy children, the contest of ath-
> letic youths and the laughter of happy maidens, whose firesides would be
> forums for the wisdom of serene old age.[528]

Given that there are so many mentions in the text above of MSPs
quoting Ireland as a model for Scotland's future, it is relevant that De
Valera's dream of mythic regeneration proved to be no more than that—
a dream. It had no more reality than MacCormick's democratic barons.
Ireland continued to go downhill for another half century.

A less introverted and more generous-spirited approach might have
averted the crisis of mass emigration that followed the achievement of
Irish independence in 1922. Despite the "happy maidens" and "cosy

---

[528] Quoted in *Ireland*, Lee, *op. cit.*, p. 334. The RTE website has a recording of the speech.

farmsteads", many, many Irish men and women refused to follow the Pied Piper of Dublin and stay at home in "frugal comfort" while the fate of the world, including their own country, was being decided out on the Atlantic and in the steppes of southern Russia. In a fundamental sense, they were the *real* patriots. It is typical of the embittered nastiness of nationalist conceit that Ireland has signally failed to honour them.

I have said nothing new in this short essay, and indeed much of it is well-known to educated opinion in Scotland. The question is whether those MSPs who refused to affirm loyalty to the Crown voluntarily on 7 May 2003 knew it too. Were they culturally ignorant or politically dishonest? Did Swinney, who led the process, really understand the emptiness of MacCormick's historical fantasy? Did Sturgeon?

Source note

The *Official Report* of the Scottish parliament which I have used above is the local version of *Hansard*, which records, in a similar format and with similar rules for editing, accuracy, comprehensiveness, etc., the debates in the parliament of the United Kingdom. *Hansard* started life after the ban on reporting speeches in parliament had been partially lifted in 1771. It progressed fitfully until full freedom of reporting was established in the early nineteenth century by William Cobbett, who went to jail for his trouble. The work was taken over by a partner of his, Thomas Curson Hansard, and was "nationalised" as the official record after 1878 when professional reporters were employed to compile it.

Scotland has been lucky in that from the inception of the parliament in Edinburgh a full record of debates has been kept in a form derived directly from the modern *Hansard*. It is an underutilised resource, and deserves to be more widely consulted by citizens who want to get a glimpse of the public character of the politicians they (partially) elect. It also tells many important stories, not only about MSPs individually, but also about issues like the evolving nuclear debate or the independence saga, which will feature more prominently in volumes 2 and 3.

In the 1950s, the great historian of eighteenth-century English politics, Sir Lewis Namier, organised and oversaw the research for and work upon the now semi-official *History of Parliament*. Sir Lewis wanted to give brief background sketches of all MPs, and therefore provide raw material for research into how the parliament worked in much the same way as he had done in his own ground-breaking studies: *The Structure of Politics at the Accession of George III* (1928) and *England in the Age of the American Revolution* (1930).

Namier's most distinguished "pupil" was A.J.P. Taylor. Taylor admired him and his work, but when, in 1953, Namier resigned his Chair as Professor of History at Manchester University, where the two men had first established their professional relationship, Taylor was offered it. But he turned it down, preferring to stay in Oxford as a lecturer. In his autobiography, he says this about the offer:

> [It] came from Manchester when Lewis Namier abandoned his Chair in order to compose a so-called history of parliament, meaning in reality potted biographies of eighteenth-century MPs. I said to him light-heartedly, "Surely there is a history of parliament already, compiled by Cobbett and later called *Hansard*?" Lewis was angry, angrier than I supposed.[529]

Namier's anger at Taylor's disrespectful riposte was perhaps uncalled for. He was a man without a great sense of humour, and Taylor liked to provoke. But Taylor was right in an important sense. The ultimate history of any parliament is what is said in it by its members. Hence the focus of this book.

Sadly, it is only a "citizen" who is in a position to write freely about these matters in Scotland today. As in Putin's Russia, though as yet to a much lesser extent, the academic world is increasingly overshadowed by the gloomy penumbra of the bureaugarchy. The series editor of the 10-volume *New Edinburgh History of Scotland*, Roger Mason, has issued a warning about this. In a recent essay called "The State of Scottish History: Some Reflections", published in the *Scottish Historical Review*, Professor Mason argued that academics are almost completely subject to government priorities for research due to what he called the "absurdities of the REF", i.e. the Research Excellence Framework. The REF is a UK-wide structure which assesses on some general—i.e. not individual—basis the "excellence" of research in government-funded educational institutions (which includes almost all of them). The body's website says: "The REF outcomes are used to calculate about £2 billion per year of public funding for universities' research." The huge figure is, I imagine, intended to impress; in fact it should depress all free spirits who read it. State interference in academic research is the thin end of a bureaugarchic wedge whose thick end could be Aspirantish thought control.

Mason went on to say that "the absurdities of REF [have been] exacerbated by the apparent politicisation of RCUK." The RCUK is the Research Councils of the UK. It bills itself as a "strategic partnership".

---

[529] *A Personal History*, A.J.P. Taylor (1984), p. 264

Mason goes on: "The RCUK has created a one-size-fits-all template of university research which is already eroding the ability of academics in the humanities to pursue self-directed research." He ends by saying: "Last year [i.e. 2012], a potentially even greater threat to academic freedom emerged in the form of Open Access publication... which paradoxically threatens to empower university *managers* to decide what academic research is published, where and when."[530] (emphasis added)

When "managers" replace free human beings in deciding the limits of inquiry, thought and expression, the student of Russian history is reminded of The Institute of Red Professors in the 1920s. That was the beginning of Soviet control over the "intelligentsia" (which is being revived in the context of the war in Ukraine today). That is the future some see for modern Britain if the bureaugarchy ever manages to establish full control over university research and publication.

But that should not deter the citizen with something to say. Neither A.J.P. Taylor nor Sir Lewis Namier ever bothered writing doctoral theses, yet those men were, and are, giants in their profession. Looking further back, Adam Smith did not need to apply for a slice of a £2 billion government treasure chest in order to transform global economic history (and, eventually, the Scottish economy). The same applies to David Hume and the *History* I have mentioned above. He was rejected for work in both Edinburgh of Glasgow universities due to his anti-establishment—i.e. free—views on religion. Arguably the most important example was Edward Gibbon. He did not even have a university degree, yet he revolutionised the writing of history in English. Like Hume, he never took a penny of public money for his work. He never wrote a "research proposal" or had to send a synopsis to a potential supervisor saying why he thought his work important.

Writing as always in plain English, Gibbon has himself described his motivation in words that are now famous:

> It was at Rome, on the fifteenth of October 1764, as I sat musing amidst the ruins of the Capitol, while barefoot friars sang vespers in the Temple of

---

[530] "The State of Scottish History: Some Reflections", Roger Mason, *Scottish Historical Review* (2013), vol. 92, p. 167 at 174. Mason is Professor of Scottish History, and Director of Scottish Historical Research, University of St Andrews.

Jupiter, that the idea of writing the decline and fall of the City first started to my mind.[531]

As a citizen today, I see narratable histories, both ancient and modern, all around me. Musing amidst the ruins of democratic Scotland, while sound-bite salary-wallahs sang bullet points in the Temple of Dewar, the idea of writing a more modest story started to my mind. Happily, the *Official Report* of the Scottish parliament was to hand. The result is what goes before this, and what will follow in the next two volumes. But other citizens could utilise comparable resources in different studies. The main requirement for intellectual integrity is to stay away from state-controlled bodies which try to tramline curiosity. Bodies like the REF and the RCUK are inherently top-down, homogenising and prescriptive in an old-fashioned, Dewarish sort of way. History faculties are increasingly staffed by "memory managers" whose priorities are more political than academic—and rarely human.

The joy of discovery cannot be expressed digitally and therefore cannot feature in any "research plan". Neither can enthusiasm be quantified. History without personal, imaginative input is a Soviet-style abomination. We need more barefoot friars, so to speak, and fewer prosaic memory managers so that everyone can write in their own, individual way about subject that interest or amuse them.

Let a thousand histories bloom!

Citizen biographers of the world, boot up! You have nothing to lose but your leisure!

---

[531] *Memoirs of my Life*, Edward Gibbon (1984), p 16

Acknowledgements

I would like to thank all those generous friends who put up with endless discussion of the themes addressed in this book. Most prefer that they are not mentioned publicly for reasons that any student of bureaugarchy, both Western (evolving) and Soviet (undefeated yet), will be uncomfortably aware. Among those who have not "taken the Gobson" but who have read drafts of the text are: Mark Davey, Mark Cresswell, Gilly from Islay, Curstaidh à Colla, Billy from "Southern Sun", Gavin the "three drammer", Kevin Drummond KC, the ubiquitous Roddy Martine, Margie Currie, Jim Sillars, Tom Walker, Nick Ritchie, "Baas Leesh", Sheila from Cambridge, Brian from the Ailsa Bar, Brian from Shore Street and, of course, Professor Alan Page, who is the expert.

I am also deeply indebted to the many Russians with whom I have discussed politics generally over the years, including the dangers of authoritarian leaders and sheep-like followers. They include Vladimir from Kiev, Ilya from Vasilyevo, and Vladimir from Skolkovo. Отдельно, я хочу поблагодарить Таню, которая терпела Шотландские политические глупости, и дискуссия об этом без конца, с улыбками и юмором. Она понимает что в жизни главное.

Finally, I wish to make particular mention of the Scottish parliament information office in Holyrood, who were at all times a model of practical co-operation. Unlike civil servants who make it as difficult as possible for the citizen to find out what the bureaugarchy is up to, and MSPs who usually seem to resent any intrusion in their "top table" existence from mere voters, the staff at the Public Information office were always helpful, candid and prompt in their replies.

Of course, however great my debt to all these people, I alone am responsible for any mistakes, omissions or inexpertisms in the text above. I am a citizen, not a computer.

Sustainability statement

by Hamish Gobson

Everyone who lives in the Highlands and the Hebrides knows that "you can't eat the scenery". That is one of the economic problems which face those of us who like to keep a healthy distance from the black hole of bureaugarchy. Ian Mitchell has found a way to turn this situation round for any literate Highlander who values reciprocity. The citizen's biography enables the author to "eat the politicians."

One of the uncovenanted benefits of political devolution has been that we now have a *sustainable* supply of subject matter—namely all those who sit, have sat or will in future sit in the Holyrood parliament attempting to eat the taxpayer.

Seaweed Cottage
by Crab Quay
Isle of Great Todday

Volume 2

Any reader who would like to be notified about publication of volume 2 of this book, covering the years 2007-14, should email an expression of interest to: sturgeonbook@gmail.com

Comment, information and offers of help with the marketing effort would be very welcome too.

Also available on www.amazon.co.uk –

THE JUSTICE FACTORY:
Can the Rule of Law Survive in 21st Century Scotland?

In this book, many of the ideas about Scottish public life which feature above first emerged. In some ways, that book was this book in embryo—but in other ways not.

Part I (Judges) describes from actual interviews the sort of people who have served as judges in Scotland since the turn of this century. What sort of people are the upholders of our law, who hold the ring between the bureaugarchy and the rest of us?

Part II (politicians) describes threats to the rule of law which are emerging from the political world. It is uncertain whether the judiciary will be allowed to retain its institutional independence. What price then, the rule of law?

The main threat to liberty in Scotland today is, as in many other countries, the desire of the politicians to replace the **rule *OF* law** with **rule *BY* law**. That is the dream of authoritarians everywhere. It is the negation of reciprocity. Our only defence is an independent judiciary.

The Foreword is by **Lord Hope of Craighead**, ex-Deputy President of the UK Supreme Court.

The Introduction to Part II was contributed by **Alan Page, Professor of Public Law** at the University of Dundee, author of the standard reference work, *Constitutional Law of Scotland*.

"Read this wonderful book. Our rulers are afraid you do."
Ian Hamilton QC

"We must all be grateful to Ian Mitchell for his controversial but very interesting book."
Lord Hope KT

The

JUSTICE FACTORY

"Show me the judge, and I'll tell you the law"

Can the Rule of Law Survive
in 21st Century Scotland?

Ian Mitchell

Second edition: updated, expanded with new Part II

65

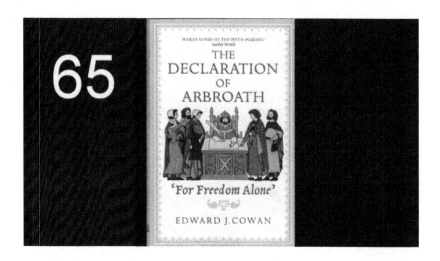

'MAKES SENSE OF THE MYTH-MAKING'
Sunday Herald

THE
DECLARATION
OF
ARBROATH

'For Freedom Alone'

EDWARD J. COWAN

Readers might also be interested in subscribing to **YouTube** *channel:*

"Ian Mitchell's Book Recommendations"

I have been reviewing books for thirty years, and in 2020 during the Covid lockdown I started to make films of my reviews. Most are recommendations of books I think other readers might find as interesting as I did.

Occasionally, I cover a book I do not like, an example of which is directly relevant to the Appendix to this book, "Popular *versus* parliamentary sovereignty". It is review 65 in the list and is entitled "The Declaration of Arbroath" by Edward J. Cowan. Professor Cowan's book was first published in 2003. Might it have been what provoked so many SNP MSPs to try to disrupt the oath-taking ceremony in May 2003, as mentioned in chapter 4 and the Appendix?

This is discussed in the film, which was made on the beautiful island of Coll. It also contains an interesting discussion from a friend of mine who is a Gaelic-speaking Collach. She doubts the fact that people in the Highlands and the Hebrides would have had any input into the "popular sovereignty" Cowan attempted to suggest existed in medieval Scotland. The idea of reciprocity between the clansmen on Coll and the barons at Arbroath, when the Declaration was signed in 1320, seems to her fanciful.

Watch the film, and make up your own mind. Enter "Ian Mitchell's Book Recommendations" in either Google or YouTube and the list of video reviews should appear. Look for number 65. Be aware: I am not a professional film-maker. This is very much "citizen's film-making". This review, sadly, suffered a glitch in the sound recording. Most are easier to listen to, so persevere!

By far the most popular of the films in the channel was the one I made about the Hate Crime Act (2021), a measure which will be covered in detail in volume 3 of this book. It is designated "Short 04".

Printed in Great Britain
by Amazon

17420737R00190